A Musician's Guide to Desktop Computing

with the Macintosh

Benjamin Suchoff

University of California, Los Angeles

PRENTICE HALL, Englewood Cliffs, New Jersey 07632

Library of Congress Cataloging-in-Publication Data

Suchoff, Benjamin
  A Musician's guide to desktop computing with the Macintosh / Benjamin Suchoff.
      p. cm.
  Includes bibliographical references and index.
  ISBN 0-13-605726-8
  1. Music—Data processing. 2. Musicology—Data processing.
  3. Macintosh (Computer). I. Title
ML74.S93 1992
780′.285′4165—dc20   93—20276
                                            CIP
                                            MN

11-24-93ds

Editorial/production supervision: Jean Lapidus
Interior design: Benjamin Suchoff
Cover design: Devine Design
Prepress buyer: Herb Klein
Manufacturing buyer: Bob Anderson
Acquisitions editor: Bud Therien

 © 1994 by Prentice-Hall, Inc.
A Simon & Schuster Company
Englewood Cliffs, New Jersey 07632

Printed in the United States of America

10 9 8 7 6 5 4 3 2 I

ISBN 0-13-605726-8

PRENTICE-HALL INTERNATIONAL (UK) LIMITED, *London*
PRENTICE-HALL OF AUSTRALIA PTY. LIMITED, *Sydney*
PRENTICE-HALL CANADA INC., *Toronto*
PRENTICE-HALL HISPANOAMERICANA, S.A., *Mexico*
PRENTICE-HALL OF INDIA PRIVATE LIMITED, *New Delhi*
PRENTICE-HALL OF JAPAN, INC., *Tokyo*
SIMON & SCHUSTER ASIA PTE. LTD., *Singapore*
EDITORA PRENTICE-HALL DO BRASIL, LTDA., *Rio de Janeiro*

To my wife, Eleanor

Contents

Preface

During my student days as a budding composer at the Juilliard School of Music, our orchestration class undertook a semester-long project, based on the ingenious, two-volume set of piano variations on *Mary Had a Little Lamb,* by the American composer Edward Ballentine (1896–1971). The stylistic range of these amusing pieces, from Bach to Stravinsky, required our preliminary study of the characteristic orchestral forces employed by the composers represented in the collection. Each student then selected a variation and began work on a full score, for evaluation and approval by the instructor. Since the project would culminate in a special reading by the Juilliard Orchestra, we had to prepare a holographic fair copy of the conductor's full score and each of the instrumental parts. I still have vivid memories of the inordinate amount of time and effort needed to complete the work. Today—at my Macintosh desktop!—I am able to quickly and easily sample and reassess instrumental combinations, notate and audio proof scores, automatically transpose and extract parts, and, above all, produce high-quality copy suitable for the most exacting publication purposes.

The second memorable incident happened many years later, during my tenure as curator of the New York Bartók Archive. While I was editing Bartók's monumental, five-volume Rumanian folk music collection for publication, I noticed the numeric lacuna in this marginal note to many melodies: "Cf. Variant No." Since a primary objective of Bartókian ethnomusicological research is the location of variants, in order to classify melodies according to style as well as determine art-music "contamination" and the influence of foreign characteristics, I set to work in an attempt to find the missing variants among the 3,404 melodies in the collection. This proved to be an impractical task, since the peasant music of East Europe contains many instances where one or more sections of a given folk song appear in a substantial number of other melodies.

Fortuitously, when I thought I would have to abandon the undertaking as overly time-consuming, a seminar in computer-oriented music research was offered in 1966 by the Music Department of the State University of New York at Binghamton, under the direction of Harry B. Lincoln and the guidance of Stefan Bauer-Mengelberg, Allen Forte, and other specialists. Thus began my introduction to batch-mode data processing for IBM mainframe computers, from the preparation of punched cards to the mysteries of the programmer's world, where such inadvertencies as erroneously keypunched characters and misplaced cards resulted in seemingly endless delays. By the end of the seminar, however, I was able to construct and process a pilot database of the seventy-five melodies contained in Bartók's published collection of Serbo-Croatian folk songs, which revealed variant relationships among the melodies that had escaped Bartók himself. The next year my essay about the project and its findings appeared in *Tempo* (London) No. 80.

Another outcome of this successful undertaking was the opportunity to continue my work under the supervision of Jack Heller, beginning at New York University and later, jointly with Lewis Lusardi, Director of the Center for Contemporary Arts and Letters at the State University of New York, Stony Brook, for database construction of larger Bartók folk music collections and other music materials. Yet the problems involved with punched card preparation and batch-mode data processing continued and were further aggravated when the IBM hardware at Stony Brook was replaced with other equipment. When in 1984 the first Apple Macintosh computer appeared, I purchased a machine and found myself in a radically new computer environment, where user-friendly interactivity is based on a graphics-oriented user interface and mouse-driven command functions. Today—thanks to my Macintosh desktop!—I, a musician, am able to quickly and with little difficulty work with the different kinds of software that are annotated in this book.

A special note: I have assumed that the reader has a working knowledge of Macintosh computers, such as choosing commands in the File and Edit menus; selecting buttons, locating files, and typing responses in dialog boxes; and is comfortable with the Finder in general and window management in particular.

CHAPTER OVERVIEW

Chapter 1 opens with a set of questions concerning software acquisition and my responses to them, in terms of the specific needs of musicians. Step-by-step tutorials for constructing choral scores are presented, from "getting started" to printed output, for the *ConcertWare+MIDI, Deluxe Music Construction Set, MusicProse, Finale,* and *Encore* applications. Each tutorial ends with a summary of the pros and cons of the application, and a Conclusions section compares street prices and offers additional advice to help the reader interested in acquiring suitable music software.

Chapter 2 is devoted to processing music-oriented graphics with the *SuperPaint 2* and Aldus *SuperPaint 3* applications, where the Adobe *Sonata* music font and certain drawing tools are employed, individually or in combination, to construct rhythm patterns, mensural notation, and font-exclusive music scores; enhance scores produced by the *Deluxe Music Construction Set* application; and create pictorial notation and non-notational graphics with shape, line, and arc tools.

Chapter 3 explores four types of databases—Thematic Index, Catalogue of Musical Works, Tabulation of Folk Music Material, and Graphic Bibliography—and provides tutorials for their quick and easy construction, with Microsoft *File* for the first three types and *FileVision IV* for bibliographic purposes.

Chapter 4 describes the techniques I use with Microsoft *Word* to produce electronic manuscripts for scholarly journals and then convert them to high-quality offprints for personal distribution. The chapter concludes with a tutorial for creating a book with Aldus *PageMaker,* in the form of camera-ready reproduction proofs, based on my experiences in preparing the complete *A Musician's Guide to Desktop Computing*—front matter, chapters, and appendices—for Prentice Hall.

Chapter 5 illustrates the procedures involved in scanning images with the Light Source *Ofoto* software for the flatbed Apple *OneScanner,* and the *ThunderWorks* software for the hand-held *Lightning 400* scanner and the *Thunderscan* cartridge scanner. The tutorials show how to scan partially obliterated music manuscripts for reconstruction of the original notation, and describe the procedures for scanning published music, line art, and photos for publication and other purposes.

Chapter 6 demonstrates the use of the *HyperCard 2* application for creating Play buttons and their typewritten scripts, which can be exported to multimedia database stacks to play the incipits of indexed or catalogued melodies. Tutorials are also given for working with the *Maestro, Sound Scripter,* and *Canary* stacks, where Play scripts are constructed, respectively, by means of music notation, a graphic piano keyboard, and an optional MIDI keyboard as the input medium. The last tutorial explains how to scan images with the *HyperScan* desk accessory and the Apple *OneScanner,* to produce bitmapped images for graphics-intensive database stacks.

Chapter 7 examines the contents and unique technological achievements of Warner New Media's *Audio Notes* CD-ROM disc, *The Orchestra,* based on Benjamin Britten's *A Young Person's Guide to the Orchestra.* The illustrated narrative is intended to serve users—teachers, students, and the lay public—as a supplementary guide for optimizing the study and appreciation of Britten's masterpiece.

Chapter 8 returns to the applications presented in the first chapter; now, however, to emphasize the value of MIDI keyboards as the ancillary means for quick, easy, and accurate notation of music scores. The tutorials are preceded by an introduction to the Opcode Systems *The Book of MIDI* stack, and my suggested layout for adding a MIDI keyboard, interface, amplifier, and speaker to the desktop.

Chapter 9 offers brief tutorials to emphasize the importance of what I consider to be the most helpful if not indispensable utilities, namely, *DiskDoubler, DiskTop, Norton Utilities, Now Utilities, PopChar, QuickKeys II, Retrospect,* and *Suitcase II.*

OF HARDWARE AND SOFTWARE

Other than a power supply replacement and a later upgrade to Macintosh Plus equivalency (2 megabytes), my 1984 Macintosh (originally 128 kilobytes) continues in service. And, to avoid incessant floppy-disk swapping, a 20-megabyte hard disk drive was added. In 1987, when the Macintosh II computer arrived, I believed myself ready to integrate word-processing, music notation, and graphics, within a Multi-Finder environment, for the production of electronic manuscripts and offprints of my scholarly essays, and camera-ready copy of music examples and scores for various publication purposes.

At the present writing, my desktop—actually a U-shaped set of three wooden tables—consists of Apple Macintosh II (8Mb) and Plus (2Mb) computers, Apple ImageWriter I and LaserWriter Plus printers, Apple internal and other external hard disk drives (Alliance Peripheral Systems, Mirror Technologies: 237Mb total capacity), DriveSavers *DataStream* tape drive (40Mb), Apple 13" RGB monitor, Sigma Designs *L-View Multi-Mode* 19" monochrome monitor, Apple *OneScanner*, ThunderWare *ThunderScan*, Toshiba CD-Rom drive, *Zoom/Modem*, Casio *CZ-101* synthesizer, and Radio Shack *Realistic* stereo amplifier with 12" speakers.

The computers intercommunicate by means of *MacTOPS* LAN (Local Area Network) software. The modem is used to download shareware and freeware programs from CompuServe Information Service, for evaluation purposes, as well as free upgrades and bulletins from commercial vendors. The installation of a PMMU (Paged Memory Management Unit) coprocessor and Connectix *Virtual* software increased Macintosh II memory to its present 13 megabytes. It should be noted that all applications used in this book for annotation, construction of tutorials, or general description were processed with Macintosh System Software version 6.0.7.

ACKNOWLEDGMENTS

Grateful acknowledgment is made to all those who have assisted in the preparation of this book. First and foremost is my wife, Eleanor, for her editorial suggestions, patience, and above all, sympathetic understanding. I am deeply indebted to my son, Michael, head of Suchoff and Associates, Los Angeles, California, who supervised the building of my electronic desktop, unstintingly provided necesssary technical advice, and introduced me to that "other world" of personal computers, including the Microsoft DOS (Disk Operating System) and Windows environments. Special thanks are due Dr. Elliott Antokoletz, Professor and Chair of the Department of Musicology, The University of Texas, Austin, for his constant support and encouragement.

I am most appreciative of the opportunity provided by Norwell F. Therien, Jr., Publisher, Art and Music, Prentice Hall, who entrusted me with the preparation of the reproduction proofs of this book, from cover to cover. The cooperation of his assistants, Barbara Barysh and Lee Mamunes, is noted with many thanks.

I would like to emphasize that this book would not have achieved its eclectic character without the interest and assistance of: Bill Adams, Peter Bartók, Carolyn P. Bekamis, Tom Burns, Larry Davis, David M. Dempsey, Jeannie Ditter, Gabriel Dotto, Scott Docherty, Michael Eusey, Rachel E. Famighette, Sue Fenstermaker, Bernard Fisher, Sylvia Goldstein, John Grimes, Lynn Halloran, Cleo Huggins, Penny Kaiserlian, David Kaplowitz, Anastasia Lanier, Tami Letsinger, Lenore Mamer, Joan Miller, Rand Miller, Michael Moore, John Nelson, Keith Pentecost, Daniel S. Rampe, Linda Rich, Christine E. Seutter, Kim Sudhalter, David Thornburg, Cynthia Woll, and the anonymous resource personnel of the companies listed further below.

For permission to engrave, reconstruct, or scan excerpts from copyrighted material, acknowledgment is gratefully made to

Taplinger Publishing Company, Inc., for excerpts from Gardner Read: *Music Notation.*

Peter Bartók, for excerpts from Béla Bartók's Slovak folk music collection.

Boosey & Hawkes, Inc., New York, N.Y., for excerpts from Bartók: *String Quartet No. 4;* Britten*: A Young Person's Guide to the Orchestra;* and Purcell: *Sound the Trumpet,* transcribed by Benjamin Suchoff.

Editio Music and Kultura, Budapest, Hungary, for excerpts from Bartók: *Two Rumanian Dances,* with commentaries by László Somfai.

Florian Noetzel Verlag, Wilhelmshaven, Germany, for excerpts from Benjamin Suchoff: "The Ethnomusicological Roots of Béla Bartók's Musical Language," in *The World of Music* (1987).

Corvina Press and Kultura, Budapest, Hungary, for excerpts from *L'Art populaire en Hongrie* (1958), edited by Edit Fél, Tamás Hofer, Klára K.-Csilléry.

Martinus Nijhoff, The Hague, for excerpts from Bartók: *Rumanian Folk Music,* vols. IV, V (1975), edited by Benjamin Suchoff.

Dr. Mantle Hood, for excerpts from Mantle Hood: *The Ethnomusicologist* (1971).

Plymouth Music Company, Inc., Ft. Lauderdale, Florida, for excerpts from Bartók: *Evening in Transylvania,* text and transcription by Benjamin Suchoff; Caldera: *Serve The Lord With Gladness,* edited and revised by Benjamin Suchoff; Emma Lou Diemer: *Homage to Cowell, Cage, Crumb and Czerny;* Fauré: *After A Dream,* English version and arrangement by Benjamin Suchoff; Haydn: *Sanctus (Heilig-Messe,* 1796), edited by Benjamin Suchoff.

Sam Fox Publishing Company, Inc., Santa Barbara, California, for excerpts from Bartók: *Pieces and Suites,* transcribed by Benjamin Suchoff; Bartók: *Four Pieces for Band,* transcribed by Benjamin Suchoff.

State University of New York Press, Albany, New York, for excerpts from Bartók: *Yugoslav Folk Music* (1978), edited by Benjamin Suchoff; Bartók: *The Hungarian Folk Song* (1981), edited by Benjamin Suchoff.

The University of California Press, Berkeley and Los Angeles, California, for excerpts from Elliott Antokoletz: *The Music of Béla Bartók: A Study of Tonality and Progression in Twentieth Century Music* (1984).

I am indeed appreciative of the hardware and software provided for review purposes. Listed below are the vendors and the products they contributed. The screen displays printed in this book are used by permission.

Adobe Systems Inc. *Sonata.*

Aldus Corporation. *PageMaker* and *SuperPaint.*

Blaschek, Günther. *PopChar.*

CE Software, Inc. *QuicKeys* and *DiskTop.*

Claris, Inc. *MacPaint.*

Coda Music Software. *Finale* and *MusicProse.*

Cyan, Inc. *Maestro.*

Dantz Development Corporation. *Retrospect.*

Electronic Arts, Inc. *Deluxe Music Construction Set.*

Fifth Generation Systems, Inc. *Suitcase.*

Great Wave Software. *ConcertWare+MIDI.*

Lyon, Tim. *Sound Scripter.*

Merel, Steve. *Maestro.*

Microsoft Corporation. *Microsoft Word.*

Now Software, Inc. *Now Utilities.*

Opcode Systems, Inc. *The Book of MIDI.*

Passport Designs, Inc. *Encore.*

Sitka Corporation, *MacTOPS.*

Thunderware, Inc. *LightningScan 400, LightningScan* DA, and *ThunderWorks.*

TSP Software. *FileVision IV.*

Warner New Media. *The Orchestra.*

Trademarks

The names listed below are recognized as registered trademarks or service marks associated with products mentioned in this book.

Adobe, Adobe Illustrator, FreeHand, Postscript, and Sonata are registered trademarks of Adobe Systems Inc.

Aldus, the Aldus logo, FreeHand, PageMaker, and SuperPaint are registered trademarks of Aldus Coporation.

Apple, the Apple logo, AppleTalk, Finder, Font/DA Mover, HyperScan, HyperTalk, Imagewriter, LaserWriter, Macintosh, Multifinder, OneScanner, StyleWriter, and System are registered trademarks of Apple Computer, Inc.

Audio Notes is a registered trademark of Warner New Media.

Canary is a registered trademark of Cyan, Inc.

Casio is a registered trademark of Casio, Japan.

ConcertWare, InstrumentMaker, and Great Wave Software are registered trademarks of Great Wave Software.

DataStream is a registered trademark of DriveSavers, Inc.

Deluxe Music Construction Set and Electronic Arts are registered trademarks of

Deluxe Music Construction Set and Electronic Arts are registered trademarks of Electronic Arts, Inc.

DiskDoubler, DDExpand, and DiskDoubler SEA are trademarks of Salient Software, Inc.

DiskTop and DiskTop.Extras are registered trademarks of CE Software, Inc.

FileVision IV is a registered trademark of TSP Software.

Finale is a registered trademark and MusicProse, ExtractParts, HyperScribe, Petrucci, and Seville are trademarks of Coda Music Software. Copyright © 1991 by Coda Systems Music Software. Illustrations used by permission.

HyperCard, MacPaint, and Claris are registered trademarks of Claris, Inc.

LaserFrench German Spanish is a registered trademark of Linguist's Software, Inc.

L-View is a registered trademark and Multi-Mode is a trademark of Sigma Designs, Inc.

LightningScan, SnapGuide, ThunderScan, ThunderWorks, Thunderware, and the Thunderware logo are registered trademarks of Thunderware, Inc.

MacTOPS is a trademark of Sitka Coporation, a Sun Microsystems, Inc.-owned business.

Microsoft, the Microsoft logo, Microsoft File, and Microsoft Word are registered trademarks of Microsoft Corporation.

Now Utilities, Now Software, NowMenus, NowSave, and WYSIWYG Menus are registered trademarks of Now Software, Inc.

Ofoto is a registered trademark of Light Source Computer Images, Inc.

Passport and Encore are registered trademarks of Passport Designs, Inc.

QuicKeys and CEToolbox are registered trademarks of CE Software, Inc.

Radio Shack and Realistic are registered trademarks of Tandy Corporation.

Retrospect is a registered trademark of Dantz Development Corporation.

Suitcase is a trademark licensed to Fifth Generation Systems, Inc.

The Book of MIDI and MIDI Translator are registered trademarks of Opcode Systems, Inc.

The Norton Utilities, Norton Disk Doctor, and UnErase are registered trademarks, and Norton Backup, DiskLight, Fast Find, FileSaver, KeyFinder, Speed Disk, and Symantec are trademarks of Symantec Corporation.

Virtual is a registered trademark of Connectix Corporation.

Zoom/Modem is a trademark of Zoom Telephonics, Inc.

CHAPTER 1

Music Notation

Desktop computing for music output—audio, video, or hard copy—extends from the construction of simple melodies to complex transcriptions which may require special fonts, symbols, and graphics (Figure 1). The tutorials provided in this chapter are suitable for entry level or advanced users and amateur or professional musicians, and are intended to serve as a practical introduction to the *ConcertWare+MIDI*, *Deluxe Music Construction Set*, *MusicProse*, *Finale*, and *Encore* applications.

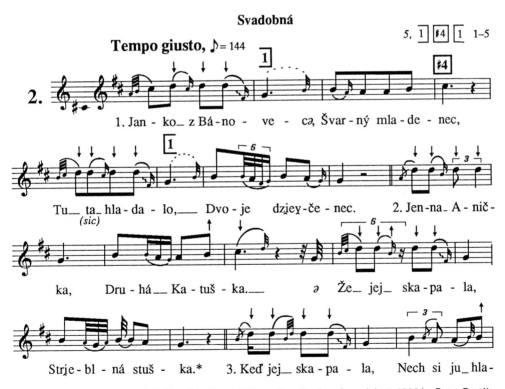

Figure 1. Transcription from Béla Bartók's Slovak folk music collection. Copyright © 1992 by Peter Bartók.

The question of choice depends on a number of factors which the prospective user should carefully consider before a decision is made:

- What kind of output is wanted?
- How friendly is data input?
- Will the music program alone be adequate?
- What are the hardware requirements?
- Is the manufacturer reliable?
- How much will it all cost?

TYPES OF OUTPUT

Electronic Copy.—Computer files intended for personal visual or audible (playback) use are usually saved on a hard disk and backed up on floppy disks or other storage media (see Chapter 9, below). When the saved files are intended to serve as "electronic manuscripts," a second set of floppy disks is prepared for processing by publishers and commercial printers. The publisher or printer may also require a copy of the music application and its special screen and printer fonts.

Camera-ready Copy.—High quality printouts, usually by a laser printer or its equivalent, for photo-offset processing.

Other Printed Copy.—Laser, inkjet, or dot-matrix printouts, produced by the user or commercial printer, for such varied purposes as conductor's scores, dissertations, handouts, overhead projection transparencies, thematic catalogues, and so forth.

DATA ENTRY AND RETRIEVAL

Notation.—Input is facilitated when the main screen provides an uncluttered facsimile of appropriate music manuscript paper. If palette bars containing music symbols and related graphics are also displayed, the palettes should be movable or removable and logically organized. The menu bar should closely follow the Macintosh interface and offer a wide range of editing functions with command-key equivalents.

Mechanics.—There is less fatigue and quicker data input when the application provides computer keyboard operation in addition to or together with the mouse. The quickest and most accurate method of notation is the use of a MIDI (Musical Instrument Digital Interface) keyboard, in tandem with the mouse or the computer keyboard, in Step-time mode (see Chapter 8, below).

Proofreading.—Playback capability offers the advantage of aural error detection of the graphic score by the computer speaker or external high fidelity equipment. Useful features are computer checking of rhythm and instrumental range, and provision for the verification of tone quality by a MIDI instrument.

Automation and Other Attributes.—A desirable feature is automated transposition of the score in whole and in part. Certain programs are capable of extracting parts from the full score as well as providing special graphics tools.

Exporting Music Files.—If the score requires hand finishing or special enhancements, the program should provide file formats (Paint, PICT) for export to an appropriate graphics application (e.g., Aldus *SuperPaint*: see Chapter 2, below). Furthermore, a number of programs include a proprietary PostScript music font, for laser printer output, that closely approximates music engraving of the highest quality. If the user intends to produce offprints or books, the progam should provide an EPS (<u>E</u>ncapsulated <u>P</u>ost<u>S</u>cript) file format capability for export of the document to a word processor or page layout application (e.g., Microsoft *Word* or Aldus *PageMaker*: see Chapter 4, below).

Ancillary Software

Some manufacturers provide a proprietary music font for printing high quality output from a laser printer, others require the user to purchase the Adobe *Sonata* printer font for that purpose. Fonts with special diacritics may be needed to produce vocal scores (see Figure 1). And there may be instances where a separate MIDI application will better serve certain purposes than the MIDI capability provided in music programs.

Special Hardware

Memory.—The Suggested Memory Size (in kilobytes) is listed in the Get Info window of each application described below. Under certain circumstances, however, music notation and other software can function with less than the suggested number of kilobytes.

MIDI and Sound.—The music programs described in this chapter have MIDI capability, for use with MIDI keyboards and other MIDI instruments which are connected to the computer with a MIDI interface (see Chapter 8, below). The sound produced by computer speakers is adequate at best. A marked improvement in output quality is obtained when the computer is connected to an amplifier with larger speakers.

Other Factors

Manufacturer's Reliability.—Important indicators include the time the product has been on the market, the number or type of upgrades that have been issued, and whether customer support services are offered.

Cost.—The estimated price given in the Summary for each program described below was derived from the quotations of mail-order vendors in *MacUser*, *Macworld*, and other Macintosh-oriented computer magazines. The cost-conscious user interested in producing orchestra or band full scores should note that inexpensive entry-level programs usually have a limited number of staves available for input in the New window. In this event, however, additional files can be constructed and printed for hard copy paste-up of the score.

CONCERTWARE+MIDI

ConcertWare.bmap

ConceWar

Music Writer

The software consists of three programs: *Music Writer, Music Player,* and *Instrument Maker*. Install the proprietary screen font (and laser font, if needed). To begin notation, double-click the Music Writer icon.

MUSIC WRITER

Main Window.—When **New** is selected from the opening dialog box, a window opens with fixed palette bars above and on the left (Figure 2). Their boxes and buttons are activated by mouse clicks, for entering or editing music. At the center of the New window is the default "music manuscript paper"—a piano system with a flashing vertical line as the insertion point. The page layout, however, can be freely formatted by way of the multi-function Ruler palette and its dialog box, to provide different staff and system combinations.

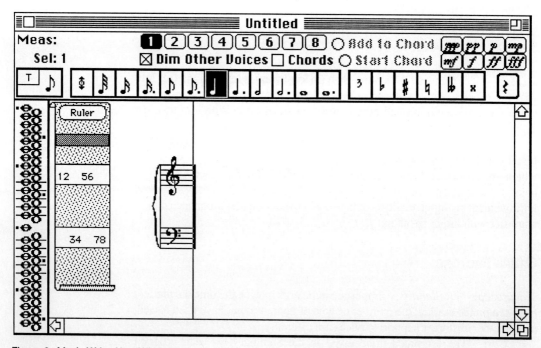

Figure 2. *Music Writer* New Window

A click on the Ruler button opens a dialog box with default selections—connector boxes, clef types, and voice distributions—for the piano system displayed in the New window (Figure 3).

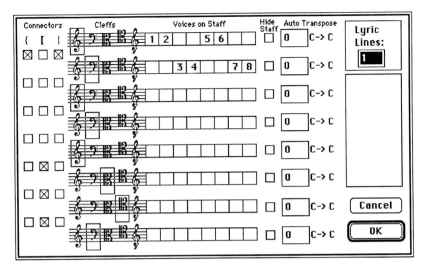

Figure 3. Ruler dialog box: default selections.

The next step is score construction: a maximum of eight staves per page is available in *MusicWriter* files. Figure 4 shows the Ruler format for a typical four-part chorus of mixed voices and accompaniment.

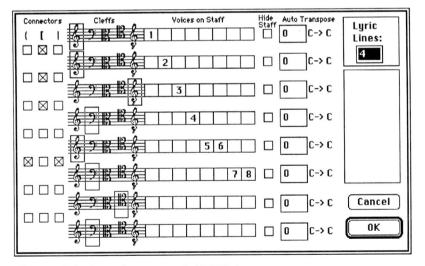

Figure 4. Ruler format for accompanied SATB chorus.

When the **OK** button is clicked, the New window reappears with a display of six staves, the related Ruler, and the assignment of Voices 1–8 to their respective staves (Figure 5). The white staff button for Voice 1, however, is temporarily hidden by the four gray lyric-line buttons.

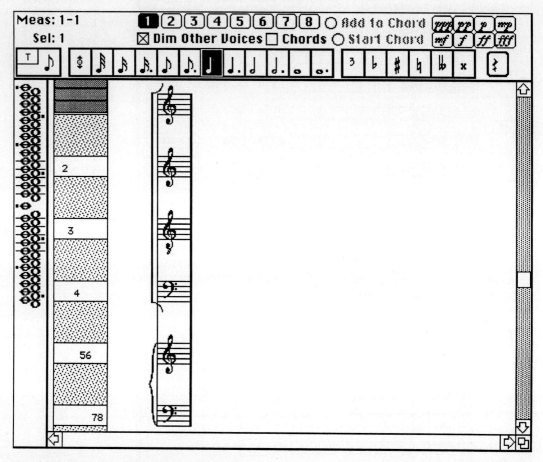

Figure 5. New Window Choral "Manuscript" Display.

The next step is insertion of key and time signatures. When **Key Signature...** is clicked in the Insert menu, a dialog box opens with C Major (A Minor) as the default radio button selection. The **Time Signature...** dialogue box has 4/4 as its default selection, which is entered if the **OK** button is clicked. The symbols for Common Time or *Alla Breve* can be entered if the related **Use...** box is selected together with the 4/4 or 2/2 radio buttons. When **Tempo Change...** is selected, a dialog box opens with options for placing a metronome mark at the insertion point (the default is M.M. $\bullet$ = 100).

Figure 6 illustrates the appropriate selections for insertion of the key of B♭ and *Alla Breve* time (refer to Figure 10 as an optional tutorial model).

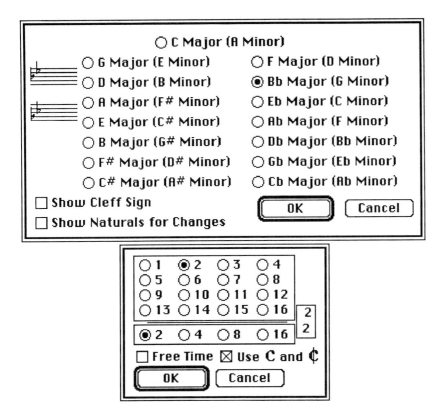

Figure 6. Dialog box selection of key and time signatures.

Entry of notation should begin with Voice 1—the default selection assigned to Staff 1—which may be a single note or a chord of up to eight notes. Although the flashing insertion point includes all staves, selection of a specific Voice button enables the automatic placement of notation on its assigned staff.

If the entry method is by mouse,

 1a. Click the desired note length box and, if needed,

  b. click the appropriate accidental box.

 2a. Click the pointer on a pitch class "button" (one of the vertical whole notes: the • symbol marks the pitch of C, from CC to c⁵), or

  b. click the Rest button (indicated by ⌡) to insert the appropriate rest length.

Each Voice may be entered separately or in alternation. Since each of the vocal staves is linked to a single Voice (1, 2, 3, 4), notate them in numeric order.

Part writing in the accompaniment is enabled by the Ruler assignment of Voices 5 and 6 to the treble staff and Voices 7 and 8 to the bass staff. These assignments, however, do not automatically align the Voices with their stems pointing in opposite directions. It is therefore necessary for the user to change stem directions after one or more Voices are entered.

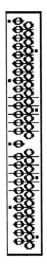

Notate

Remove Beam ⌘Y
Beam Up... ⌘U
Beam Down... ⌘I

Stems Up
Stems Down
Stems Mixed

To create four-part notation in the accompaniment:
1. Enter Voice 5.
2. Select the note or notes (click-drag).
3. Pull down the Notate menu.
4. Select **Stems Up.**

Voice 6 is entered the same way, but the menu selection is **Stems Down.** Repeat the same procedure for the bass staff.

The choral score in Figure 7 incorporates the basic input techniques discussed thus far, with the exception of the Voice 1 and 5 slurs in the second measure. To add slurs to notes:
1. Click on the Voice 1 button.
2. Select the two quarter-notes.
3. Pull down the Change menu.
4. Select **Slur Above.**
5. Repeat Steps 2–4 in Voice 5.

Change

Slur Above ⌘H
Slur Below ⌘J
Slur Both ⌘K
Remove Slur ⌘L

The arrows in the piano system are default editing options, to indicate stem direction in the window (see the **Preferences...** dialog box in the Edit menu), and are not printed. The slurs are automatically positioned by the program and can be deleted but not moved or reshaped.

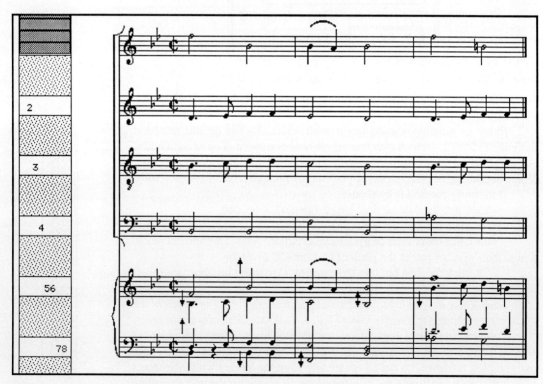

Figure 7. SANCTUS (Joseph Haydn, *Heilig-Messe*, 1796). Copyright © 1982 by Plymouth Music.

8

Text Insertion.—After the basic notation is completed, the next step is positioning of lyrics. The text menus and tools are located in the alternate palette (Figure 8) which is switched on when the **T** box is selected.

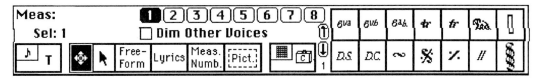

Figure 8. Text palette tools.

1. Select the desired text attributes from the **Font** and **Size** menus.

2. In addition to font style the Style menu has two options for placing text. **Gap Text** appears as the default style (that is, with a check mark), which provides automatic note and text spacing for variable word lengths, so that the first letter of each word or syllable is placed under its associated note. If **Centered** is also selected, the word or syllable will be centered under that note.

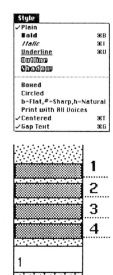

3. Select the **Mover** tool: a lyric-alignment ruled line appears for each gray lyric band and the pointer changes to four-way arrows. Reposition the uppermost (unnumbered gray) lyric band on the Ruler (= Voice 1 lyric) by dragging it with the **Mover** tool to the desired point below the Voice 1 (white) staff band. Then move the other lyric bands, in order, below their respective Voices 2, 3, 4.

4. Select the **Lyrics** box (the pointer changes to an I-beam), then click the I-beam on the Voice 1 lyric-alignment ruled line, directly under the first note. The I-beam changes to a flashing text-insertion point, inside a dashed rectangle.

5. Type the first word or syllable to be linked to the first note, then press the Tab key to move to the next note (or click the insertion point under the next note). Complete Voice 1 text entry.

6. Select the Voice 2 button and repeat steps 4 and 5 on the Voice 2 lyric-alignment ruled line. Follow the same steps for Voices 3, 4.

Entering Music Symbols.— The Music Symbol Library consists of fourteen numbered displays, each one containing fourteen boxed symbols. Move the pointer toward the adjoining vertical-arrow buttons next to the boxed music symbols, and place it on the upper or lower arrow. Click and hold until the appropriate symbol appears (Figure 9).

Select the desired symbol (the pointer will change to a cross), then click the pointer at the appropriate spot in the score. The symbol appears (enclosed by a temporary dotted rectangle) while the pointer changes to the **Mover** tool. When the symbols have been properly positioned, print a copy of the completed score for proofreading purposes (cf. Figure 10).

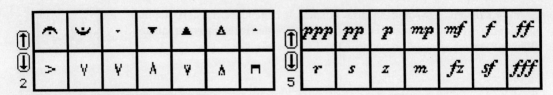

Figure 9. Music Symbol Library pp. 2 and 5.

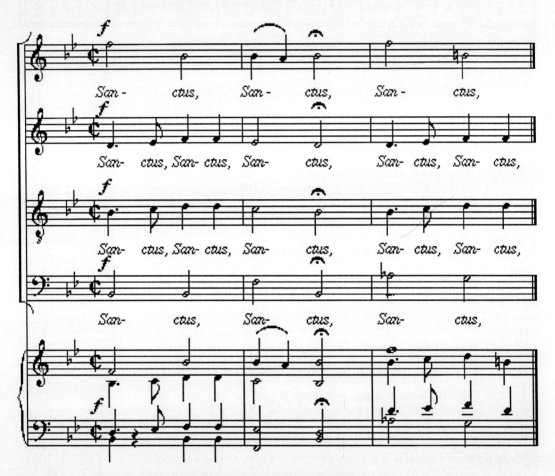

FIGURE 10. *Sanctus* window with added symbols and text (**Times** 12 italics).

Proofreading the Score.—Audiovisual proofreading is a particularly useful feature of desktop music processing. The following steps provide quick and easy error detection:

1. Select **Print...**from the File menu.

2. Click the **Print** button in the dialog box. When the printed score is

displayed, return to the notation palette (click ♪ in the **T** box) and pull down the Sound menu.

   3. Select the default (checked) **MIDI** option to uncheck it and thereby enable playback through the computer speaker.

   4. Pull down the Sound menu again and select **Play...** to begin playback and simultaneously open the related dialog box (Figure 11).

Stop Playing	Pause	☐ Repeat	☒ Vc1 ☒ Vc3 ☐ Vc5 ☐ Vc7
Stop and Move Insertion Point			☒ Vc2 ☒ Vc4 ☐ Vc6 ☐ Vc8

Figure 11. **Play...** dialog box (maximum non-MIDI selection: any four Voices).

   Title Page Layout.—When **Headers&Margins...** is selected in the File menu, a dialog box is displayed for entering titles (headers) and similar text matter; copyright notice, date, and other entries (footers); and instructions for pagination and margin format (Figure 12).

Title:	◉ Print Title, Comp., & Info
Composer:	
Information:	◯ Use on Player Screen Only
Copyright / Footer:	

Page Number Position		Margins	(Inches)
First Page: ◯ Left ◯ Right ◉ None		Music Left Margin:	0.500
Even Pages: ◉ Left ◯ Right ◯ None		Music Right Margin:	0.250
Odd Pages: ◯ Left ◉ Right ◯ None		Extra Indent for First Line:	0.500
First Page Number: 1 (Inches)			
Page Number Side Margin: 0.000		Cancel	OK
Page Number Top Margin: 0.000			

Figure 12. **Headers&Margins...** dialog box

   Only one font can be used for text entry and page numbers, which is selected in the **Preferences...** dialog box. Header text is automatically centered at the top of p. 1 of the score. Footer text, on the other hand. is placed at the bottom of each page. Since headers and footers are not displayed in the score window, text matter must be proofread by printing the page or previewing it by way of the

File menu **Print...** dialog boxes. An alternative approach to text handling, that can provide high-quality output (Figure 13), is transfer of the file to a graphics program for enhancement of the score (see Chapter 2, below).

Figure 13. *SuperPaint*-enhanced Apple LaserWriter output.

Keyboard Entry of Notation.—Notes, rests, accidentals, and triplets can be entered from the computer keyboard—as an alternative to or together with mouse input—when **Step Time Entry** is selected in the Sound menu (Figure 14). Keyboard entry is disabled, however, if **MIDI** is also selected.

MUSIC NOTATION

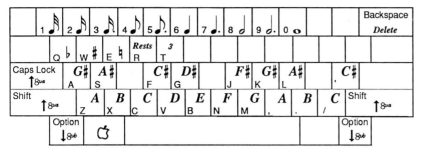

Figure 14. *MusicWriter*-Macintosh keyboard input equivalents.

SUMMARY

The first version of *ConcertWare+MIDI* appeared in 1984 and the present upgrade (Version 5), in 1989. The proprietary screen and printer fonts, and the Adobe *Sonata* screen font, are included in the package. For practical reasons, an illustrated presentation of the *Music Player* and *Instrument Maker* programs could not be included.

The Pros.—*MusicWriter* is an inexpensive, entry-level program for music notation, and it is useful for various individual, classroom, or non-professional publication purposes. Music can be entered with the mouse alone or by combining it with the computer keyboard and/or a MIDI keyboard. The various menus offer powerful editing features, such as transposition, duration changes, and much more.

The Cons.—Ledger-line notes have identical stem lengths, except when flagged notes are beamed together. Flagged-note groupings are connected with straight beams. The program enters slurs and ties, which have the same contour and cannot be moved or altered after they are placed. Only two slurs or ties (one above, one below the notes or stems) can be placed when chords with three or more notes are linked. The precise placement of text—other than lyrics—and placement of certain graphics in the Music Symbol Library would be considerably facilitated if a Zoom In/Out command or tool were available.

DELUXE MUSIC CONSTRUCTION SET

The application includes the Adobe *Sonata* screen font, the *DMCS* proprietary fonts, and the Font/DA Mover for installing the fonts in the System Folder. There is, too, a Voice Editor subprogram, activated by pressing a special key combination in the *DMCS* program, which could not be included here. If laser printer output is intended, the *Sonata* printer font is needed for high quality copy. Since the printer font is not included in the package, the user can obtain it from the

DMCS Fonts

Deluxe Music v.2.5

manufacturer (Adobe Systems) or a software vendor. To begin notation, double-click the *DMCS* icon.

Main Screen.—The default display consists of three active windows: (New) Score, Note Palette, and Piano Keyboard. The scrolling Score window contains a double-staff system, with the insertion point flashing on the treble staff, the non-printing < > marks (= **Begin Section**, **End Section**; see the Play menu) at the top of the score, and the bar number below the bass staff (automatically inserted by the program in the first bar of each system). When the arrow pointer is moved onto the score, it changes to a quarter note as the default Note Palette selection (Figure 15).

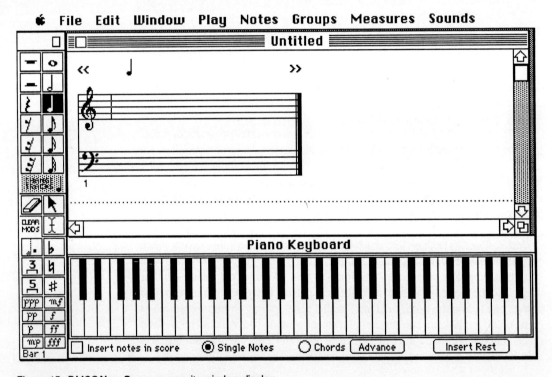

Figure 15. *DMCS* **New Score** composite window display.

If the arrow pointer is selected in the Note Palette, each window can be clicked—to display its title bar—and freely positioned elsewhere, or closed and thereafter reopened from the Window menu. The Score window also can be resized to the dimensions of the full screen. When **Score Setup** is selected in the menu, a dialog box—partitioned in two sections by a ruled line—is displayed as an independent fourth window for formatting purposes. Figure 16 shows the

MUSIC NOTATION

dialog box default settings, where the upper section has slider, box, and button controls for global settings, and the the lower one has similar controls, including radio buttons, which affect specific staves only.

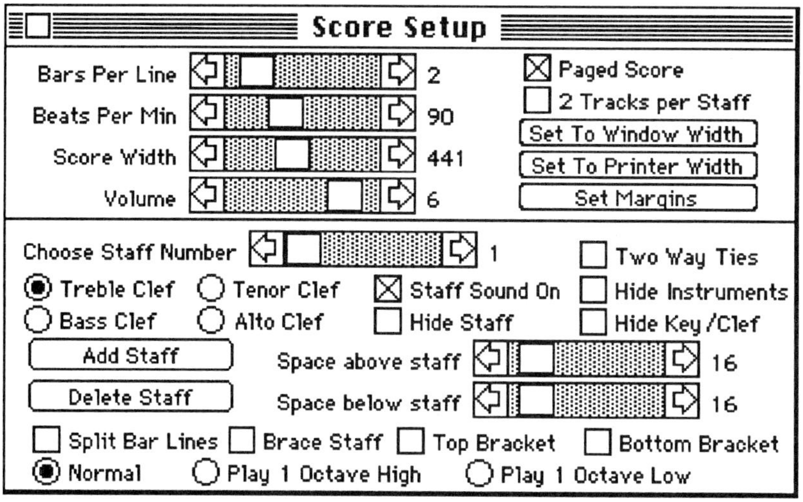

Figure 16. **Score Setup** dialog box with default settings.

In order to compare *DMCS* with *Concertware+MIDI*—they are the only entry-level, inexpensive programs currently available for music notation—the following procedures (illustrated in Figure 17) will provide a similar type of score for four-part chorus of mixed voices and accompaniment. The suggested measurements, beginning with the upper section of the **Score Setup** dialog box, are entered as follows:

1. Select **Score Setup** in the Window menu.

2. Change the four sliders in the upper section of the dialog box by clicking their right or left arrows or dragging their scroll boxes, to read:
   •Bars Per Line: **3**.
   •Beats Per Minute: **72**.
   •Score Width: **556** (or click the Set to Printer Width button).
   •Volume: **6**.

3. Keep the default Paged Score selection and click the 2 Tracks per Staff box. Whenever the Set to Printer Width button is clicked, the Score Width slider will read **556** (pixels) and the system(s) will extend accordingly.

4. Click the Set Margin button to display its dialog box, type **108** in the Title Space box and **72** in both Left Indent boxes, then click the **OK** button.

Since upper-section settings affect the entire choral score, change in the number of bars, width of the score, tracks per staff, or margin values should only be made when global revision is necessary.

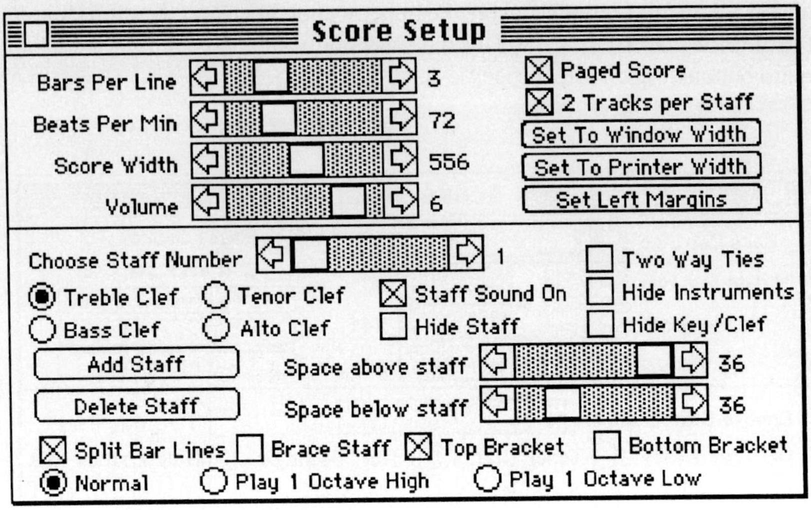

Figure 17. Dialog box settings for accompanied SATB chorus.

The lower section of the Score Setup dialog box is devoted exclusively to the format of individual staves and systems. Most of the formatting controls are specifically linked to whatever staff number is displayed on the right side of the Choose Staff Number slider. During notation, this slider also displays the number of whatever staff contains the flashing insertion point. It should be noted that *DMCS* allows a maximum of 48 staves for notation purposes.

Precede score construction by resizing the Score window to the full length of the screen (the window will temporarily cover the dialog box and the Piano Keyboard), and bring the hidden dialog box to the front by selecting **Score Setup** in the Window menu. The following steps will format a typical single-system title page, including the copyright notice:

1. Choose Staff Number **1** (= Soprano voice).
   •Click Treble Clef button, Split Bar Lines box, and Top Bracket box.
   •Space Above Staff: 36, Space Below Staff: 36.
2. Choose Staff Number **2** (= Alto voice).
   •Click Treble Clef button and Split Bar Line box.
   •Space Above Staff: 36, Space Below Staff: 36.
3. Click Add Staff button to display Staff **3** (= Tenor voice, treble clef).
   •Click Split Bar Line box.
   •Space Above Staff: 36, Space Below Staff: 36.
4. Click Add Staff button to display Staff **4** (= Bass voice).
   •Click Bass Clef button, Split Bar Line box, and Bottom Bracket box.
   •Space Above Staff: 36, Space Below Staff: 36.
5. Click Add Staff button to display Staff **5** (= Piano voice, treble clef).
   •Click Brace Staff box.
   •Space Above Staff: 52, Space Below Staff: 20.

6. Click Add Staff button to display Staff **6** (= Piano voice, bass clef).
   •Click Bass Clef button and Brace Staff box.
   •Space Above Staff: 20, Space Below Staff: 90.

Figure 18. Reduced view of **Score** window printout.

Since the program lacks reduction capability or a preview display of the Score window, a printed copy (see Figure 18) is the only way the user can evaluate the settings in the Score Setup dialog box.

Measures
Set Time Signature ...
Set Key Signature ...
Set Clef ...
Set Instrument   ⌘;
Erase Instrument
Set Tempo
Erase Tempo
Insert Measure
Split Measure
Join Measures
Delete Measure
ReAlign Measure

The insertion of key and time signatures begins in the Measures menu. When **Set Key Signature...** is selected, a dialog box opens with C maj/A Min as the default. The **Set Time Signature...** default is 4/4. It should be noted that Common Time and *Alla Breve* symbols are not provided.

If **Set Tempo** is selected, the metronome mark, ♩ = **72**, appears above the first staff, as set in the Beats Per Min. slider in the Score Setup dialog box (see Figure 17; the default number in Figure 16 is **90**). In order to change the M.M. value in the Score window, select **Erase Tempo** to delete the mark, set the new value in the dialog box, and select **Set Tempo** again.

Figure 19 illustrates the appropriate dialog box selections for insertion of the key of F and 3/4 time.

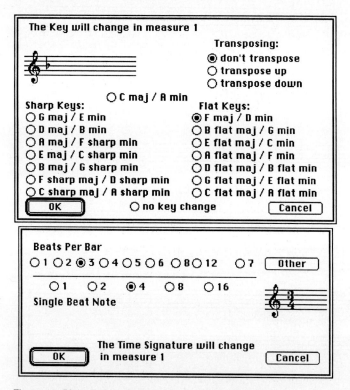

Figure 19. Dialog box selection of key and time signatures.

Notation begins at the default insertion point which flashes in Staff 1. Since the global 2 Tracks per Staff was previously checked in the Score Setup dialog box, all note stems should point up as the default selection in the Palette Window (if not, click the **Change Tracks** icon).

Although the steps outlined further below are limited to mouse selection of notes, rests, and dynamics in the Note Palette, users with keyboard experience

18   MUSIC NOTATION

may prefer to experiment with mouse selections in the Piano Keyboard window (MIDI keyboard input is discussed in Chapter 8, below). And it should be noted that:

•When an icon is clicked, the pointer changes to the selected symbol. If the pointer is a note, and the notehead is clicked on a staff (or ledger) line or space, the related pitch will be sounded.

•Notes and rests temporarily appear in Outline font style as they are inserted—to indicate they are selected—and can be removed by pressing the Delete (Back Space) key, or freely moved vertically and horizontally.with the Arrow pointer. Each successive entry reverts the preceding outlined symbol to Normal font style.

•When an entered value exceeds the designated meter, the outlined symbol appears in gray and therefore should be deleted.

Referring to Figure 20 as the tutorial model:

1. Notate Staff 1, select notes on or above the middle staff line, then choose **Flip Note Stem** in the Notes menu. Select the rests and drag them down to their proper position (when the pitch sounds b♭!).

2. Notate Staff 2 and Staff 3 (the Choose Staff Number slider in the Score Setup dialog box automatically displays the number of the staff containing the insertion point). Drag the whole rests in Staff 3 to the center of the bar.

Notes	
Up Half Step	⌘U
Down Half Step	⌘J
Up Level	⌘I
Down Level	⌘K
Up Octave	⌘O
Down Octave	⌘L
Invert Chord Up	
Invert Chord Down	
Half Time	⌘H
Double Time	⌘D
Flip Note Stem	⌘F
Set Play Style ...	⌘V

Figure 20. *Serve The Lord With Gladness* (Antonio Caldera).

3. Since Staff 4 is in the bass clef, each rest should be dragged down till the pitch sounds D. Drag the whole rests to the center of the bar.

4. Notate the chords in Staff 5 by clicking the pointer notehead directly above or below a note. After entering the upper part in Bar 3:

  •Select **Change Tracks.**
  •Click the insertion point at Beat 1.
•Select the ♩ icon and enter the chord.
  •Select the 𝄽 icon and enter the rests.

5. To adjust the position of the rests in the lower part, select the Arrow pointer and drag each rest down till the pitch sounds b♭.

6. Select **Change Tracks**, then the rest on Beat 1, and drag upwards till it sounds g².

7. Notate Staff 6.

Insertion of Lyrics.—After the basic notation is completed, the next step is entry and positioning of text lines. The text tool is the I-beam icon in the Palette Window; when it is selected, the Sounds menu is replaced by the Fonts menu. Before entering lyrics, it is important to note that:

•The default size for all fonts is 9 Point, and the default font is Geneva. Whether Geneva or the suggested New York font is selected, pull down the Font menu, choose **Set Size…**to display its dialog box, and click the **12** radio button.

•The Page Setup… dialog box—displayed when **Print Score…** is selected in the File menu—shows all Printer Effects as default choices. Deactivate the **Font Substitution?** box by clicking it.

1. Scroll the Score Window to display the three bars of Staff 1.

2. Select the text tool icon in the Palette Window.

3. Place the I-beam pointer below the staff and to the left of the note head, then click and drag the dotted-line text box to the end of Bar 3.

•Release the mouse button. Two text-box handles (■) appear: the upper-left handle freely positions the box; the lower-right handle resizes it.

4. Enter the first word at the flashing insertion point.

5. Place the I-beam on the upper-left handle, press and hold down the mouse button, and note the present-position readout at the upper-left corner of the Score Window.

•Using the readout as the guide, drag the text box to **left:32, top: 25**.

6. Carefully release the button (do not move the mouse!). The word should be more or less centered under the first note (Figure 21).

•Enter the other words, using the Space Bar to center them under the respective note heads (the Tab key has the same function as the Space Bar).

7. Staff 2 option: instead of repeating the procedure, select and copy the Staff 1 lyric.

  •Execute Step 3.
  •Paste the lyric (Edit menu or Command-V).
  •Execute Step 5.

8. Staff 3 and Staff 4 option: copy the first two words of the Staff 1 lyric, then follow the Execute and Paste procedure in Step 7.

Fonts

▲
✓**New York**
 Palatino
 Petrucci
 Shpfltnat
 Sonata
 SuperFrench
 Symbol
 Times
 TSuperFrench
 Venice
 Zapf Chancery
 Zapf Dingbats

 Set Size ...
 Set Style...

Figure 21. Text box location procedure.

The readout is based on positive and negative numbers, where 0 is:

•A horizontal point slightly to the left of the first note or rest in each bar.

•A vertical point, when the positioning handle is anywhere on the middle line of the staff (as if the handle were a half rest).

•(A negative number indicates a position to the left or above 0.)

Other Text Blocks.—The following font specifications and location readouts are suggested:

•Voices: Times 12; left: -103, top: -6; Piano and Organ: the same, except top: -51, Staff 6.

•Tempo mark: Times Bold 14; left: -19, top: -49.

•Title: Times 24; left: 2, top:-170.

•Subtitle: Times 10; left: 73; top: -145.

•Composer and Editor or Arranger : Times 12 Caps; left: 77, top: -103 (or -82 if composer only),
Staff 1, Bar **2**.

•Copyright footer (Staff **6**, Bar 1): Times 12; left: -61, top: 60.

If a laser printer is unavailable for the production of high quality copy, use the New York font instead of Times. In this case, however, some minor adjustment of the location readouts will be necessary.

Entering Music Symbols.— Select the *p* icon: the pointer changes to that symbol. Enter it in the piano system and above the vocal staves.

Proofreading the Score.—The Play menu contains useful commands to control playback. Specific notes or bars can be played or repeated: click the insertion point at the desired location and select **Begin Section** <<, then click elsewhere and select **End Section** >>.

Figure 22 illustrates the title page of the tutorial score, processed without need for a supplementary graphics program. In the event graphic enhancement or other procedure is necessary, the *DMCS* file can be exported by choosing **Select All**, followed by **Copy** (Command-C) in the Edit menu, then **Paste** (Command-V) in the Scrapbook, a graphics program, and/or a word processor.

Play	
✓Play Song	⌘P
Play Section	⌘S
Stop Play	⌘Q
Resume Play	⌘R
Begin Section <<	⌘<
End Section >>	⌘>
Flash Notes	
Player Piano	
Repeat Play	
External Speaker	⌘E

Figure 22. Apple LaserWriter output of *Deluxe Music Construction Set* file.

Keyboard-Assisted Notation.—Other than **Change Tracks**, each icon in the Note Palette has one or two keyboard equivalents (Figure 23). And the keyboard can be operated in tandem with the mouse (the most efficient method in terms of quick error correction and other editing functions), the Piano Keyboard window, or a MIDI instrument.

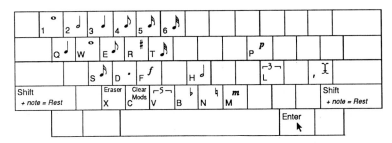

Figure 23. Note Palette keyboard equivalents.

SUMMARY

The first version of *Deluxe Music Construction Set* appeared in 1985 and the present upgrade (Version 2.5), in 1989. The proprietary bitmapped fonts and the Adobe *Sonata* screen font are included in the package.

The Pros.—Deluxe Music Construction Set is an inexpensive, entry-level program for music notation and an excellent example of user-friendly music software. Page layout is easy to control or change, and the ingenious use of graphics is apparent when the pointer assumes the shape of whatever symbol is selected from the Note Palette. Individual notes can be dragged to new staff positions, sounding identifying pitches and simultaneously flashing their respective keys on the Piano Keyboard. Chords can be restructured and repositioned the same way, and text matter can be precisely inserted, resized, and freely moved at any time. Angled beams connect ascending or descending flagged notes. The various menus offer powerful editing features, such as transposition, duration changes, beaming flagged notes, slur insertion, free repositioning of bar lines, and much more.

The Cons.— The Note Palette ranges from whole notes to thirty-second notes and rests. Additional palettes are not provided for other music symbols: the user must rely on time-consuming exploration and selection of needed characters from the Sonata font. Slurs and ties cannot be moved or altered after they are placed by the program. Bar numbers—automatically placed by the program under the first bar in each staff or system—cannot be deleted or moved elsewhere. Among other needed additions are a Ruler, Insert Column command, and Preview Window option.

MusicProse™

MusicProse
Screen Fonts

Petru

Sevil

MusicProse

The application includes the proprietary *Petrucci* music fonts and *Seville* guitar fingerboard fonts. Install the Petrucci font (and *Petru* laser font, if needed). In addition, many kinds of instrumental and vocal scores are available in the *MusicProse* Templates Folder. This tutorial, however, opens with the suggested procedure for score construction from the onset. To begin notation, double-click the *MusicProse* icon.

Main Screen.—The default display consists of two active windows: the **New** window and the **Main Tool Palette**. The default staff is one measure with a treble clef, Common Time signature, and whole rest. The palette can be independently opened and closed or freely positioned elsewhere (Figure 24).

Staff

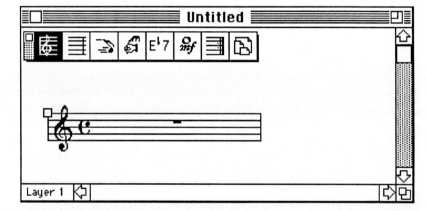

Figure 24. *MusicProse* **New** window composite display.

Since the Staff icon is the default selection, its related menu appears at the end of the Menu Bar.

    1. Select the staff by clicking the arrow pointer in the square handle on the fifth line.

    •If the mouse button is held down, the staff can be freely dragged. Alternatively, it can be erased with the **Delete (Back Space)** key.

    •Either action is restored to its original state if **Undo** is immediately chosen in the **Edit** menu.

    2. Choose **Add Staves...** in the **Staff** menu, to display its dialog box, type **5**, and click the **OK** button to construct a six-stave system for accompanied mixed chorus.

    3. Select the third staff and choose **Staff Attributes...** in the **Staff** menu, to display the dialog box (Figure 25).

    •Select the treble clef with joined **8**.

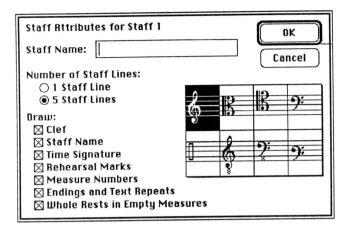

Figure 25. **Staff Attributes...** dialog box.

4. Select the fourth staff and repeat Step 3. Exception: select the bass clef.

5. Select the sixth staff, then repeat Step 3 and select the bass clef.

6. The last step is addition of system brackets. Select the the fifth staff and choose **Brackets...** in the **Staff** menu. When the dialog box is displayed, click the Brace icon to select it, then the **OK** button.

Brackets

•The brace appears in small size, with two handles. Select and drag the lower handle down, until the horizontal crosshair of the insertion point is hidden by the bottom line of the sixth staff. Release the mouse button.

•Select the **Soprano** staff handle and repeat the procedure, this time clicking the square Bracket (middle icon) and dragging its lower handle down to the bottom line of the **Bass** staff. **Save** the file and name it **Tutorial**.

Figure 26. Choral score with default signs and rests.

Measure

Measure	
Add Measures...	⌘M
Insert Measures...	
Change Key...	
Change Meter...	
Change Clef...	
Change Barline...	

Click the Measure icon to replace the the **Staff** menu with the **Measure** menu. Choose **Add Measures...** to display its dialog box, and type **2** to construct a three-measure system (Figure 26). Be sure to **Save** the file now and at frequent intervals during the Tutorial.

Select the first measure in the Soprano staff and choose **Change Key...** in the **Measure** menu.

1. When the default dialog box appears, click once on the down arrow in the Scroll box to display the F key signature, then click the radio button marked **Selected Region Through End of Piece** (Figure 27).

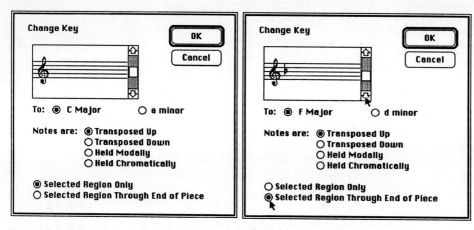

Figure 27. **Change Key...** dialog box C Major (default) and F Major signatures.

Now choose **Change Meter...** in the **Measure** menu. The default dialog box opens with the Common Time sign.

2. Click the **Abbreviate Meter** box to uncheck it and thereby replace the sign with 4/4 (Figure 28).

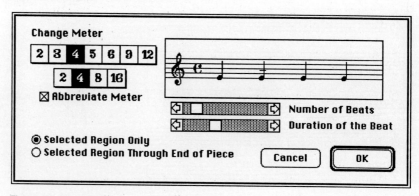

Figure 28. **Change Meter...** default dialog box.

Select the second and third measures in the Soprano staff.

3. Drag the arrow pointer to enclose the measures in a marquee (that is, a dotted-line selection rectangle) or hold down the Shift key and click them.

Choose **Change Meter...** to display its dialog box and change the meter sign from 4/4 to 3/4.

•Click the **3** box or click once on the left arrow in the **Number of Beats** Scroll box.

Music Notation.—Click the Entry icon to replace the the **Measure** menu with the **Entry** menu. If the **Simple Entry** palette (Figure 29) is not displayed, choose **Show Simple Entry Tools** in the **Entry** menu.

Entry

Figure 29. **Simple Entry** palette.

Select the Half-Note tool and move the arrow pointer to the first measure of the Soprano staff.

1. Click the tip of the pointer on the fourth line to enter the note D.

2. The default rest is replaced by the note.

3. If the entry is incorrect, select the eraser tool and click above or below the note head to delete it, then enter the note again.

Complete the choral notation illustrated in Figure 30.

Figure 30. Simple entry notation of Béla Bartók, *Evening in Transylvania.* Copyright © 1981 by Plymouth Music.

1. The eighth-note pairs are automatically beamed while the notes are entered. To create a beamed group of four eighth-notes, select the Beam tool and click the third eighth-note in the first two measures (A and C, respectively).

2. A dot can be added to the half-note by selecting the Dot tool and clicking the note. To remove the dot, select the Half-Note tool and click the dotted note.

3. Two notes can be tied when the Tie tool is selected and the first note of the pair is clicked.

Since the opening measures of the piano accompaniment are intended for rehearsal purposes only, each piano staff will require part-writing, that is, in two layers. Clarity is achieved if (a) Staff 5 has the Soprano part with stems pointing upward and whole rests placed under the first line, and (b) Staff 6 has the Alto and Tenor.parts, also pointing upward but notated in thirds, and whole rests placed under the first line.

1. Select **Layer Attributes...** in the **Edit** menu to display its dialog box.

2. Type **-6** in place of **0** in the Layer 2 **Steps** box (Figure 31).

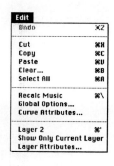

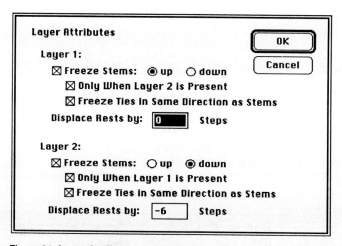

Figure 31. **Layer Attributes...** dialog box.

3. Notate the Soprano part, including beaming and tie signs, in Staff 5.

4. Click the Layer 1 box at the bottom left corner of the window to switch to Layer 2.

•Select the Whole-Note tool and enter the note in the first measure.

•Click the whole note to transform it to its displaced position as a whole rest (Layer 1 is automatically transformed to upward-pointing notation).

5. Notate the Alto and Tenor parts as ledger-line parallel thirds in the bass, in Staff 6.

•Repeat Step 4 (Figure 32).

Figure 32. Simple entry of the piano score for rehearsal purposes.

Text Insertion.—The underlying principle in *MusicProse* is to link text matter according to function.

    1. Words or syllables are inserted by clicking specific notes, have extensor handles attached to them, and are movable as such or as textlines.

    2. Staff Names are fixed attributes, that is, they are attached to specific staves and cannot be repositioned.

    3. Text Expressions and Rehearsal Marks are inserted by clicking specific measures and can be repositioned.

    4. Text Blocks, Headers and Footers are page entries that can also serve as an alternate method for inserting the other types of text matter listed above.

    Figure 32 illustrates the following preliminary steps to replace the default Geneva font:

    1. Select the **Edit** menu, choose **Global Options...** to display its dialog box, then click the **Lyrics** button to display the **Set Font** dialog box.

    2. Scroll the Font list until **Times** (laser printers) or **New York** (other printers) is selected.

    3. Select the same font for the **Text Blocks** button.

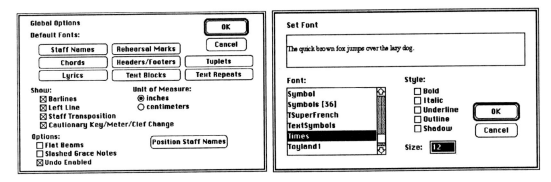

Figure 33. **Global Options...** and **Set Font** dialog boxes.

    Next follows placement of the lyrics in the score.

    1. Select the Lyric icon, to display the **Lyric** menu.

    2. Choose **Mass Create...**, to display its dialog box, and type this lyric:
In the vil-lage chil-dren sing-ing, Zm! sing-ing, (Figure 34).

Lyric

Lyric
Click Assignment...
Position Adjustment
Word Extension
Lyric Shift

✓Mass Create...
Lyric Options...

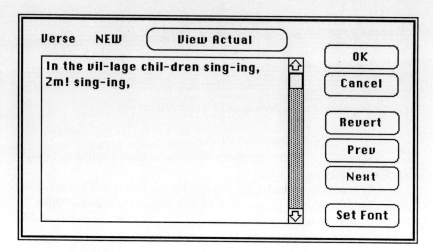

Figure 34. **Mass Create...** dialog box with lyric (note the insertion of hyphens).

     3. Click and hold down the **View Actual** button to verify that the lyric is set in Times or New York font (if not, see Figure 33 and the instructions concerning Global Options).
     4. Choose **Click Assignment** in the **Lyric** menu.
         •The lyric, set in Times font, appears in a special window (Figure 35).

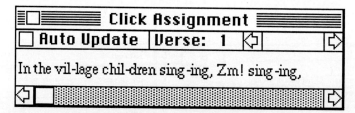

Figure 35. **Click Assignment** window for lyric placement.

     5. Position the arrow pointer on the first note of the Soprano part and click once. The first word of the lyric, "In", appears under the note.
     6. Referring to Figure 36, click the eighth-notes that are to be assigned a word or syllable.
     7. Click the first measure of the Alto staff.
         •The Base Line Position box moves down to Staff 2, with its triangle pointing at the insertion path.
         •Click the half-note and two eighth-notes with "Zm! sing-ing,".
     8. Click the first measure of the Tenor staff.
         •The Base Line Position box moves down to Staff 3.

•Be sure to click the right arrow or drag the box in the lower Scroll Bar of the **Click Assignment** window until "Zm! sing-ing," is displayed.

9. Click the half-note and two eighth-notes.

•If the Base Line Position triangle is dragged, the entire text line moves with it.

Lyrics that underlie tied or slurred notes should have extensions (that is, ruled lines) added to the related text. The program provides them by way of a handle at the end of each word and syllable, that can be dragged to variable lengths.

1. Select **Word Extension** in the **Lyric** menu, press and hold down the Option key, and click the arrow pointer in the first measure of Staff 1.

•Word Extension handles are displayed.

2. Click and drag the handle of the first word to a position under the tied eighth-note.

3. Referring to Figure 36 as a guide, option-click the other measures and drag the relevant Word Extension handles accordingly.

Figure 36. The choral score with assigned lyrics.

Page Layout.—The default position of the staves within the system is too close and requires additional leading (that is, vertical space) to provide room for needed articulations, dynamics, and text expressions. Since the program does not include a ruler, the following procedure should provide fairly accurate leading.

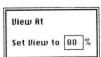

1. Choose **View at X%...** in the **View** menu and type **80** in the dialog box.

2. Select the Staff icon to display the six staff handles.

•The bracket and brace handles also appear.

3. Press and hold down the Shift key while the arrow pointer is clicked in the handles of Staff 2–6. A dot appears in each selected handle.

4. Release the Shift key and select **Group Staves** in the **Staff** menu, to lock the selections for movement in unison.

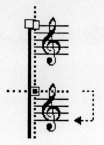

5. Click the Staff 2 handle again, holding down the mouse button.

•A dotted crosshair cursor appears, whose horizontal line is positioned on the top line of the staff.

6. Drag the crosshair down to the bottom line of the staff and release the mouse button: the handles are deselected and ungrouped.

7. Repeat Steps 3–6 for each of the lower staves, beginning with Staff 3 (Tenor).

•Exception: Staff 5 (Piano Treble) should be given extra leading, to provide space for the tempo expression.

8. Carefully drag the bottom handle of the bracket and the brace until the crosshair is positioned on the bottom line of Staff 4 and 6, respectively.

Figure 37 pictures the expanded system, ready for the additional formatting necessary to create the first (title) page of a choral score.

Figure 37. Reformatted system with additional leading.

32

1. Choose **Adjust Staff Systems...** in the **Page** menu, to display its dialog box (Figure 38).

•The dotted rectangle pictures the position, width, and length of the expanded system in relation to the solid rectangle. And the latter represents the print area of letter-size (8-1/2 X 11-inch) paper.

2. Click the already selected upper handle of the rectangle and slowly drag it down toward the lower handle. Release the mouse button when the upper readout is about **-1.87** and the left readout, **0.66**

•The lower and right readouts should read **0**. If not, click-drag the lower handle of the rectangle accordingly.

Page

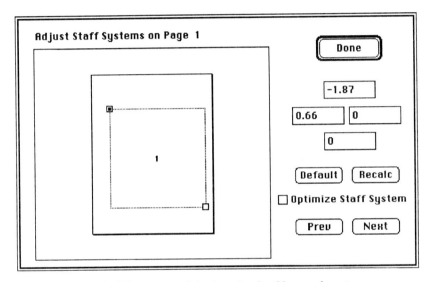

Figure 38. **Adjust Staff Systems...** dialog box showing title page format.

The next procedure is insertion of articulations, dynamics, and text blocks. Select the Expression icon to display its menu, then choose **Show Articulation Palette** and **Show Dynamics Palette**. Also choose **View at 100%** in the **View** menu (Figure 39).

Expression

Figure 39. **Expression** menu with Articulation and Dynamics dialog boxes.

1. Click the arrow pointer in the *marcato* accent (>) icon, then click directly above the half-note in Staff 1.
  •If necessary, click-drag the accent handle to reposition it.
2. Repeat Step 1 for the first eighth-note in Staff 2 and 3 and the same half-note and eighth-notes in Staff 5 and 6
3. Referring to Figure 40 as a guide, click and place the *mf*, *sfz*, and *mp* signs in the score.

Figure 40. Choral score with articulations, dynamics, and text expressions.

Although the same menu provides a list of Text Expressions which require one dialog box for editing purposes and another for inserting the expressions into the score, the following Text Block method is suggested as an alternative:

1. Select the Page icon and choose **Add Text Block...** in the **Page** menu.

Page

2. Click the **Set Font** button in the dialog box to display the **Set Font** dialog box.

•The Font list and Size box should show Times or New York 12, as previously selected in the **Global Options...** procedure (see Figure 33). Click the **Italic** box, then click **OK** to return to the **Add Text Block** dialog box.

3. Type **espressivo**. Use the **View Actual** button to verify the font attributes, then click **OK**.

4. The expression with its handle appears in the left margin of the score, above Staff 1.

•Click-drag the handle to position the text after the *mf* sign in Staff 1 and 5.

5. Repeat Steps 1–4 for each of three occurrences of **dim.** and two of **Lento, rubato.**

•Exception: set the tempo expression in **Bold 14**.

The last procedure is insertion of titles, subtitles, staff names, and a copyright notice. Here, too, the **Add Text Block...** insertion method can replace headers, footers, and the Staff Name placement option in the **Staff Attributes...** dialog box (see Figure 25).

When the score is completed, it can be saved as an EPS (Encapsulated PostScript) file for high quality laser printing. Choose **Compile PostScript Listing...** in the **File** menu, click the boxes and radio buttons as shown in Figure 42, then click the **Compile** button.

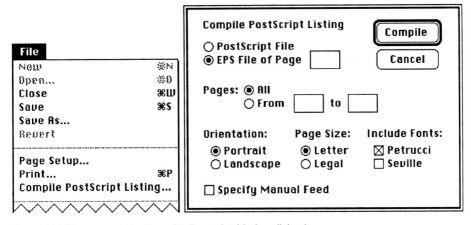

Figure 41. **File** menu and its **Compile Postscript Listing** dialog box.

Figure 42 displays the EPS file of the completed tutorial which, if printed on laser paper, is suitable as a reproduction proof for publication purposes. The additional text blocks are also set in Times font, and the styles and point sizes listed below are the same as they appear in the original publication.

- •Composition Title: **24.**
- •Type of Chorus and Composer: **14.**
- •Transcriber: **12 Caps.**
- •Other Text Matter: **12 Italic.**
- •Staff Names: **12 Bold.**
- •Copyright Notice: **12.**

Figure 42. Final copy of the choral tutorial in EPS file format.

Keyboard-Assisted Notation.—Figure 43 indicates the keys and related palette tools as an alternative to mouse selection in Simple Entry mode. The same tools are selected by the numeric keypad, with the addition of the Clear key for selecting the Eraser tool and the dual-function Plus (♯ or ✕)and Minus (♭ or ♭♭) keys.

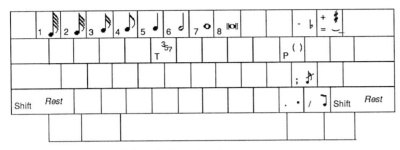

Figure 43. Simple Entry Palette keyboard equivalents.

In Speedy Entry mode—including MIDI input—a click of the arrow pointer in a measure places a cursor with its pitch insertion bar on the middle line of the staff. The Arrow Up and Arrow Down keys, certain letter keys, or the arrow pointer may be used to reposition the insertion bar to the desired pitch. Thereafter, the number keys (see Figure 43) are pressed to insert the durations.

SUMMARY

The first version of *MusicProse* appeared in 1989, and the present upgrade (Version 2.1), in 1991 The proprietary bitmapped and printer *Petrucci* fonts are included, and registered owners receive *Coda Notes,* a quarterly newsletter.

The Pros.—*MusicProse* is a moderately priced, intermediate-level program for music notation. Page layout is easy to control, text attributes can be freely intermixed in lyrics or text blocks, and one or more ledger lines are added to the cursor for precise entry of notes above or below the staff. Handles are provided to freely reposition notational entries, text blocks, expressions, and other elements. Slurs are adjustable, and the construction and the insertion of lyrics are quick and easy.

The Cons.—The reduction capability of the Grace Note Tool is not applicable to the notation of small-head groupings. A graphic Ruler is needed for precise alignment of text blocks or staff spacing in Page View. Ties cannot be adjusted nor handles grouped. Editing commands, such as Cut, Copy, and Paste are applicable only in conjunction with the Measure and Lyric tools, and *MusicProse* files cannot be saved in MacPaint or PICT document formats.

Finale

Finale Screen Fonts

Petru

Sevil

NewStaff

FINALE

The application shares many features with its offshoot *MusicProse*, including the proprietary *Petrucci* music fonts, *Seville* guitar fingerboard fonts, and several instrumental and vocal score templates. This tutorial provides the suggested procedure for score construction from the onset. Install the *Petrucci* fonts and double-click the *Finale* icon to begin notation.

Main Screen.—The New window display has a fixed Main Tool Palette.and a default staff consisting of one measure with a treble clef, Common Time signature, and whole rest. An additional default selection is the New Staff Tool, which adds a square selection handle on the top line of the staff. (Figure 44).

Figure 44. *Finale* New window display.

The following procedures will create a score for five-part chorus (SSATB) with keyboard accompaniment.

1. While the Option key is depressed, click the crosshair cursor on the staff handle to display the Staff Usage List dialog box.
   •Click the **Add...** button to display the New Staves dialog box.
   •Type **6** in the Number of Staves box and click the **O.K.** buttons to return to the Main Screen. (Figure 45).
   •**Save** the file and name it **Tutorial**.

(An alternative method of construction is to reformat the SATB Choral/Piano Template in the *Finale* Templates Folder.)

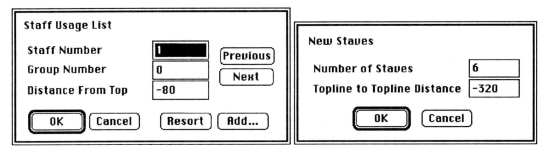

Figure 45. Staff Usage List and New Staves dialog boxes.

2. Select the Staff Attributes Tool.
   •The staff handles are repositioned.
3. Click the Staff 4 (Tenor voice) handle to display the Staff Attributes dialog box.
   •Click ***Starting Clef*** to display the Clef Selection palette.
   •Select the treble clef with joined **8** (Figure 46).

Staff
Attributes

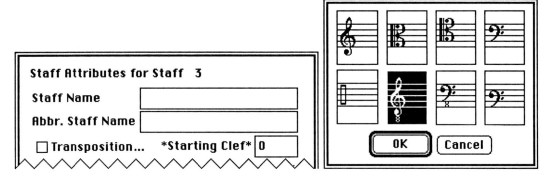

Figure 46. Staff Attributes dialog box and its Clef Selection palette.

Key Sig.

4. Repeat Step 3 for Staff 5 and Staff 7. Exception: click the bass clef in the Clef Selection palette.

5. Select the Key Signature Tool
   •Click the Staff 1 handle to display the scrolling list of key signatures.
   •Click the **Down Arrow** once to display the **F** key signature, then click the **OK** button.
   •The Key Change Information box appears: click the **This Measure Through End of Piece?** box (Figure 47).

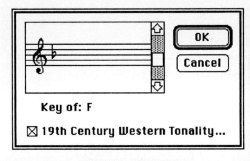
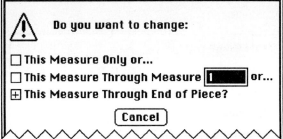

Figure 47. Key Signature dialog boxes.

New Staff

Bracket

6. Select the New Staff Tool to enable the placement of a system bracket for the vocal staves.
   •Group these staves: hold down the Shift key and click the Staff 1–5 handles (a dark circle appears in each handle), then release the shift key and double-click one of the selected handles.

7. Select the Bracket Tool.
   •Click any grouped staff to display the Bracket dialog box.
   •Click ***Bracket I.D.*** to display the Bracket palette.
   •Double-click the center bracket, then click **OK** to exit (Figure 48).

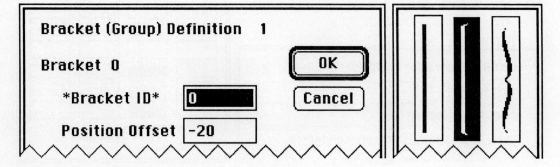

Figure 48. Bracket dialog box and palette.

8. Follow Steps 6–7 to group and place a Brace for the keyboard staves.
When vocal and keyboard staves are grouped, their bar lines are extended accordingly. The next procedure, therefore, is to break the bar lines connecting the vocal staves and, in the same dialog box, add the staff names to the choral parts. A suggested preliminary step, however, is to select an appropriate font.

9. In the Special Menu choose **Font Selection...** to display its dialog box.

•**Click the Name...** button to display the default font attributes (10-point Italic Chicago font) dialog box.

•Choose **Times** and click the **Italic** box to uncheck it. The text display shows 10-point Times Normal font. Click **OK** to return to the Font Selection dialog box.

•Change the default measurement in the ***X Offset*** box to **-220**, to provide adequate space for the longest staff name (Figure 49).

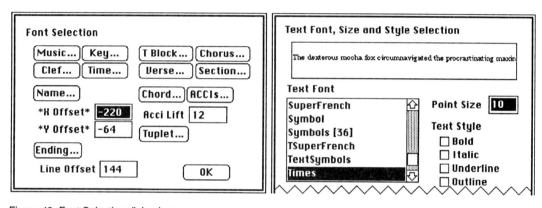

Figure 49. Font Selection dialog boxes.

10. Select the Staff Attributes Tool and click on the Staff 1 handle to display its dialog box (see Figure 46, above).

Staff Attributes

•Type **Soprano I** in the Staff Name box.

•Click the **Break Barlines** box.

•Click the **Next** button to bring up Staff 2 in the dialog box, type **Soprano II**, and click the **Break Barlines** box.

•Repeat the process, designating Staff 3 **Alto**, Staff 4 **Tenor**, and Staff 5 **Bass**. Since the keyboard designation requires three textlines, its processing is described further below, under the Text Block heading.

11. Click the Measure Add Tool **twice**, to format a three-bar system (Figure 50).

Measure Add

Music Notation.—Including the use of a MIDI keyboard, *Finale* offers five different methods of entering music. In order to compare the application with

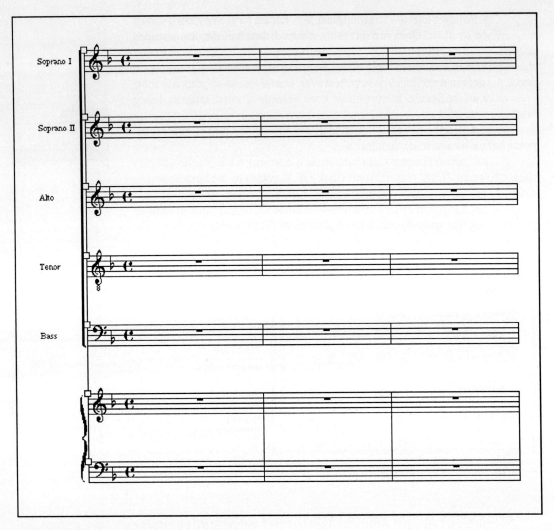

Figure 50. SSATB choral score ready for note entry.

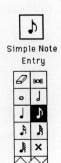

Simple Note Entry

MusicProse, this tutorial follows the same approach to music entry.

1. Click the Simple Note Entry to replace the Main Tool Palette by a notation palette.

•Click the Whole-Note icon and move the cursor to the third measure of the Soprano I staff.

•Click the cursor cross hair on the third line to enter the note C.

•The default rest is replaced by the note.

•If the entry is incorrect, select the Eraser Tool and double-click the note head to delete it, then enter the note again.

2. Complete the choral notation illustrated in Figure 53.

MUSIC NOTATION

•Eighth-note rests are entered by choosing the eighth-note icon, clicking the cursor in the measure, then clicking the head of the newly-placed note.

3. Begin the keyboard notation with the ostinato pattern in Staff 7. Since the default mode is beamed pairs during eighth-note entry, the following procedure will transform them into beamed quartets.

•Click the Exit icon in the palette to return to the Main Tool Palette.

•Choose the Mass Mover Tool (the Mass Mover menu is placed in the menu bar), use the cursor to enclose Staff 7 in a marquee, then release the mouse button to select the three measures (the Mass Edit menu also appears in the menu bar).

•Referring to Figure 51, choose **Modify Entries...** in the Mass Edit menu to display the Entry Modifications dialog box.

•Click the **Rebeam...** box to display the Time Signature dialog box.

•Click the **Decrease** button for the **Number of Beats** until 2/4 ♩ ♩ appears.

•Click the **Increase** button for **Duration of Beat** until ¢ ♩♩ replaces the display. Click the **OK** button to exit the dialog boxes.

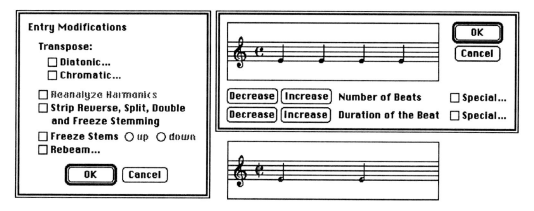

Figure 51. Entry Modifications dialog box and Time Signature dialog box displays.

4. Notate the first and third measures of Staff 6.

•Chords are constructed by clicking a line or space directly above (or below) a note head.

5. The two independent voices in the second measure of Staff 6 require use of the Layer 1/Layer 2 mechanism. Choose **Layer Attributes...** in the Edit menu to display the Layer Attributes dialog box (Figure 52).

•Layer 1: Select the **Freeze...** and **Do Only...** boxes, and the **Up** radio button.

•Layer 2: Select the **Freeze...**, **Do Only...**, and **Offset...** boxes, and the **Down** radio button. Type **-2** in the **Offset...** box.

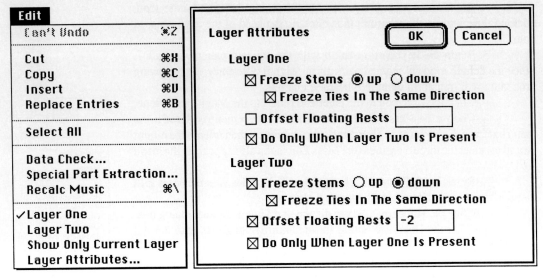

Figure 52. Edit menu and **Layer Attributes...** dialog box.

Speedy Note
Entry

Simple Note
Entry

Over-Slur

6. The box below the icon palette should read "layer: 1" (the default setting). If "2" is the numeral, double-click the box to switch to Layer 1.

• Enter the four eighths and the two quarter-note dyads.

7. Double-click the Layer box to switch to Layer 2.

• Enter the quarter note, quarter rest, and four eighths, then double-click the Layer box to return to Layer 1.

8. Referring to Step 3, select the second measure and rebeam the eighth-note pairs to quartets.

9. The quarter-note dyads need to be repositioned, to offset them from the adjoining D and C beamed eighths. Click the Exit icon to return to the Main Tool Palette.

• Click the Speedy Note Entry Tool, then the second measure.

• When the editing frame appears, hold down the Shift key, click the F notehead and drag the dyad slightly to the right.

• Shift-click-drag the E notehead similarly.

10. The basic notation is completed by entering the tie and slur in the third measure of Staff 1 and the tie in each layer of the second measure in Staff 5. Although the application provides different tools and icons for entering ties and slurs, the Smart Shapes method can be used for either symbol. Return to the Simple Note Entry palette and click the **Over-Slur** icon.

11. Position the cursor in the third measure of Staff 1, so that the vertical cross hair (note the down arrow) adjoins the right edge of the whole note and the horizontal cross hair bisects the fourth space.

• Hold down the Shift key, double-click to display the bounding box, and drag to the right until the bar line is reached. Release the mouse button.

Figure 53. Simple Note Entry of the choral score, *Sound the Trumpet* (Henry Purcell). Copyright © 1964 by Hawkes & Son (London) Ltd; Copyright Renewed. Reprinted by permission of Boosey & Hawkes, Inc..

•Reposition the cursor arrow above the midpoint of the slur, click and drag down the arc until it it reaches an imaginary sixth staff line (Figure 54).

12. Click the **Over-Slur** icon and position the cross hair over the center of the whole note and exactly on the top line of the staff. Repeat the procedure in Step 11, but drag down until the arc reaches a point above the tie.

•Click the cross hair above the right endpoint and drag slightly upward. Redraw the screen (Command-**D**).

13. Draw slurs over and under the beams of the eighths in Staff 6.

Under-Slur

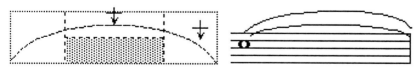

Figure 54. Smart Shape bounding box and related music example. The box shows a symmetrical tie/slur and the proper cursor placement for shape modification. The gray area enables dragging of the whole shape.

Repeat

14. The last step is to create a forward repeat barline in the third measure of the system. **Exit** the Simple Note Entry palette and click the Repeat Tool in the Main Tool Palette.

•Click the third measure in Staff 1 to display the Repeat Selection box.

•Double-click the (default) Forward Repeat icon (Figure 55) and redraw the screen.

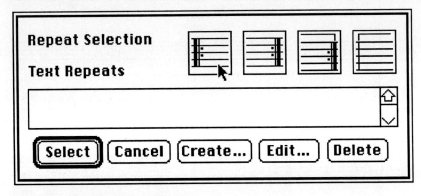

Figure 55. Repeat Selection dialog box.

Lyrics

Entering Lyrics.—Click the Lyrics Tool to display the Lyrics menu, and choose **Mass Create...** to display its text processing dialog box.

1. Type the following lyric (be sure to enter the punctuation and the space between each word): **Sound Sound, O sound, O** (Figure 56).

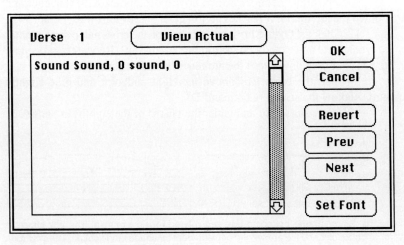

Figure 56. **Mass Create...**dialog box.

•Click the Set Font button to display the Font Selection dialog box (see Figure 49, above).

•Type **12** in the Point Size box.

•Return to the lyric display and click the View Actual button to verify that the font is Times 12 point.

2. Choose **Click Assignment...** in the **Lyric** menu.

•The lyric is displayed in a special, movable window (Figure 57). The Baseline Position box also appears, at Staff 1, with its triangles pointing to the baseline position where text will be placed.

☐☐≡ **Verse 1 Click Assignment** ≡	☐☐≡ **Verse 1 Click Assignment** ≡
☐ **Auto Update**	☐ **Auto Update**
Sound Sound, O sound, O	Sound, O sound, O

Figure 57. Click Assignment windows. The left window is applicable to Soprano I and II; the right window shows the scroll position for the Alto and the Bass.

3. Click in the first measure of Staff 1, then position the cursor crosshair on the staff and in the third measure, directly above or below the whole note C, and click once.

•The word **Sound** appears under the note and the Click Assignment box scrolls to the next word.

4. Click Staff 2: the Baseline Position box moves down to Staff 2.

•Position the cursor as before and click each of the four notes once.

•The Click Assignment window scrolls to the end. Drag the scroll box to the left until the display reads **Sound, O sound, O.**

5. Repeat the procedure in Step 4 for Staff 3 and Staff 5.

6. Since the ♪♩ notation results in text overlap in Staff 2, 3, 5, choose **Position Adjustment** in the Lyrics menu, position the cursor above or below the second quarter-note, and click to display the handle of the word **sound**.

•Click the handle to select it, then press the right arrow key three times.

•An alternate method is to click-drag the handle and position it slightly to the right.

7. A word or syllable that underlies tied or slurred notes should have an extension (that is, a ruled line) added to the related text, which extends to the next word or syllable. The program provides extensions by means of a handle, at the end of each word or syllable, which can be click-dragged to draw ruled lines.

•Select **Word Extension** in the Lyrics menu, and click the cursor above or below the whole note in Staff 1 to display its Word Extension handle.

•Click and drag the handle to the barline.

Page Layout.—The default position of the staves between the vocal parts and the keyboard accompaniment requires additional leading (that is, vertical space) between Staff 5 and Staff 6 to provide room for a text expression and metronome mark. Since the program does not include a ruler, the following procedure should provide fairly accurate leading.

New Staff

1. Select the New Staff icon to display the six staff handles.
2. Press and hold down the Shift key, then click the handle of Staff 7 to select it for grouping with Staff 6.
   •Click-drag the handle of Staff 6 downward until the horizontal line of the cursor is positioned on the first line of the staff.
   •Release the Shift key and click outside the handle to ungroup the two staves.

The next procedure is formatting the score as the first (title) page.

Page Layout

1. Select the Page Layout Tool to display the Page Layout menu, and choose **Group Measures...** to display its dialog box.
   •Type **3** to freeze the layout during the formatting procedure (Figure 58).

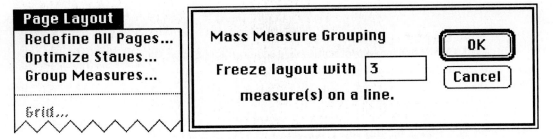

Figure 58. Page Layout menu and Group Measures... dialog box.

2. Click anywhere on the score to display the Page Layout dialog box, then click the **Show Music** box to view the default position of the score on the page (Figure 59). The four numeric boxes indicate the page size in EVFUs (*Finale* measurement units: 288 per inch). Thus, bottom (0) to top (3168) of the page measures 11 inches, and left (0) to right (2448) measures 8.5 inches. Note that the Staff Names will not print, since they extend beyond the left margin of the page, and that the position of the system does not provide adequate space for the insertion of titles and other text matter.

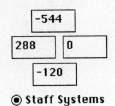

3. Click the **OK** button to exit, then click again on the score to bring back the dialog box for editing the layout.
   •Click the **Staff Systems** button.
   •Type **-544** (negative number!) in the upper box, **288** in the left box, and **-120** in the lower box (the right box remains 0).
4. Choose **Recalc Music** in The Page Layout menu.
   •If necessary, readjust the position of lyrics and slurs.

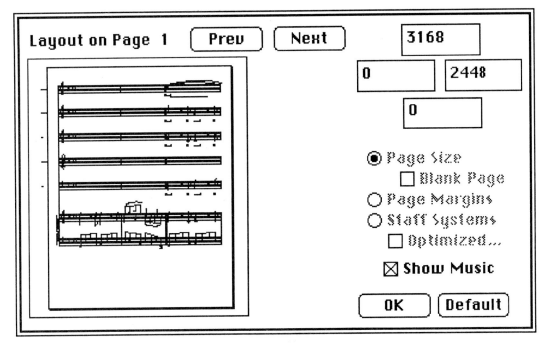

Figure 59. Page Layout dialog box with default Show Music display: the Staff Names extend beyond the left margin of the page and will not be printed.

Entering Dynamic Marks and Staff Expressions.–The preliminary procedure is to choose **Load Library...**in the File menu, then **Open**, in turn, the *Finale* folder, Libraries folder, and Text Expressions Library file.

Staff
Expression

1. Select the Staff Expression Tool and click the whole note in Staff 1 to display the Staff Expression Selection dialog box, then double-click the *f* symbol.

•The default Expression Assignment dialog box is displayed (Figure 60). Since it is quicker to position the symbol manually, click **OK** to exit the dialog box.

•Click the note again to display the symbol handle, click the handle to select it, and drag the symbol or use the arrow keys to position the *f* slightly above the Staff 1 double-bar line.

2. Repeat Step 1 for the *mf* symbol, which is to be placed above the first quarter-note in the third measure of Staff 2, 3 and 5, respectively.

3. The same procedure is used to enter the *f* symbol in the first measure, between Staff 6 and Staff 7. Exception: place the cursor in Staff 6, click the lowest note (F) of the first chord, then drag the symbol handle down.

4. The Staff Expression Selection dialog box also can be used to create the tutorial tempo mark, **Moderato marziale**, and place it above the first measure in Staff 1 and 6. Since the Staff Expression Tool is not applicable to rests, double-click the whole note in Staff 1 to display the dialog box..

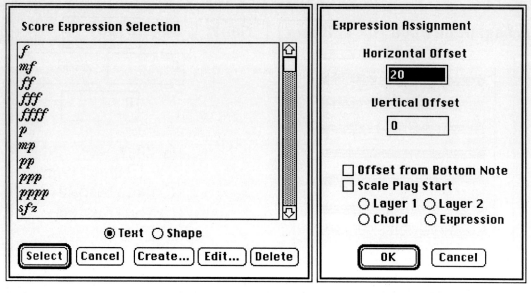

Figure 60. Text Expression and Expression Assignment dialog boxes.

•Click the **Create...** button in the Staff Expression Selection dialog box to display the Text Expression Designer dialog box.
•Type **Moderato marziale** in the Expression Text box.
•Click the **Set Font...** button to display the Text Font, Size and Style Selection dialog box.
•Select **Times 14 Bold** (Figure 61).

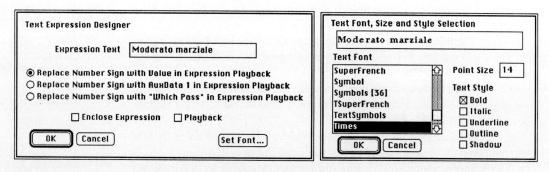

Figure 61. Text Expression Designer and Font Selection dialog boxes.

5. Scroll to the end of the list of expressions to display the newly-created tempo mark.
•Follow Step 1 to display and select the tempo mark handle.

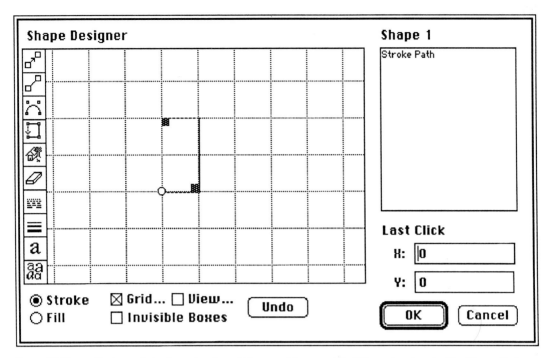

Figure 64. Shape Designer dialog box, showing grid lines and the completed Shape 1 rectangle. The Shape Designer is a subprogram for creating graphics.

Figure 67 illustrates the position of the five text blocks, the Header, and the Footer in the completed score. Since construction of the other text blocks (GROUP ID nos. 2–5) follows the same procedure as described above, for GROUP ID 1, the following instructions refer only to the changes to be made in Text (Block) Steps 1 and 3, and Shape Steps 4 and 5.

GROUP ID 2: Composition TITLE.
•Text Step 1: Horizontal **1032**, Vertical **-172**.
•Text Step 3: **24** Caps (Normal; be sure to select the typed text before the font is changed).
•Shape Step 4: Form a rectangle eight squares in width and one square in height.
•Shape Step 5: Justification is **Left**.
GROUP ID 3: Type of Chorus.
•Text Step 1: Horizontal **1456**, Vertical **-636**.
•Text Step 3: **12** (Normal).
•Shape Step 4: View at **75%**. Form a rectangle ten squares in width and one square in height.
•Shape Step 5: Justification is **Left**.
GROUP ID 4: COMPOSER/Transcriber
•Text Step 1: Horizontal **956**, Vertical **-360**.

•Text Step 3: COMPOSER **14** Caps, "Transcribed by" **12** Italic, Transcriber **12** (Normal).

•Shape Step 4: View at **100%**. Form a rectangle five squares in width and two squares in height.

•Shape Step 5: Justification is **Center**.

GROUP ID 5: Legend.

•Text Step 1: Horizontal **16**, Vertical **-632**.

•Text Step 3: **11** (Normal).

•Shape Step 4: View at **100%**. Form a rectangle five squares in width and two squares in height.

•Shape Step 5: Justification is **Center**.

Header/
Footer

Headers and Footers.–Although page numbers and copyright notices can be created as text blocks, it is quicker and easier to use the Header/Footer construction method (alternatively, one-line titles and other text matter—not exceeding 42 characters, including spaces—also can be entered as headers or footers). Since the inside cover page of a choral octavo is usually printed as the title page and numbered as the second page of the score, complete the following steps in Page View:

1. Click the Header/Footer Tool.

2. Double-click the score to display the Header/Footer Designer dialog box The Header and Justification Left radio buttons are default selections (Figure 65).

3. Type **2** in the Text box, **64** in the Horizontal Offset box, and **16** in the Vertical Offset box.

4. Select the **Only on this Page** radio button.

5. Click the **Set Font...** button to display the Font Selection dialog box, and choose **Times 12**.

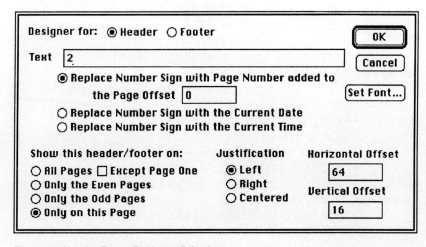

Figure 65. Header/Footer Designer dialog box.

The Designer text-line limitations necessitate five footers to properly format the Copyright Notice.

    1. If the Header/Footer Tool is already selected, double-click the score in the left margin of the page, below Staff 7, to display the Header/Footer Designer dialog box.

    2. Click the **Footer** and **Only on this Page** radio buttons.

    3. Type © **Copyright Boosey & Hawkes, Inc.**

     •Press Option-G to produce the copyright symbol.

    4. Type **64** as the Horizontal Offset, **20** as the Vertical Offset.

    5. Click the **Set Font...** button to display the Font Selection dialog box, and choose **Times 11**.

The other footers require the same procedure, except Step 3 and Step 4, as follows:

    Text: **Copyright for all countries.**

     •**64** Horizontal, **-32** Vertical.

    Text: **All rights reserved.**

     •**720** Horizontal, **-32** Vertical.

    Text: **Octavo 5540**

     •**1250** Horizontal, **-32** Vertical.

    Text: **Printed in the U.S.A.**

     •**1272** Horizontal, **-32** Vertical.

When the Tutorial is completed, it can be saved as an EPS (Encapsulated PostScript) file for high quality laser printing. The procedure is similar to the *MusicProse* File menu command, **Compile PostScript Listing**.

Keyboard-Assisted Notation.—In Speedy Entry mode—with or without a MIDI keyboard—a click of the cursor in a measure places the cross hair within an editing frame, with its pitch insertion bar on the middle line of the staff (Figure 66). The Arrow Up and Arrow Down keys, certain letter keys, or the cursor may be used to reposition the insertion bar to the desired pitch. Thereafter, the keypad or keyboard number keys are pressed to insert the durations, the plus and minus keys add accidentals, the Delete key serves as an eraser, and so forth (see Figure 43, above).

Speedy Note
Entry

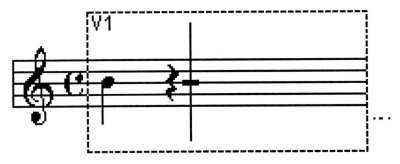

Figure 66. Speedy Note Entry: Voice 1 editing frame.

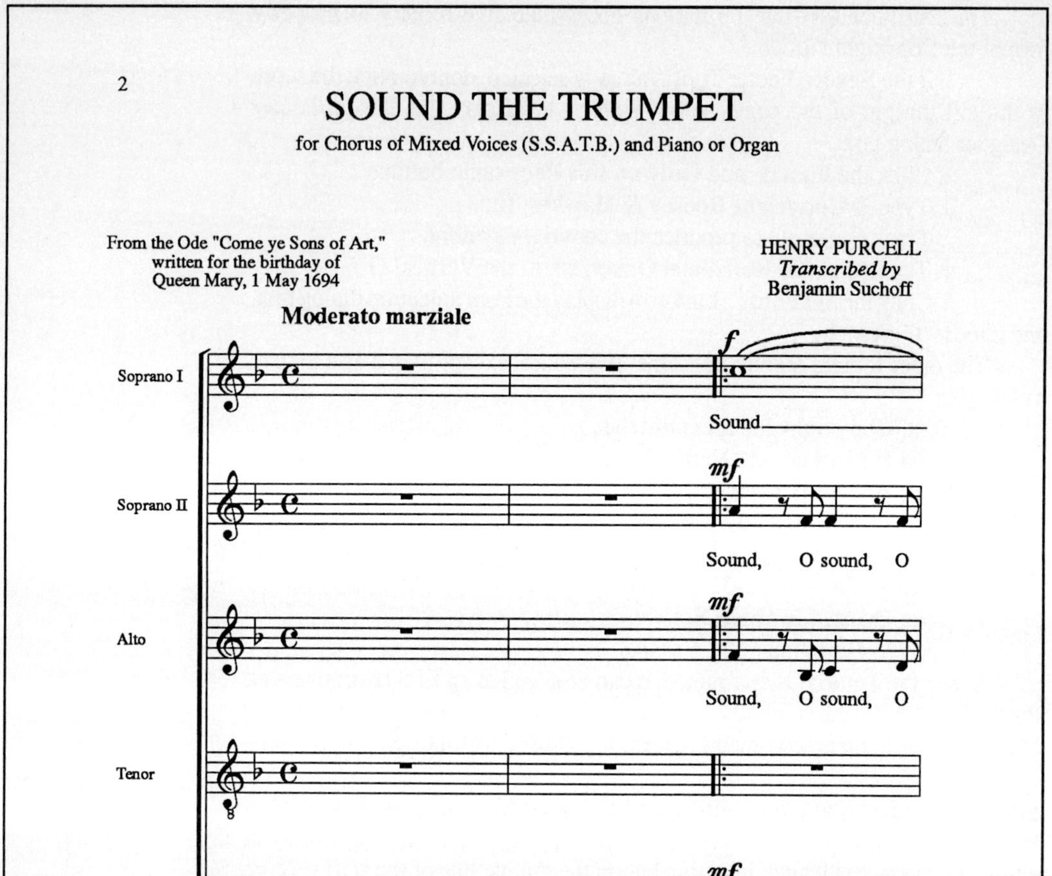

Figure 67. Final copy of the Tutorial in EPS file format.

SUMMARY

The first version of *Finale* appeared in 1988, the present upgrade (Version 2.6) in 1991. The proprietary *Petrucci* and *Seville* bitmapped and printer fonts are included in the package. Although list and street prices are higher than the other music applications discussed in this chapter, *Finale* also includes a PostScript processor for graphics enhancement of the score, a high-level, sequencer-like step time/real time MIDI capability, and three excellent manuals (Tutorial, Reference, Encyclopedia) and other supplements (Startup Guide, upgrade advisories, keyboard and font charts) that total more than 970 pages. Registered users also receive the quarterly, *Coda Notes,* and other useful materials.

The Pros.—Finale stands alone as the only comprehensive, professional music program for Macintosh computers. Note entry is possible with the mouse, the computer keyboard, a MIDI instrument, or in various combinations. In addition to standard note-head shapes are diamonds, boxes, triangles, and other symbols that are selected from a special *Petrucci* font chart. Cue-size notes (appogiaturas and grace notes) and strings of variable-size small-head notes (cadenzas and melismata) are easy to construct. Slurs and ties can be quickly placed and moved, or adjusted with regard to their arc or the position of end segments. Insertion of lyrics and assignment of different font attributes on the same text line are, to a certain extent, similar to procedures followed in word processing applications.

A noteworthy inclusion is a group of Macros which provide regional insertion of Note Expressions (accents, mordents, bowings, etc.), doubling and halving of values (including a dialog box for changing the time signature), note size reduction by percent, respacing staves, repositioning Staff Names, and other shortcut functions.

Among the scores in the *Finale* Templates Folder are Accompanied SATB Chorus, Small Orchestra (Woodwinds, Horns, Strings, and Grand Staff), Piano-Vocal, and String Quartet. The Libraries Folder contains the various collections of repeats, expressions, and shapes that are available for insertion in the score.

*The Cons.—*In brief: overcomplication of means. There are too many icons, some of them non-mnemonic; a plethora of dialog boxes, including multiple-layered ones for text block construction, are involved in many procedures; and "user unfriendly" inconsistencies with regard to standard editing commands, where selection of certain objects or regions does not also permit group/ungroup, cut, copy, paste, and other functions. The program is lacking a Page View ruler for manual alignment of objects, text blocks, and staves. Among the other needed improvements are a multiple-line Staff Names dialog-box capability; juxtaposition of text blocks and their handles; and the ability to open two or more *Finale* files for comparative purposes or interchange of data.

Encore

Sonata Plain

ENCORE

This MIDI-oriented application is based on the Adobe *Sonata* screen font. The printer font, not included in the package, can be purchased from Adobe Systems or a software vendor. To begin notation, double-click the *Encore* icon.

Main Screen.—The default display consists of two active windows: the Notes palette and the New window with 4/4 Grand Staff (Figure 68).

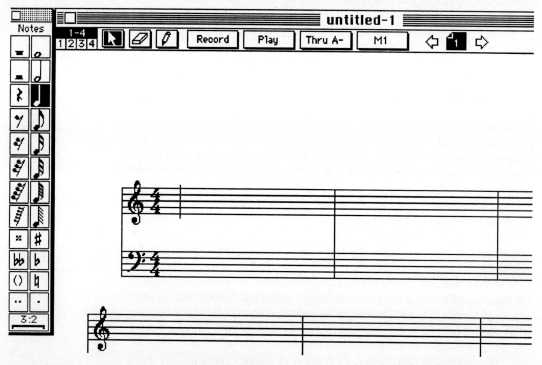

Figure 68. *Encore* default New window and Notes palette.

Under the Title bar are the the Arrow pointer (the default selection), Eraser and Pencil icons. When the Pencil icon is clicked, the cursor assumes the shape of the default quarter-note. The shape-cursor not only reflects the music symbol but also one or more ledger lines, depending on the position above or below the staff. Selection of the parentheses icon is made in conjunction with an accidental, dot and double-dot icons with notes or rests, and the triplet icon with notes.

This Tutorial creates the first (title) page for a choral score (Solo or Soli, SATB and Piano accompaniment), consisting of five bracketed and two braced staves, with four measures in each staff.

58

1. Choose **New** in the File menu to display the Choose Page Layout dialog box.

2. Type **7** for the number of Staves, **1** for Systems and **3** for measures.
•Click **OK** to exit the dialog box. (Figure 69).

3. Hold down the Shift key and click the Arrow pointer in the left margin of Staff 1–5.
•The five staves are selected.

4. Choose **Connect Staves...** in the Page Layout menu to display the Connect Staves dialog box.

5. Click the **Break barline** and **Bracket** boxes.

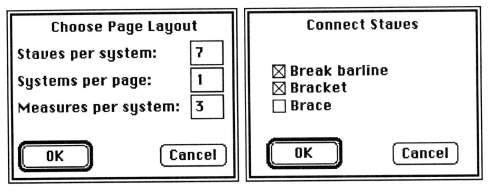

Figure 69. Choose Page Layut and Connect Staves dialog boxes.

6. Repeat Steps 3 and 4 for Staff 6–7.
•Exception: click the **Brace** box only in the Connect Staves dialog box.

7. Repeatedly click on the **Notes** caption of the palette until the **Clefs** palette is displayed.

8. Select the Treble clef with joined **8** icon.
•The cursor assumes the clef shape.

9. Click the cursor on the Treble clef in Staff 4.

10. Select the Bass clef icon and click the cursor on the Treble clef in Staff 5 and 7.

11. Repeatedly click on the **Clefs** caption of the palette until the **Notes** palette is again displayed.

12. Click in the left margin of Staff 1 to select it.

13. Choose **Key Signature...** in the Change menu to display the Key Signature dialog box (Figure 70).
•Click once on the Down arrow in the Scroll box to display the **F Major or D Minor** key signature, then exit the dialog box.
•The key signature is entered in all staves, and Staff 1 remains selected.

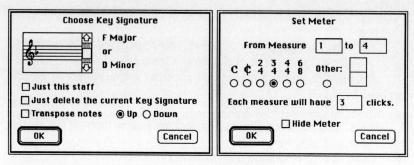

Figure 70. Choose Key Signature and Set Meter dialog boxes.

14. Choose **Time Signature...** in the Change menu to display the Set Meter dialog box.
   •Click the **3/4** radio button and exit the dialog box.
   15. Save the file and name it Tutorial (Figure 71).

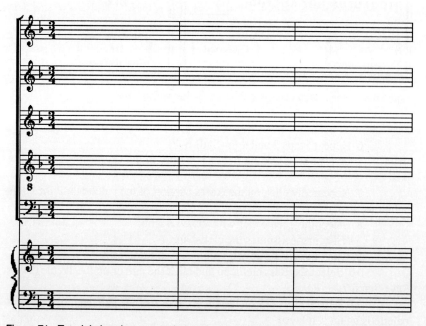

Figure 71. Tutorial choral score ready for title page formatting.

Title page format.— Since *Encore* is MIDI-oriented (see the discussion in Chapter 8, below), score margins and spacing between staves should be adjusted before note entry. If **Preview** is selected in the Windows menu, it will be obvious that only one system of the displayed choral score will fit on the page and, moreover, that its default placement does not provide adequate space for needed text blocks (title, subtitle, composer, etc.).

1. Choose **Show/Hide...** in the Goodies menu to display the Show/Hide dialog box.

2 Click the **Rulers, Control Points** and **Page Margins** boxes, then exit the dialog box.

• Rulers, measured in inches, are displayed at the left and top sides of the window, together with the page margins.

• A dotted line is displayed in each ruler, indicating the precise vertical and horizontal positions of the cursor.

3. Close the **Clefs** window (click the small square at the top of the palette) to clear the left margin of the page.

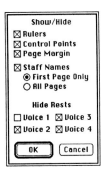

4. Position the Arrow pointer on the top line of Staff 1, on or to the left of the staff line, click and hold down the mouse button.

• A dotted rectangle encloses the staff (clicking elsewhere in the margin selects it).

5. Drag down until the dotted line in the vertical ruler indicates 3-1/2 inches, then carefully release the mouse button.

• All staves below Staff 1 move down simultaneously, without changing interstaff spacing.

6. Repeat Steps 4 and 5 for Staff 2, dragging it to the 4-1/2 inch mark.

• This will provide the extra spacing needed to enter two lines of lyrics for Staff 1.

7. Repeat Steps 4 and 5 for Staff 6, dragging it to the 7-1/2 inch mark.

8. Choose **Staff Sheet** in the Windows menu to display the Staff Sheet dialog box (Figure 72).

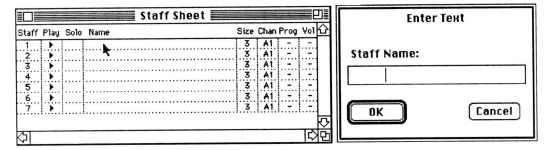

Figure 72. Staff Sheet and Enter Text dialog boxes. Note the Enter Text cursor position in the **Staff Name** box.

9. Click in the Staff 1 **Name** area to display the Enter Text dialog box.

10. Using the Space Bar, move the flashing Insertion point **10** spaces to the right, then exit both dialog boxes.

• The left margin of the score is now adjusted to accommodate the entry of staff names (Figure 73).

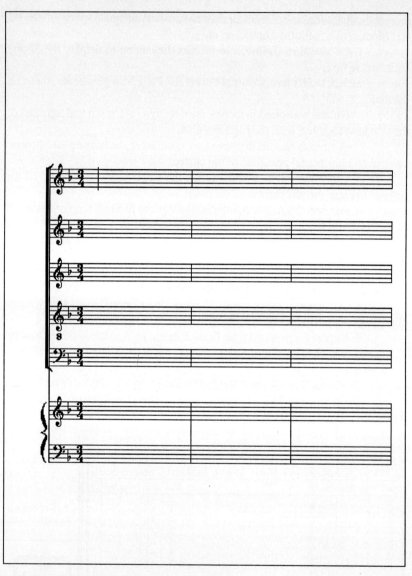

Figure 73. Preview window of formatted title page.

Music Notation.—Choose **Palette** in the View menu to display the Palette sub-menu, hold down the mouse button and drag the arrow pointer onto **Notes** to display the Notes palette.

    1. Click the Pencil icon to enable palette selection.

       •The cursor assumes the shape of the default eighth-note and adds or subtracts ledger lines while the shape moves above or below the staff.

    2. Referring to Figure 74, click the whole rest icon.

62   MUSIC NOTATION

3. Click the rest in the first measure of Staff 1–5.

    •The rest is positioned automatically.

4. Enter the rest in measures 2–3 in Staff 5.

5. Select the half-note icon, then the dot icon, and enter the dotted note in the first space of measures 2–3, Staff 3.

6. Repeat Step 5 in the second space of measure 2 in Staff 2 and on the third line of measure 3, Staff 4.

7. Select the natural icon and carefully click its shape on the note head **B** in Staff 4.

8. Select the quarter-note icon and enter **A D E** in measure 2, and **F** in measure 3, Staff 2.

9. Select the eighth-note icon, then the triplet icon. Enter **F E D** twice.

    •The two sets of notes are automatically beamed as triplets.

    •If the beams are positioned too far below the staff, click the tip of the Arrow pointer at the center of the beam and drag upward until the leading edge of the beam rests on the first staff line.

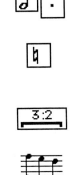

Figure 74. Note entry of the vocal parts: *After A Dream* (Gabriel Fauré). Copyright © 1990 by Plymouth Music.

The Piano accompaniment calls for beamed groups of six chords in each measure (Figure 75).

1. Select the eighth-note icon and carefully click the shape to form the triad **D F A** in measure 1, Staff 6.

2 Click the Arrow icon and drag the pointer over the triad to select it.

3. Copy (Command-C), click to the right of the triad and paste (Command-V).

    •The second triad also appears as a flagged entry.

4. Click the pointer to the right side of the second triad and paste again.

•Repeat pasting until there are six flagged triads in the measure.

5. Select the six triads, then choose **Beam Group** in the Notes menu.

•If eighth-note triads are individually notated, the program beams them in pairs during entry.

6. Double-click the first measure to select the beamed triads, copy and paste them in measures 2 and 3.

7. Click the Eraser icon, place the cursor cross-hair on the note head **D** of the last two triads in measure 2, and click to delete the note.

8. Click the Pencil icon (the eighth-note icon should still be selected) and add **E C** to form the chord **A F E C**.

•The program automatically re-beams the six chords in paired groups.

9. Double-click measure 2 to select it, then choose **Beam Group** in the Notes menu.

•The beamed pairs are replaced by individually flagged chords, and the measure remains selected.

10. Choose **Beam Group** again: the six chords are beamed together.

•The beam should form a straight line. If not, click-drag with the tip of the Arrow pointer at the left or right edge of the beam.

•The height of the beam should be aligned with the beam in measure 1. If not, click-drag with the tip of the Arrow pointer at the center of the beam.

11. Enter ledger-line **B** below each triad in measure 3.

•The program automatically re-beams the six chords in paired groups.

12. Erase **A** in the last two chords and add **G** to form the chord **G F D B**.

13. Add a natural to **B** (click the sign on the note head) in the first chord of the measure.

•The program erroneously adds a flat to the same note in the next chord. Click that note head with the natural-sign cursor: the flat is shifted to the **B** in the third chord.

•Click the cursor on each **B** in the remaining four chords to remove the erroneous flat sign from the measure.

14. Enter **G** as a dotted half-note octave in the third measure of Staff 7.

Figure 75. Note entry of the piano accompaniment.

15. Choose **Select All** in the Edit menu (or Command-A), then choose **Justify Spacing** in the Change menu (or Command-J).

Entering Lyrics.—Choose **Font Selection** in the Goodies menu to display the Font submenu, hold down the mouse button and drag to select **Lyrics**. The default Choose Font dialog box is displayed with "Welcome to Encore!" set in Geneva 10-point Normal style font.

1. Click the left selection box to change the font to **Times** (or **New York**), then click the center one to change the size to **12** (Figure 76).

Choose Font

| Times | | 12 | | Style |

Welcome to Encore!

OK   Cancel

Figure 76. Choose Font dialog box.

2. Click the Notes palette once to display the Graphics palette, then select the **L** icon. The cursor changes to an I-beam, and a lyric-baseline Position Arrow points to the insertion path below Staff 1.

3. Click the I-beam under the first note in measure 2 to position the flashing insertion point.

4. Referring to Figure 78, type **'Twas in my sleep, in a hap-py de-.** Each word or syllable, including its hyphen, must be followed by pressing the Tab key to move the insertion point to the next note. Thus entered, they are attached to their respective notes and move along the baseline when the notes are repositioned horizontally.

  •The single quotation mark is entered by holding down the Option and Shift keys while the }/] key is typed.

  •Since the first two notes in measure 3 are tied, tab twice after **sleep,** is typed, then type **in** under the note **E**.

5. Click the I-beam under the first note in measure 2 of Staff 2. Type the capital letter **M**.

6. Repeat Step 5 in measure 2 of Staff 3 and 4.

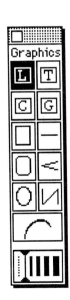

7. The crowded lyrics of the last triplet in measure 3, Staff 1 will need to be separated by manual adjustment of their overlying notes. Click the Arrow pointer and select as one region—those triplet notes, their lyrics, and the quarter note in Staff 2.

•Hold down the Command key and tap the }/] key continuously, to nudge the selected region to the right until the lyrics are properly spaced.

•Excepting chords, any note, word or syllable can be selected and nudged the same way.

•A chord can be repositioned by carefully click-dragging one of its notes horizontally.

8. Select the **L** icon and click the I-beam cursor on measure 1, Staff 1 to display the baseline Position Arrow.

•Click-drag the Position Arrow down until the lyrics clear the triplet **3** numeral.

9. Choose **Show/Hide...** in the Goodies menu to display its dialog box.

•Click the **Rulers**, **Control Points** and **Page Margin** boxes.

•The Control Points (that is, "handles") are displayed when graphics and text blocks are entered.

10. Select the Arrow pointer and drag it over the quarter note and eighth note (**F**) in measure 3, Staff 1 to select them, then choose **Tie** in the Notes menu (or Command-**T**).

•The arc of the Tie can be adjusted when its handle is dragged with the Arrow pointer.

11. Select and **Tie** the half notes in measures 2–3, Staff 2 and 3.

12. Lyric extension lines can be entered after selection of the Line icon in the Graphics menu. The Line Weight (that is, thickness) icon at the bottom of the Graphics palettes should indicate the default selection of the second line from the left. If not, click that line: the cursor changes to a cross hair.

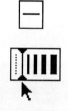

•Click-drag the cross hair after the word **sleep,** to a position under the first eighth-note of the triplet in measure 3, Staff 1.

•If the line is too short or long, or not straight, adjust it by click-dragging either of its two handles. And the line can be repositioned horizontally or vertically by a click-drag on the line, at its center.

•Add the long extension lines to the letter **M** in Staff 2–4.

Entering Music Symbols.— Click the **Graphics** caption in the palette window until the **Dynamics** palette is displayed.

1. Select the *p* icon. The cursor changes to a cross hair.

•Position it near the top line of Staff 1, center the cross hair above the first notehead, and click to insert the symbol (see Figure 78).

•If necessary, select the Arrow pointer and click-drag the symbol to reposition it.

2. Repeat Step 1 for Staff 2–4.

3. Select the **pp** icon and click the cursor under the first chord in measure 1, between Staff 6 and Staff 7.

4. Display the Graphics palette and select the **crescendo** icon. The cursor changes to a cross hair.

•Position the cross above Staff 1, between **D** and **E** in measure 2, click-drag until the moving pair of handles are positioned between the barline and the quarter note in measure 3, then release the mouse button.

•The Arrow pointer can change the hairpin angle or length by, respectively, a vertical or horizontal click-drag on any handle. The hairpin itself can be freely moved by a click-drag on its shape, anywhere between the left and right pair of handles.

5. The original score requires a Tie in Staff 2, from the quarter-note **G** in measure 3 to the same pitch in measure 4, p. 2. To insert the Tie but still limit the title page to three measures, choose **Linear View** in the Windows menu and scroll to measure 4.

•Display the Notes palette, select the half note and dot icons, and entered the shape on the second line (**G**) in measure 4 of Staff 2.

•Click-drag the Arrow pointer over the quarter note–dotted half-note in measure 3–4, then type Command-T (or choose **Tie** in the Notes menu).

•Choose **Linear View** again to uncheck it and return to Page View format.

Entering Text Blocks.—Music expressions, staff names, titles, and other text matter can be freely positioned in the score, similar to procedures used in a number of other applications. When the **T** icon is selected, the Text menu replaces Goodies and Notes in the menu bar, and the cursor changes to an I-beam. (Be sure that **Rulers, Control Points**, and **Margins** are selected in the Goodies menu **Show/Hide...** dialog box.)

1. At the top of the score, click-drag the I-beam to the right, about an inch, to display a bounding box with its flashing insertion point and sizing handle.

•The handle can be freely dragged with the I-beam cross bar, to resize the bounding box in the event of unwanted text wrap, etc.

2. Type **dolce**.

3. Drag down the Text menu and choose **Times** (or **New York**) in the font submenu, **12** in the size submenu and **italic** in the style submenu.

•The text expression changes to reflect the three submenu choices.

4. Select the Arrow pointer: the text bounding-box is replaced by four sizing handles.

•Place the pointer on **dolce** and click-drag it to the right of the **p** sign in measure 2, Staff 1 (see Figure 78).

5. Following the same procedure in Steps 1–4, type **Andantino**. Exception: choose **14 Bold**.

•Drag the expression to a position slightly above measure 1, Staff 1, so that its first letter is aligned with the Time Signature.

•Create a text bounding-box above Staff 6, re-type the expression and drag it until it is aligned with the Time Signature.

6. Return to the Text menu and choose **12 Plain**.

7. Type **SOLO (one or more voices)** and drag the block to a position above the dynamic signs in measure 2, Staff 1.

8. Add the Staff Names as caps (**SOPRANO, ALTO, TENOR** and **BASS**)to Staff 2–5, respectively.

•Add **PIANO** at the midpoint of the Staff 6–7 brace.

9. Click the I-beam below Staff 7 and drag the bounding box to the width of the score for the two-line copyright notice below Staff 7.

•Use the Space Bar to evenly separate the three individual entries in the second line.

10. Choose **Align Middle** in the Text menu for the two-line text blocks which designate the poet/translator and composer/arranger, type the text blocks and position them at the left and right margins of the page, respectively,.and about two inches below the top margin.

•Choose **Align Left** and type the text block description of type of chorus. Position the block as a centerhead, about a half-inch above the text blocks described in Step 10.

11. Type **2** as the page number, then drag it to the upper left corner of the margin bounding-box.

12. The title, **After A Dream**, is a **24**-point centerhead. Separate **A** with two spaces preceding and following the letter, and position the block about an inch below the top margin.

Headers and Footers.—This Tutorial employs an alternative, text-block approach to construction of a sample title page. It should be noted, however,that the Goodies menu provides special dialog boxes for creating headers, footers, title page text blocks and a copyright notice. Additionally, the Staff Sheet dialog box (see Figure 72, above) is useful for inserting one-line Staff Names.

Keyboard-Assisted Notation.—Although the focus of *Encore* is the interaction of a MIDI instrument with the computer keyboard for data input and output, the same computer keys are operational with the mouse to expedite selection of Arrow, Eraser, Pencil and palette icons (Figure 77). Exceptions: Lyrics and Text icons and, in these modes, the Arrow and Eraser icons. Extended-keyboard left and right arrow keys can be used to select specific staff events.

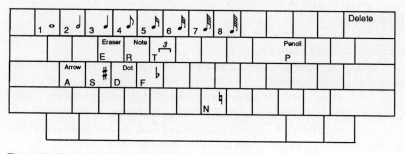

Figure 77. Note palette and other keyboard equivalents.

Figure 78. Final copy of the Tutorial in bitmapped (*Sonata* screen font) file format.

SUMMARY

The first version of *Encore* was copyrighted in 1989, Version 2.0 (used in this chapter) appeared in 1991, and the current Version 2.5 (see Chapter 8, below) was upgraded in 1992. The proprietary *Frets* guitar chord font, Adobe *Sonata* screen and printer fonts, and Adobe *Type Manager* are included in the package. *Encore* is suitable as an entry level or higher application.

The Pros.—Multiple files can be opened for cross-referencing, and their data, including text matter, edited in accordance with standard Macintosh commands. Up to sixty-four staves are available per page and can be organized into one or more systems. Ties, slurs, beams, lyrics, and text blocks can be treated as if they were objects in a sophisticated graphics application. Individual notes and chord members are easily selected, deleted, freely dragged, or precisely nudged. Page layout is facilitated by the use of rulers, page margins, control points, the Staff Sheet, and the Preview window. Nested dialog boxes are limited to typographical attributes. Variable font sizes are for notation, and they can be intermixed to construct cue-size and full size staves on the same page. Cadenzas and other small-head melismata are easy to notate.

The Cons.—*Encore* files require a MIDI instrument to playback the score, and they cannot be imported by other applications such as Microsoft *Word*, Aldus *PageMaker,* and Aldus *SuperPaint.* Nudge commands and Shift-key constrain functions should be applicable to graphics and text blocks, and there is no provision for entering metronome marks or inserting a column between previously notated events. Zoom capability, grouping function, and a set of score templates would be useful additions.

CONCLUSIONS

This chapter provides five "getting started" tutorials, designed to guide the user through the basic steps necessary to produce a choral score, including music notation, lyrics, titles, and other text blocks in the *ConcertWare+MIDI, Deluxe Music Construction Set, MusicProse, Finale,* and *Encore* applications.

As of this writing, the approximate street price of the *Deluxe Music Construction Set* package is $85, but the additional purchase of the Adobe *Sonata* printer font (about $60) is recommended. The *ConcertWare+MIDI* package street price is about $98, including a proprietary printer font. *DMCS* is recommended for users who need an entry-level music program which can produce good quality, camera-ready scores. *MusicProse* (street price: $190) and *Encore* ($400) provide higher-quality scores. The choice here depends on three variables: cost, learning curve, and ultimate destination of the printed scores. *MusicProse* output is, to a certain extent, similar to that of *Finale; Encore,* on the other hand, is much easier to learn. *Finale* (street price: $550; specially priced for qualified students and teachers at about $190) is the only music application that can produce top-quality, professional scores with Macintosh computers.

It is indeed noteworthy that all the above-listed applications have MIDI capability and are the products of reliable manufacturers who have consistently provided the public with enhanced upgrades and technical support services.

CHAPTER 2

Music and Graphics

Creating scores for performance or sheet music distribution is only one instance of the many kinds of files that musicians can produce. A graphics program and a music font can serve as a substitute for music applications, a tool for enhancement of scores, or a medium for construction of drawings and other illustrations. Among the many graphics-oriented products are rhythmic patterns, scales or modes and other schemata, music examples in combination with line art and other drawings, and illustrations in which music notation is minimal, replaced by special symbols or completely omitted. All these products can be accomplished by the *SuperPaint* graphics application, with or without the convenience of an inexpensive, entry-level program such as *Deluxe Music Construction Set.*

SUPERPAINT

SuperPaint

SuperPaint is arguably the most suitable graphics program for musicians, since it provides painting and drawing layers which are quickly and easily interchanged, combined, or transformed from one layer to the other.

    The Paint Layer is the default mode when the program is opened: the Paint Brush icon overlaps the Compass icon, to indicate the Paint layer and its movable windows are active. The painting tools create bitmaps, that is, individual dots or pixels assembled into lines, curves, font characters and other images which are related only to their screen position and not to each other. Thus, for instance, to move a bitmapped line from one position to another, its collection of pixels must be enclosed by one of the five selection tools. Although the Paint layer allows the user to freely add or delete individual pixels (usually with the Pencil tool, most bitmapped images (especially music font characters!) cannot be scaled without some distortion or loss of resolution. It is therefore advisable to create music-oriented graphics in the Draw layer as the basic design mode.

    The Draw Layer, shown in Figure 79, is activated when the Compass icon is clicked to bring it to the front. Each shape created by the drawing tools is a discrete object which, when selected, displays its handles: a small black square at each end of a line or at the corners of other shapes. Thus displayed, objects can

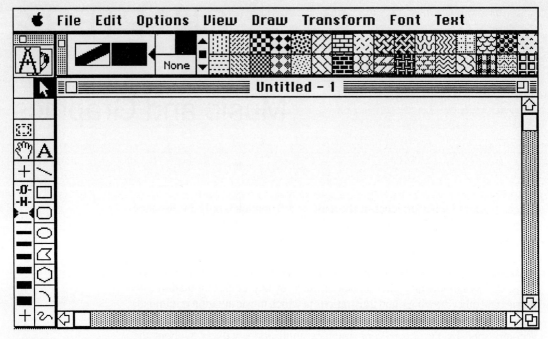

Figure 79. *SuperPaint* New window in Draw mode.

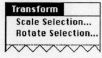

Draw
Bring to Front	⌘=
Send to Back	⌘-
Group	⌘G
Ungroup	⌘U
Edit SuperBits	⌘R
Align Objects...	⌘M
Object Info...	⌘I
Convert to Bezier	▶
Bezier to Polygon	▶
Join Beziers	
Bezier Settings...	
✓Opaque	
Transparent	
✓Unlock	
Lock	

Transform
| Scale Selection... |
| Rotate Selection... |

be freely moved, rotated, scaled proportionately, filled with patterns, enlarged, grouped together, and transformed or edited in various ways. Note, however, that when the handles of neighboring objects are in close proximity or overlap, it is difficult to isolate the desired object during the selection process. In this case the unwanted objects can be locked—the handles are then displayed as gray boxes to indicate their shapes are non-selectable—or the **Send to Back** command can be invoked to move them to a plane "underneath" those to be edited. It is also important to note that objects can be resized, but not proportionately, when they are dragged by one of their handles: proportional resizing is calculated in the Transform menu **Scale Selection...** dialog box. Therefore, when it is necessary to reposition an object, the Arrow pointer must be placed between the handles on a line or within the area bounded by the corner handles of a shape, and then click-dragged elsewhere.

FONT-EXCLUSIVE SCORE CONSTRUCTION

Sonata

The popular Adobe *Sonata* font is the recommended typeface for creating music notation in graphics applications. While it is frequently easier to edit music characters in the *SuperPaint* Paint Layer, the printed output shows the typical "jaggies" that mark MacPaint file bitmaps (see Figure 78, above). The Draw

Layer, on the other hand, based on built-in Macintosh QuickDraw routines which use mathematical formulas to construct smooth characters, exports PICT format files for high-quality reproduction by QuickDraw or PostScript printers (Figure 80).

Figure 80. Proportional reduction of QuickDraw and bit-mapped font characters.

The rhythmic pattern in Figure 81 illustrates the kind of music example that can be created for publication in a book, article, or classroom handout, using the *Sonata* font instead of a music application.

Figure 81. Rhythmic pattern created as a music font graphic.

The following Tutorial outlines the suggested steps for creating the pattern or similar schemata.

1. Choose **Grid & Rulers...** in the Options menu to display its dialog box.

2. **Grid spacing: 6.00 points** (= 0.08).

3. Click the **Show grid** and **Show rulers** selection boxes (Figure 82).

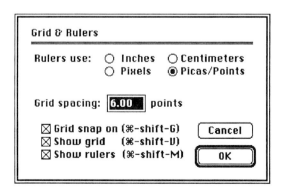

Figure 82. **Grid & Rulers** dialog box.

4. Choose **Sonata** in the Font menu and **18**-point size in the Text menu. Note that the Apple menu Key Caps display will verify the following keyboard equivalents: e = ♪, q = ♩, h = ♩, l = l, and option-shift-{ = final double-bar.

5. Select the text icon to display the I-beam cursor, then click on the 12-point grid pixel and drag to draw a text box to the 36-point grid pixel.

6. Create the pattern with proportional spacing, as shown in Figure 83, typing the following number of spacebar additions after each character: ♩ + 8, ♩ + 4, ♪ + 2 and l + 3.

The 3/4 time sign is constructed with the same font.

1. Click the I-beam and type **3**.

•Choose **Lock**, then **Send to the Back** in the Draw menu (the handles change from black to gray).

2. Click elsewhere and type **4**.

•Click the Arrow tool and drag the number slightly under and aligned with the **3**.

3. In the View menu choose **Zoom In** three times to display the numbers in Fat Bits (that is, enlarged to a collection of individual pixels).

•It may be necessary to move the screen with the Hand tool, to bring the numbers into view.

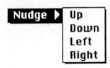

4. Choose the Nudge commands in the Edit menu (or the arrow keys on an extended keyboard) to precisely align the numerals as well as position them one or two pixels apart.

5. Click the Two-layer selection tool and select the numerals.

6. Choose **Unlock**, **Bring to the Front**, and **Group** in the Draw menu.

7. **Zoom Out** three times and click-drag the completed time sign to the position shown in Figure 83.

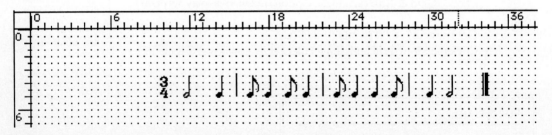

Figure 83. Proportionately-spaced rhythmic pattern with displayed Rulers and Grid pixels.

GRAPHICS AND SCORE RECONSTRUCTION

Figure 84 is another example of font-exclusive score construction, where the staff, clef, and whole notes of the lower tetrachord are assembled and grouped as one object; and the upper tetrachord is likewise assembled and grouped, and replicated three times. The latter tetrachords are then grouped as a four-stave system and attached to a staff line. The final steps are juxtaposition of the lower tetrachord with the upper ones, construction of an interval bracket, and typing the text blocks.

Drill

Add half-step brackets and accidentals to the upper tetrachords

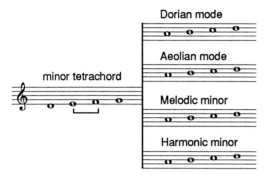

Figure 84. Font-exclusive score construction with *SuperPaint*.

A less tedious and exacting method is entry of the tetrachords in a music application such as *Deluxe Music Construction Set*, which permits copy to the Clipboard for pasting into the *SuperPaint* Draw Layer as QuickDraw graphics (Figure 85). The following Tutorial may require additional reference to *DMCS* (pp. 13–23, above).

Drill

Add half-step brackets and accidentals to the upper tetrachords

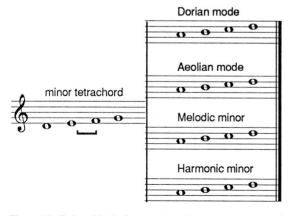

Figure 85. *DeluxeMusic Construction Set* score reconstruction with *SuperPaint*.

Deluxe Music v.2.5

Window
Score
Piano Keyboard
✓Score Setup ⌘W
Note Palette
Memory Usage

Open the *DMCS* application and choose **Score Setup** in the Window menu to display the Score Setup dialog box (the default settings are shown in Figure 16, above). Change the sliders in the upper section of the dialog box by clicking their right or left arrows or dragging their scroll boxes, to read: Bars Per Line: **1**, Score Width: **170** (Figure 86).

Score Setup

Bars Per Line ◁▦▶ 1		☒ Paged Score
Beats Per Min ◁▦▶ 90		☐ 2 Tracks per Staff
Score Width ◁▦▶ 170		[Set To Window Width]
Volume ◁▦▶ 6		[Set To Printer Width]
		[Set Margins]

Choose Staff Number ◁▦▶ 1   ☐ Two Way Ties
◉ Treble Clef   ◯ Tenor Clef   ☒ Staff Sound On   ☐ Hide Instruments
◯ Bass Clef   ◯ Alto Clef   ☐ Hide Staff   ☐ Hide Key /Clef
[Add Staff]   Space above staff ◁▦▶ 16
[Delete Staff]   Space below staff ◁▦▶ 16
☐ Split Bar Lines ☐ Brace Staff ☐ Top Bracket ☐ Bottom Bracket
◉ Normal   ◯ Play 1 Octave High   ◯ Play 1 Octave Low

Figure 86. *DMCS* Score Setup dialog box settings.

The lower section of the Score Setup dialog box enables the formatting of individual staves and systems. Most of the slider controls and selection boxes and buttons are specifically linked to whatever staff number is displayed on the right side of the Choose Staff Number slider.

The lower tetrachord in Figure 87 is entered as follows :
1. Choose Staff Number **2**.
2. Click the Hide Staff box to select it.
   •The default Bass staff disappears.
3. Click the whole-note icon in the Note Palette and enter **D E F G**.
4. Close, Save and name the file "Lower Tetrachord."

Figure 87. *DMCS* "Lower Tetrachord" notation.

Construction of the upper tetrachord system begins with the same Bars per Line and Score Width settings illustrated in Fugure 86.

    1. Open a **New** file.

    •The Score Setup dialog box changes to its default settings. Reset to Bars Per Line **1** and Score Width **170**.

    2. Click the Hide Key/Clef box to select it.

    3. Set Space below staff to **20**.

    4. Choose Staff Number **2**.

    •Repeat Steps 2–3.

    5. Click the Add Staff button.

    •Repeat Steps 2–3

    6. Repeat Step 5 to complete a four-stave system

    7. Enter the whole notes **A B C D** in each staff (Figure 88).

    8. Close, Save and name the file "Upper Tetrachords."

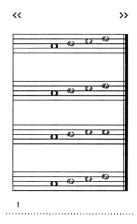

Figure 88. *DMCS* "Upper Tetrachords" notation.

Transfer of the *DMCS* files to *SuperPaint* follows the standard Macintosh Copy/Paste procedure. Referring to Figure 89 as a visual guide:

    (a) Open the "Lower Tetrachord" *DMCS* file, select the Arrow tool, and click-drag it diagonally, from left to right, to enclose the staff with a selection box.

    (b) The whole notes are displayed in outline form, indicating the staff and its contents are selected.

    •**Copy** the selection (Command-**C**).

    (c) Open a New file in the Draw Layer of *SuperPaint*.

    •**Paste** the selection (Command-**V**): each discrete object (staff line, staff section, clef, whole note, and ending barline) displays its handles.

    (d) Click the Arrow tool elsewhere to hide the handles.

    •Save the *SuperPaint* file and name it "Tutorial."

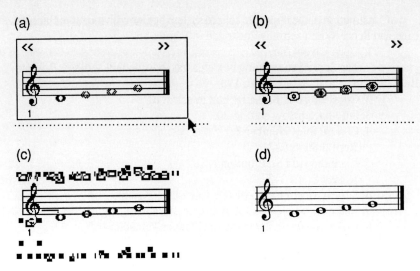

Figure 89. *DMCS* file transfer to the *SuperPaint* Draw Layer.

The next procedure is removal of superfluous objects and grouping of the remaining ones (in the event of a selection error, choose the **Undo** command in the Edit menu or type Command-**Z**).

1. Click the page number **1** to display its handles, and delete it.

2. Click to the right of the ending double-bar line to display its handles, and delete it.

3. Click-drag as described in (a) above, to display all the remaining handles, and choose **Group** in the Draw menu.

•The assembled notation displays four handles, indicating it is now a discrete object..

Following the steps in (a) to (d) above, transfer the *DMCS* "Upper Tetrachords" notation to the *SuperPaint* Tutorial file.

1. Referring to Figure 85, click-drag the lower tetrachord to the midpoint of the upper- tetrachord system.

2. Place a bracket under **E** and **F**.

•Choose **Times 24** (or **New York 24**) and type [(left bracket).

•Select the bracket, choose **Rotate Left** in the Transform menu, and drag it into position.

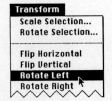

3. Type the text blocks.

•Header: **Times 14**.

•Subhead: **Times 12**.

•Captions: **Helvetica 12** (or **Geneva 12**).

MENSURAL AND PICTORIAL NOTATION

Graphics programs provide an ideal medium for creating tabulations which contrast mensural notation and standard font characters, or for designing pictorial characters which symbolize pitch, rhythm, tone color and peculiarities of performance.

The table of note shapes illustrated in Figure 90 is constructed in the Draw (or Paint) Layer—for the most part by simple alteration of *Sonata* font characters—in four stages:

•A four-line staff is drawn and replicated, followed by construction and placement of mensural note-symbols.

•Ruled lines are drawn to form the tabular framework.

•Columnar headings are typed and dragged into position.

•The modern notation is added to the table.

Maxima (duplex long)	Longa (long)	Brevis (breve)	Semibrevis (semibreve)	Minima (minim)	Semi-minima	Fusa	Semifusa

			Double whole-note	Whole note	Half note	Quarter note	Eighth note	Sixteenth note

Figure 90. From the Table of Note Shapes (13th to 20th centuries) in Gardner Read, *Music Notation*. Copyright © 1969 by Crescendo Publishing, New York.

Creating and Replicating a Four-Line Staff.—**Open** a New file in the Paint Layer of *SuperPaint* and choose **Sonata** in the Font menu.

1. Choose **Other** in the Text menu.

•Type **28** in the Other Font Size dialog box.

2. Select the **A** (Text) tool in the Tool window and click the I-beam cursor to position the flashing insertion point.

•Type = (equal sign) twice to produce an extended five-line staff.

3. Select the **Eraser** tool and delete the bottom line of the staff.

4. Select the **Lasso** tool and encircle the staff to select it.

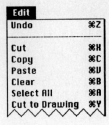

Edit	
Undo	⌘Z
Cut	⌘H
Copy	⌘C
Paste	⌘U
Clear	⌘B
Select All	⌘A
Cut to Drawing	⌘Y

•Choose **Cut to Drawing** in the Edit menu to transform the (bit-mapped) four-line staff into a discrete (QuickDraw) object.

5. Activate the Draw Layer (click the Compass icon at the upper left side of the Tool window).

•The staff displays four handles to indicate it is selected.

6. **Save** the file and name it "Table Tutorial."

The following steps will clone the four-line staff in tabular format, as shown in the upper portion of Figure 90.

1. Choose **Grid & Rulers...** in the Options menu to display its dialog box (see Figure 83).

•Rulers Use: **Centimeters.**

•Grid spacing: **0.20.**

•Select **Show grid.**

•Select **Show rulers.**

2. Exit (**OK**) the dialog box and select the staff (if its handles are not displayed).

3. Choose **Replicate...** in the Edit menu to display its dialog box.

•No. of copies: **2.**

•Measure in: **Cm.**

•Move each copy: **1.69** cm Down (Figure 91).

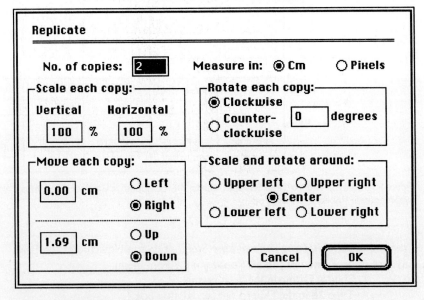

Figure 91. **Replicate...** dialog box.

Three staves are now displayed in precise vertical alignment, and the lowest one displays its selection handles.

1. Hold down the Shift key and click the upper two staves to select them.

•The three staves are ready for horizontal replication.
2. Choose **Replicate...** in the Edit menu to display its dialog box.
•No. of copies: **7**.
•Measure in: **Cm**.
•Move each copy: **0.00** Down and **1.87** cm Right (Figure 92).

Figure 92. Replicated staves ready for editing.

3. Exit the dialog box, then select the upper two staves in the last three columns and the top staff staff in the fifth column.
•Press the Delete key to remove the selected staves from the display.
•In the event of an error in the selection process, choose **Undo** in the Edit menu (or Command-**Z**) to restore the deleted objects.
4. Select the remaining seventeen staves and choose **Group** in the Draw menu (or Command-**G**) to arrange them as one large object.

Creating Mensural Note-Symbols.—The upper two staves in the first three columns of the table, representing the 13th and 14th centuries, are notated with the same forms of the *maxima, longa,* and *brevis*. These forms are constructed with special 24-point symbols contained in the *Sonata* font.
1. *Maxima:* Select the Text tool and click the insertion point away from the staff area.
•Hold down the Option key and type the Hyphen key twice to form a dark rectangle.
•Type Command-**E** (or use the View menu) three times to **Zoom In** to Fat Bits mode (that is, pixel view).
•Select the **Perpendicular Line** tool (the cursor changes to a cross hair) and carefully add a seven-pixel stem below the righmost pixels of the rectangle (the stem displays its two selection handles).
•Select the **Arrow** tool, hold down the Shift key, and click the dark rectangle to select it.
•Type Command-**G** to group the stem and rectangle, then type Command-**W** three times to **Zoom Out** to Window view.
•Duplicate (Command-**D**) the note shape, and drag each one to its position on the middle space of the upper two staves in the first column.

2. *Longa*: The procedure is similar to the construction, duplication, and placement of the *maxima,* with these exceptions:

- The note shape is a dark square (type Option-hyphen once).
- The stem is added to the right side of the note shape, as a fourteen-pixel line.
- Place the note shapes in the second column of staves.

3. *Brevis*: The note shapes are stemless dark squares (Option-hyphen), and they are positioned in the third column of staves.

4. *Semibrevis*: The note shapes are stemless dark diamonds (Option-Shift-Zero), and they are positioned in the fourth column of staves.

5. *Minima*: The note shape is a dark diamond with a thirteen-pixel stem, and it is positioned in the upper staff of the fifth column.

The later (fifteenth to seventeenth centuries) note shapes are constructed by alteration of a special symbol in the *Sonata* font, using dark and "white" diamonds, and adding stems and angular flags.

1. *Maxima*: Change to the Paint Layer (select the Paint Brush icon in the Tool window).

- Continuing with the **Sonata 24** font size, select the **A** (text) icon in the Tool window.
- Click the cursor in the main window and type Option-Shift-4 to display a "white" multiple rest symbol.
- Select the **Pencil** icon in the Tool window and position it over the symbol.
- Hold down the Command key and click the mouse to **Zoom In** to Fat Bits mode.
- Click the point of the **Pencil** tool on the top and bottom pixels of the left vertical line of the symbol. The two pixels will be deleted, reducing the line length from thirteen to eleven pixels.
- Delete the top pixel of the right vertical line, and add three pixels below the line to extend it to fifteen pixels in length.
- Encircle the symbol with the **Lasso** tool and choose **Cut to Drawing** in the Edit menu.
- Drag the note shape to its position in the first column.

2. *Longa*: Follow the same steps for constructing and transforming the *maxima*, with the exception that the ten-pixel horizontal lines are reduced to six-pixel widths.

- Drag the note shape to its position in the second column.

3. *Brevis*: Same basic shape as the *maxima*, with the exception that one pixel is also deleted from bottom of the right vertical line (none are added).

- Drag the note shape to its position in the third column.

4. *Semibrevis*: Option-Shift-9 produces the "white" diamond symbol.

- Drag the note shape to its position in the fourth column.

5. *Minima*: The note shape is a "white" diamond (Option-Shift-9) with a thirteen-pixel stem, and it is positioned in the lower staff of the fifth column.

The *semiminima, fusa* and *semifusa* are similar to the *minima* forms, where the addition of flags requires longer stems.

1. Begin by producing three dark diamonds (Option-Shift-9) and three white ones (Option-Shift- Zero).

2. Select the **Perpendicular Line** tool and draw three fifteen-pixel stems, two with seventeen pixels, and one with nineteen.

3. Affix the fifteen-pixel stems to one white diamond and two dark diamonds.

    •**Group** each diamond-stem combination.

4. Repeat Step 3 with the seventeen-pixel stems affixed to a white and a dark diamond, and the nineteen-pixel stem affixed to a white diamond.

5. A flag consists of a 2-point (pixel) line, eight pixels in length, which is rotated to a 20-degree angle. Begin by clicking the **Pixels** radio button in the Grid & and Rulers dialog box.

    •Select the **Arrow** tool and click the line directly below the default selection in the Line Width Selector.

    •Select the **Perpendicular Line** tool, **Zoom In** to Fat Bits mode, and draw an eight-pixel horizontal line.

    •Choose **Rotate Selection...** in the Transform menu, type **20** in the degrees box, and click the Clockwise and Upper left radio buttons (Figure 93).

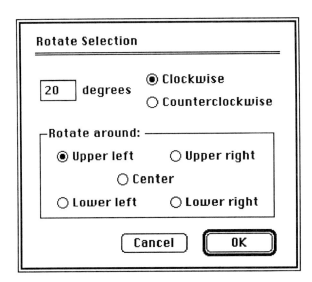

Figure 93. Rotate Selection dialog box

6. Make several duplicates of the flag (Command-**D**), and affix one of them to a short-stem white diamond and another to a short-stem dark diamond.

    •Be sure to drag the flag by clicking the **Arrow** pointer below or above it. A click-drag directly on the flag will alter its shape.

    •**Group** each note shape with its flag.

7. Select a copy of the flag and choose **Replicate...**

•Referring to the dialog box shown in Figure 90, click the Pixels and the Down radio buttons, and move **1** copy down **4** pixels.

•**Group** the two flags, **Duplicate**, and affix one double-flag to a medium-stem white diamond and the other to a medium-stem dark diamond.

•**Group** each note shape with its flags.

8. Construction of a triple flag follows the same procedure given in Step 7, but type **2** as the No. of copies.

•**Group** the three flags.

•Affix the triple flag to the long-stem white diamond,

•**Group** the note shape with its flags

9. Position the note shapes as shown in the last three columns of Figure 90.

10. Select the **Arrow** tool, position it above and to the left of the uppermost staff in the first column, and draw a selection rectangle which will enclose all staves.

•When the selection handles appear for each object, **Group** them into one object (four boundary handles will replace the individual selection handles).

Drawing the Tabular Ruled Lines.—Referring again to Figure 90 as the exemplar, the precise placement of tabular ruled lines is simplified by the use of grid lines (which do not appear on the printed output) and pixel measurements.

1. In the Grid & Rulers dialog box (see Figure 82) type **5** (pixels) as the Grid Spacing, and click the Show grid box to activate it.

2. With the uppermost staff in the first column of the tabular staves as a positioning guide, place the point of the **Arrow** tool at the left edge of the top staff line.

•The dotted lines in the rulers mark the present position of the pointer.

•Click-drag, observing the motion of the dotted lines, until they intersect the **100**-pixel line of each ruler.

•Choose **Lock** in the Draw menu to prevent inadvertent movement or editing of the tabular staves.

3. Click the **H** (hairline) in the **Line Width Selector**, and select the **Cross hair** tool.

•Beginning at the **50**-pixel mark on the vertical ruler, and the **75**-pixel mark on the horizontal ruler, draw a horizontal line to the **505**-pixel mark.

4. **Duplicate** the line and align the copy below the original, on the next grid, to form a double line.

5. Create five more duplicates from the copy, and align them below the double line, at the **85**-, **230**-,**235**-, **265**-, and **310**-pixel marks.

6. Shorten the lower three lines so that they begin at the **190**-pixel mark on the horizontal ruler.

•Click-drag the left handle only.

7. The first (short) vertical line is drawn at the **85**-pixel mark of the horizontal ruler and joins the first and third horizontal rules.

•**Duplicate** the line and align it with original at the 140-pixel mark of the horizontal ruler.

84

8. Draw a longer line at the **190**-pixel mark, so that it joins the first and last horizontal rules.

9. Create six more copies of the line and align them with the original at the **245-, 300, 355-, 405-, 460-,** and **505**-pixel marks on the horizontal ruler.

10. Draw a selection box with the **Arrow** tool to enclose all lines, and **Group** them together.

•Choose **Lock** in the Draw menu.

The column headings are **Times 12** font, typed in the Draw Layer as individual objects, with **Center** justification selected in the Text menu.

1. Drag each heading to its position (see Figure 90).

2. Draw a selection box with the **Arrow** tool to enclose all headings, and **Group** them together

•Choose **Lock** in the Draw menu.

Entering Modern Notation.—Except for the construction of a special double whole-note, the notes are unedited characters in the *Sonata* font. The computer keys and their corresponding music characters are given in Figure 94.

Figure 94. *Sonata* font characters and their corresponding keys.

1. Select **Sonata 18** font and type == to enter the proper staff length.

2. **Duplicate 5** copies.

•Position the staves about an inch apart, to avoid overlapping of their selection handles.

3. Referring to Figure 94, type the values as individual objects and place them on their assigned staves.

•Use **Nudge** commands where necessary.

•Excepting the double whole-note, **Group** the notes with their assigned staves.

•Grouping these objects is easier if the **Two-Layer Selection** tool is used, but the **Group** command will not be activated unless the **Arrow** tool is clicked after the selection handles are displayed.

4. Drag the staves to their position in the table (see Figure 90).

5. The special double whole-note is constructed by framing a whole note with single lines.

•Type **w** and **Zoom In** three times to Fat Bits mode.

•Select the **H** (Hairline) in the **Line Width Selector**, and draw two seven-pixel vertical lines.

•Place a line over the leftmost set of pixels of the note, so that the top pixel of the line is aligned with top pixels of the note.

•Place the other line, using the same alignment, so that it is over the set of pixels next to the rightmost set.

•**Group** the lines with the note.

6. Type **W** to enter the standard double-whole note, and place it on the staff (to the right of center).

•**Group** the note and staff.

•Place the special double-whole note on the staff, to the left of center, and **Group** the objects together.

7. Position the configured double whole-notes in the third column of the table.

8. **Group** the six staves.

9. Select, in turn, the mensural notation and tabular rules groupings, and **Unlock** them.

10. Hold down the shift key and click each of the three sets of grouped objects, and **Group** them together.

•The complete table can now be moved freely or locked to prevent further editing.

Pictorial notation includes non-standard note shapes and other graphics to symbolize certain peculiarities of perfomance. Figure 95 illustrates six types of symbols which are easily constructed with the *SuperPaint* program.

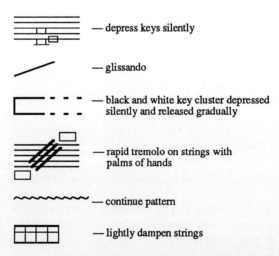

— depress keys silently

— glissando

— black and white key cluster depressed silently and released gradually

— rapid tremolo on strings with palms of hands

— continue pattern

— lightly dampen strings

Figure 95. From the Foreword to Emma Lou Diemer, *Homage to Cowell, Cage, Crumb and Czerny*, for Two Pianos. Copyright © 1983 by Plymouth Music.

The graphic representation of silent key-depression is a combination of the standard five-line staff and simple line drawings.

1. Create a **New** file in the SuperPaint Draw Layer and choose **Sonata 24** as the font size.

2. Type = (equal sign) three times to construct the staff.

•If the *Sonata* font is not available, a 24-point staff can be assembled by replicating hair lines five pixels apart.

3. Using the default line (one-pixel width) in the **Line Width Selector**, and in Fat Bits mode (**Zoom In** three times), draw two five-pixel vertical rules, eleven pixels apart, between the second and third staff lines.

4. Repeat Step 3 below the first line of the staff, so that the four rules are in alignment.

•Center a seventeen-pixel ledger line below the two vertical rules.

5. The last "note" begins two pixels to the right of the other two.

•Repeat Step 3 with seven-pixel rules, so that they are centered on the first line of the staff.

•Connect the two vertical rules with horizontal ones.

•Another method of construction is to use the **Rectangle** tool, with **None** as the Fill Pattern.

6. **Zoom Out** to normal view and choose the **Two-Layer Selection** tool to display the handles of the staff and its rules.

•Click the **Arrow** tool, then **Group** (Command-**D**) as one object.

•**Save** the file as "Pictorial Tutorial."

The glissando is also created with the **Line Width Selector** set at the default (one-pixel) width.

1. Draw a half-inch horizontal rule.

•The selection handles are displayed.

2. Choose **Rotate...** in the Transform menu to display its dialog box (see Figure 93).

•Rotate **20** degrees Counterclockwise around Center.

The graphic representing cluster-key depression is drawn in the Paint Layer, then converted to a Draw Layer object.

1. Set the **Line Width Selector** set at two-pixel width (the line directly below the default line) and choose the **Rectangle** tool.

•Choose **None** as the Fill Pattern.

2. Draw a rectangle, from left to right, one-half inch long and one-quarter inch high.

3. Hold down the Command key and double-click the **Pencil** tool to **Zoom in** to Fat Bits mode.

• Click the point of the tool on the pixels comprising the right line of the rectangle, to delete them.

•Referring to Figure 95 as a guide, add three dashes to the upper and lower lines, each dash three pixels long and two pixels in width.

4. **Zoom Out** to normal view and choose the **Lasso** (or other selection tool) to enframe the drawing.

•Choose **Cut to Drawing** in the Edit menu.

The rapid-tremolo graphic is built with the previously duplicated staff, in the Draw Layer.

1. Using the two-pixel line width in the **Line Width Selector**, draw a vertical line one-half inch long.

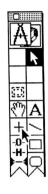

2. Choose **Rotate...** in the Transform menu to display its dialog box (see Figure 93).

　　•Rotate **45** degrees Clockwise around Center.

3. Choose **Replicate...** in the Edit menu to display its dialog box (see Figure 91).

　　•No. of Copies: **2**; Measure in: **Pixels**; Move each copy: **4** pixels Right and **4** pixels Down.

　　•**Group** the three lines as one object and position the center line of the group as shown in Figure 95.

4. The rectangles above and below the staff are drawn at the default (one pixel) line width.

　　•Choose **None** as the Fill Pattern.

　　•Select the Rectangle tool and draw a rectangle, from left to right, one-quarter inch long and one-eighth inch high.

　　•**Duplicate** the rectangle and position each one as shown in Figure 95

　　•**Group** the objects together.

The symbol for pattern continuation is constructed by replicating the ~ symbol in the *Sonata* font.

1. Choose **Sonata 24** in the Font and Text menus, then select the **A** (Text) tool.

2. Type **Shift-~** (tilde/acute-accent key).

3. Choose **Replicate...** in the Edit menu to display its dialog box.

　　•No. of copies: **8**; Measure in: Pixels; Move each copy: **9** pixels Right.

4. Using the Two-Layer Selection tool, drag it over the linked symbols to display their handles.

　　•Select the **Arrow** tool, then type Command-**G** to **Group** the symbols into one object.

The last symbol, indicating dampened strings, is constructed in the Paint Layer.

1. Select the two-pixel line in the **Line Width Selector** and **None** as the Fill Pattern.

2. Draw a rectangle, from left to right, approximately five-eighths inch long and one-quarter inch high.

3. Double-click the **Pencil** Tool to **Zoom In** to Fat Bits Mode.

　　•With the point of the tool, delete the outer set of pixels comprising the left and right sides of the rectangle.

4. Using one-pixel width vertical rules, partition the rectangle into four sections.

5. Draw a horizontal rule one-eighth inch below the upper line of the rectangle.

6. Select the rectangle and **Cut to Drawing**.

7. Align the six symbols (see Figure 95) and add the explanatory text matter (**Times** or **New York 12** font).

8. Use the **Two-Layer Selection** tool to display all graphics and text handles, then select the **Arrow** tool and **Group** the objects together.

ENHANCING THE SCORE

One of the major problems facing scholars, educators, and other authors of essays on music is the preparation of music examples with clarifying graphics, particularly when publication is the objective. The usual solution is to photocopy a score extract and add hand-drawn descriptors for processing by music engravers or professional draftsmen. Publication contracts invariably mandate the costs of illustrative material to be the responsibility of the author. And, too, there are obstructive factors to consider, such as the time element, communication problems, and proofreading tasks, until satisfactory completion of the illustrations. A solution to the problem is illustrated by Figure 96, one of any number of similar music examples that can be prepared at the desktop and submitted to a publisher as camera-ready final copy.

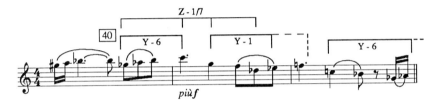

Figure 96. Example 137 in Elliott Antokoletz, *The Music of Béla Bartók*. Copyright © 1984 by the Regents of the University of California. The extract is from Bartók's *String Quartet No. 4*, Movement I, mm. 40–42. Copyright © 1929 by Universal Edition; Copyright and Renewal assigned to Boosey & Hawkes, Inc. Reprinted by permission.

The music notation was processed in *Deluxe Music Construction Set* and exported to the *SuperPaint* Draw Layer (see p. 22, above), where it was saved as a **New** file. The ancillary matter is entered as follows:

    1. The line drawings are constructed in the Paint Layer, with the **Line Width Selector** at the default (one pixel) setting and the **Rectangle** tool with **None** as the Fill Pattern.

    •After each of the four variable-length rectangles are drawn above the related notation, the **Pencil** tool is used in Fat Bits mode to delete the bottom line.

    2. The dashed lines are drawn with the crosshair cursor and the **Line Width Selector** set at the default (one pixel) line.

    •The **Line Styles** command is selected in the Options menu, to display its dialog box, and **Dashed** is checked in the submenu.

    3. The next step is selection of the **Dashes...** command, in the same menu, to display the **Edit Document Dashes** dialog box.

    •The **Pixels** radio button is clicked and **5** typed as the length of the **dash** and the **gap** between dashes (Figure 97). The dashed lines are then appended to the upper line of the related rectangles.

    4. The **Selection Rectangle** is used to enclose the painted rectangles and dashed lines, followed by the **Cut to Drawing** command in the Edit menu.

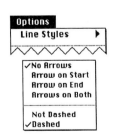

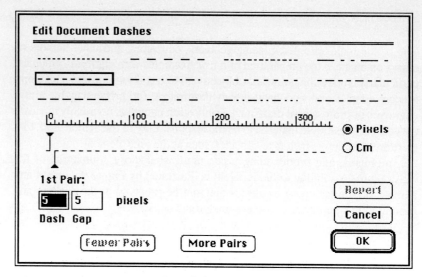

Figure 97. Edit Document Dashes dialog box.

5. The Draw Layer is activated, music and line drawings are selected with the **Arrow** tool, and **Group** is clicked in the Draw menu.

6. The last procedure is the addition of the text matter.

•The Z- and Y-cell descriptors are entered in **Times** or **New York 12** font.

•The boxed measure number and the dynamic mark are **14**-point size, and the latter is a combination of Plain and Bold styles.

•The text blocks are grouped with the graphics to form one object.

EXTRA-NOTATIONAL CONSTRUCTIONS

Figure 98 shows the kind of shape and line combinations that can be constructed in the *SuperPaint* Draw Layer, with a minimum of time and effort. The following Tutorial uses rulers and grids, with **1** centimeter as the grid spacing (see the **Grid & Rulers...** dialog box in Figure 82).

The chordophones (stringed instruments) and membranophones (drums) are represented by rectangular shapes and line objects.

1. Select the **Rectangle** tool, with **None** as the Fill Pattern, and draw the shape **4** centimeters wide and **2** centimeters high.

2. Select the **Perpendicular Line** tool, with the default (one pixel) line in the **Line Width Selector,** and draw a pair of diagonal lines which join the opposite corners of the rectangle.

3. Draw a pair of perpendicular lines which join the opposite sides of the rectangle and intersect at the junction of the diagonal lines.

•Select the **Arrow** tool, hold down the Shift key, and click each line

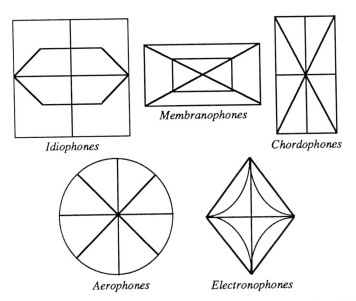

Idiophones

Membranophones

Chordophones

Aerophones   Electronophones

Figure 98. Symbolic taxonomy for musical instruments in Mantle Hood, *The Ethnomusicologist*. Copyright © 1971 by McGraw-Hill, New York.

and any side of the rectangle, to display all handles.

•**Group** (Command-**G**) the lines and shape into one object.

3. **Duplicate** (Command-**D**) the object and choose **Rotate Left** (or **Right**) in the Transform menu.

•Complete the Chordophone symbol with an intersecting third line.

4. Return to the original object and draw an inner rectangle, with **None** as the Fill Pattern, so that its corners also join with the diagonal lines.

•**Group** the two shapes and the diagonal lines into one object, to complete the membranophone symbol.

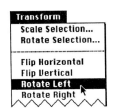

The Aerophones (wind instruments) are represented by a circular shape and line objects.

1. Select the **Perpendicular Line** tool and draw a **4**-centimeter horizontal line.

2. Choose **Replicate...** in the Options menu, to display its dialog box (see Figure 91).

•No. of copies: **3**.

•Rotate each copy: Clockwise **45** degrees.

3. Choose **Draw from Center** in the Options menu, and select the **Oval** tool with **None** as the Fill Pattern.

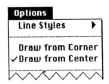

•Hold down the Shift key, place the cursor cross hair at the junction of the intersecting lines, and draw a **4**-centimeter circle.

4. **Group** (Command-**G**) the shape and lines into one object.

The idiophones (non-membraneous percussion instruments) are represented by a square, hexagon, and perpendicular lines.

1. Select the **Rectangle** tool, with **None** as the Fill Pattern.

2. Choose **Draw from End** in the Options menu, hold down the Shift key, and draw a **4**-centimeter square.

3. Select the **Perpendicular Line** tool and draw a pair of perpendicular lines that will partition the shape into four **2**-centimeter squares.

4.Select the **Multigon** tool with **None** as the Fill Pattern.

•Choose **Multigon Sides...** in the Options menu to display its dialog box.

•Click the hexagon to select it (Figure 99).

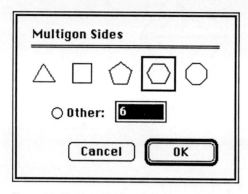

Figure 99. **Multigon Sides** dialog box with hexigon selected.

5. Choose **Draw from Center** in the Options menu and center the cursor cross hair at the junction of the perpendicular lines.

6. Hold down the Shift key and draw a **4**-centimeter hexagon.

•Drag one of the upper handles down **1** centimeter.

•Drag one of the lower handles up **1** centimeter.

7. Hold down the Shift key and click each perpendicular line and any side of the square and the hexagon, to display all handles.

•**Group** (Command-**G**) the shapes and lines into one object.

The electronophones (electronic instruments) are represented by a diamond shape, arcs, and perpendicular lines.

1. Select the **Multigon** tool with **None** as the Fill Pattern.

•Choose **Multigon Sides...** in the Options menu to display its dialog box.

•Click the triangle (default) shape to select it (see Figure 98).

2. Choose **Draw from Corner** in the Options menu.

3. Draw a triangle **3** centimeters wide and **2** centimeters high.

•If necessary, select the **Arrow** tool and drag one or another of the four handles to adjust the dimensions.

4. **Duplicate** (Command-**D**) the shape and choose **Flip Vertical** in the Transform menu.

5. Drag the duplicate by one of its sides and position it to form a diamond shape.

•The horizontal side should be placed over the one of the original shape, to maintain a common, one-pixel line width.

•If necesssary, **Zoom In** to Fat Bits mode and use the **Nudge** commands in the Edit menu (or the arrow keys) to align the shapes.

6. Select the **Perpendicular Line** tool and draw a vertical line connecting the upper and lower corners of the shape.

7. Choose the **Arc** tool, position the cursor cross hair on the upper corner of the shape, and drag downward to its left corner.

•Reposition the cursor and drag downward to the right corner.

8. Position the cursor cross hair on the lower corner of the shape and drag upward to the left corner.

•Reposition the cursor and drag upward to the right corner.

9. Choose the **Arrow** tool and drag it across the completed shape to display all handles.

•**Group** (Command-G) the shapes, lines and arcs into one object.

SUMMARY

The seven "user friendly" tutorials for creating music-oriented graphics were processed with the Silicon Beach Software *SuperPaint* (Version 2.0) application. The difference between bitmaps (Paint Layer) and objects (Draw Layer) is illustrated by comparing screen and laser-printed characters from the Adobe *Sonata* music font. *Sonata* also provides the music characters used to build rhythmic patterns, construct font-exclusive scores, reconstruct scores, or produce music examples in the *Deluze Music Construction Set* program for subsequent graphic enhancements. And certain *Sonata* symbols are used to supplement drawn characters in the construction of mensural notation. Unconventional pictorial notation and non-notational graphics, built with *SuperPaint* shape, line, and arc tools, are provided as exemplars for creative musicians and scholarly writers.

In 1991, long after this chapter had been completed, a major upgrade of *SuperPaint* appeared, following the aquisition of Silicon Beach Software by the Aldus Corporation. The new version 3.0, renamed Aldus *SuperPaint*, provides new features and a number of improvements to the previous, exceptional program. The current street price of the Aldus *SuperPaint* application is about $135 (registered owners of the earlier version have been offered the upgrade for $65), and the recommended Adobe *Sonata* screen and printer fonts can be purchased for $60 or less.

CHAPTER 3

Database Construction

A computer database (the "datafile") is comparable to a group of library index cards (the "records") which contain entries such as title, author, and subject (the "fields"). In this chapter Microsoft *File* is used to construct tutorials of music-oriented databases, namely a lexicographical thematic index, catalogue of compositions, and grammatical tabulation of folk songs. *Filevision IV* is a unique application for retrieving information from a graphic bibliography of music sources. A third approach to database construction, with the multimedia information manager *HyperCard 2,* is explored in Chapter 6, below.

THE THEMATIC INDEX

In his Introduction to *Serbo-Croatian Folk Songs (Yugoslav Folk Music,* vol. 1) Béla Bartók compares lexicographical and grammatical principles of grouping folk song melodies. He refers to the former as a system similar to the one used in lexicons and dictionaries, which enables the easy location of melodies by simple mechanical means. The structural attributes of this system are the melody section (the portion corresponding to one line of text) and its melodic contour (the pitch relation of the principal tones). In addition to its value as a theme finder the lexicographic index can serve as a guide to variant relationships within and between discrete repertories, including popular art songs (so-called urban folk music) and Western art music.

Beginning in 1965 Harry B. Lincoln successfully constructed what is probably the largest database of Italian Renaissance music, and he developed a program for lexicographic indexing of themes by an IBM mainframe computer, which required preliminary translation of music notation into machine-readable form (alphanumeric representation). Pitch is represented by numbers which indicates staff position, duration by mnemonic letters, and pitch alteration by other characters. The computer scans the numeric string and calculates the melodic contour of the first melody section (the "incipit") in terms of plus and minus digits (+2 -2, +3 -3, etc.), to indicate the sequence of ascending and descending intervals. For practical reasons (about 40,000 incipits were involved) the sequence was limited to a maximum of seven interval changes, and repeated notes as well as intervallic quality were ignored.

The processing concludes with the sorting of the interval sequence, where lesser precedes greater and plus precedes minus, as in the following sample:

+2 +2 +2 +2 +2 –2 –2
+2 +2 +2 +2 +2 –2 –3
+2 –2 –2 –2 –2 –2
–2 +2 +2 +2 +2 +2 +2
–2 –2 +2 +2 +2 +2 +2
etc.

Determination of Melodic Contour.—In conformity with the Bartók system of folk song classification, when two or more notes of different pitch are sung to one syllable they constitute an ornamental group (melisma). In such cases one of the notes can be regarded as the principal one and the others as supplementary ornamental notes. The first step in determining melodic contour, therefore, is to skeletonize the incipit according to its syllabic structure (Figure 100).

+2+2-4

Figure 100. Skeletonized incipit and its interval sequence from melody No. 33, in Béla Bartók, *Serbo-Croatian Folk Songs.* Copyright © 1951, 1978 by the State University of New York, Albany, as *Yugoslav Folk Music,* vol. 1.

The next step is analysis of the skeletonized incipit and determination of the direction and size of its interval sequence. The most economic use of a desktop computer in building a large database, particularly with regard to memory requirements and the time involved in data input and output, is to structure the file as a pointer to the original source material and not as an electronic depot for storing and processing alphanumeric representations of notated music. As Figure 100 implies, it is a relatively simple procedure to ignore the repeated note (G), treat the major second (G-A) and minor second (A-B♭) as identical signed digits (+2), and enter the derived interval sequence as a field in the record.

Construction of the Datafile.—The maximum capacity of Microsoft *File* is 65,535 records, 1,023 fields in each record, and 32,767 characters in each field. Put in another way, the application can list, find, and sort for location or comparative purposes the substantial number of incipits and related information derived from Bartók's composed works and his collections of Hungarian, Rumanian, Slovak, and Yugoslav folk music.

Figure 101 shows syllabic (non-melismatic) examples from the folk music collections, where each incipit has the same +2 +2 –2 –2 interval sequence. The program consolidates identical interval sequences during the sorting procedure, thus indicating possible variant relationships. If the related music notations are added to the datafile, it acquires duality of purpose: location of themes and determination of variants.

Bartók. *The Hungarian Folk Song*, 181

Bartók. *Rumanian Folk Music* IV, 62d

Bartók. *Slowakische Volkslieder* I, 55c

Bartók and Kodály. *Transylvanian Hungarian Folk Songs*, 56

Bartók. *Yugoslav Folk Music* III, 7b

Figure 101. Identical interval sequences (+2 +2 –2 –2) in Bartók's *The Hungarian Folk Song* (Copyright © 1981 by the State University of New York, Albany), *Rumanian Folk Music* IV (Copyright © 1975 by Martinus Nijhoff), *Slowakische Volkslieder* I (Bratislava: Slovenskej Akadémie Vied, 1959), *Yugoslav Folk Music* III (Copyright © 1978 by the State University of New York, Albany), and (with Zoltán Kodály) *Transylvanian Hungarian Folk Songs* (Budapest, Popular Literary Society, 1923).

Microsoft File

Double-click the *File* icon to display the Name for New Datafile dialog box, type **Tutorial**, and click the **New** button.

1. The active Form window is displayed in front of the Datafile window, with a flashing insertion point in its default field box (Figure 102).

96

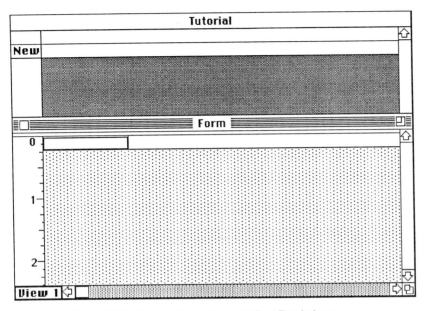

Figure 102. *Microsoft File* Form and New ("Tutorial") Datafile windows.

2. Type **Sequence** as the field name (a second field box is displayed during text entry).

3. Press the Return key (the program automatically saves all entered data)..

•The Type (of data) dialog box is displayed, with the default **Text** button selected. Click the **OK** button, since interval sequences are Text data for indexing purposes and not Number data for mathematical calculations.

•The Sequence field name appears in the Tutorial window and the insertion point flashes in the next field box in the Form window.

4. Repeat Steps 2–3 with **Source** as the field name.

5. Repeat Steps 2–3 with **Incipit** as the field name and **Picture** as the Type of data (Figure 103).

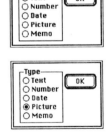

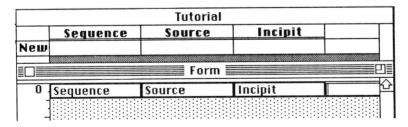

Figure 103. Field name entries in the Form window default boxes and (Chicago) font, with their counterparts as centerheads in the Datafile window.

Since the usual size of music fonts is 18 or 24 points, the default rectangular boundaries of the Incipit field box will clip the notation. It will therefore be necessary to adjust the width and height of the box, after the first incipit has been pasted. Adjustment of the Sequence and Source field boxes will depend on the number, style, and size of the characters entered in each field. Although the purpose of this Tutorial is to construct a theme locator with notated incipits for comparative analysis, the reader may wish to limit data input to text fields. In this case the Incipit field may be left blank or deleted in the Form window by clicking the cursor in the field box (the Arrow pointer changes to a multiple-arrow shape) and choosing **Clear** in the Edit menu.

1. Engrave the incipits shown in Figure 101.

•The music application must be able to Cut or Copy the notation to the Clipboard, for Paste in the *File* Incipit field.

•For economic datafile construction, the incipits can be pasted in the *SuperPaint* Draw Layer (or similar graphics application) and proportionately scaled 60% (24-point music font) or 80% (18-point) prior to field entry.

2. **Open** the Tutorial (or click on its window if the Form window is active).

•The insertion point flashes in the Sequence field box of the New record.

3. Type **+2+2–2–2** (do not use the Space Bar).

•Hold down the Option key when typing the hyphen key, to produce the minus sign.

•Press the Return key to move the insertion point to the Source field box.

4. Type **Bartók, The Hungarian Folk Song 181** (a portion of the text scrolls out of sight).

•The accented **ó** is produced when Option-**e** precedes the **o** key.

5. Position the (I-beam) cursor in the Source field header area, on the right side of its box.

•The cursor changes to a horizontal double-arrowhead shape.

•Click-drag to the right until the complete text is displayed.

6. **Copy** the incipit in the music application, return to the Tutorial, and **Paste** it in the Incipit field box.

7. Choose **Show Form** in the Form menu to display the active Form window.

8. Repeat Step 5 in the Form window Incipit box (the cursor changes from a multiple-arrow shape) to display the full width of the notation.

9. Position the cursor on the bottom side of the Incipit box.

•The cursor changes to a vertical double-arrowhead shape.

•Click-drag down until the remainder of the notation is displayed.

10. Click the Tutorial window to activate it for font enhancement.

11. Select the Sequence header with the I-beam.

•Choose **Set Font...** in the Form menu, to display its dialog box. and select **Helvetica** (or **Geneva**). The default alignment and style may be changed in the **Format Text Field...** dialog box).

98

•Repeat the procedure for the Source and Incipit headers.

13. Select the interval sequence in Record 1 and change the font to **Times** (or **New York**).

•Repeat the procedure for the text in the Source field.

Figure 104 is a screen dump of the completed Tutorial window. In order to display the records with three adequately-spaced columns, without clipping text or picture data, the Sequence and Source fonts are set in 10-point size and the 18-point Incipit notations are scaled to 80% of original size. Output from a laser printer provides high quality copy at various reduction percentages.

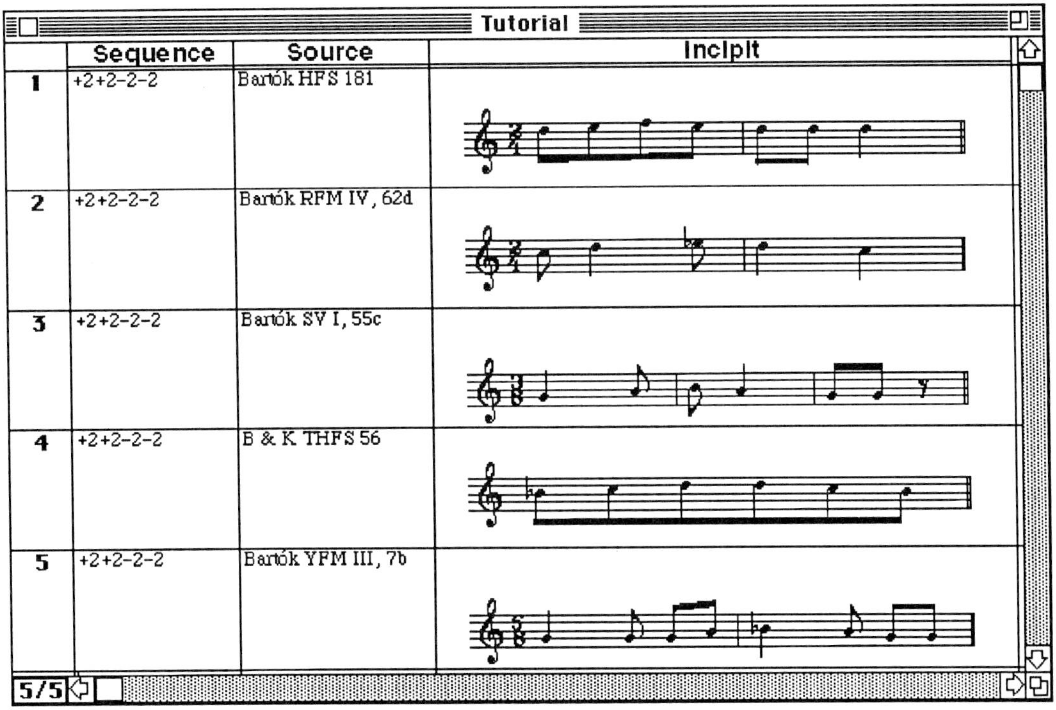

Figure 104. Completed Tutorial datafile. The distorted notation results from reduction bit-mapped music characters.

The final procedure is retrieval of information by use of commands in the Organize menu. The location of themes is implemented when **Find…** is selected and its dialog box (Figure 105) is displayed for typing the sequence wanted, including symbolic operators such as the equal sign ("match exactly what is typed"). When the sequence is found, all the related records in the datafile are sequentially displayed. It is noteworthy that Incipit fields cannot be searched, since they are non-retrievable Picture data.

The determination of possible variant relationships begins with the **Sort…** command which displays a dialog box for the alphabetical ordering of records, from A→Z (or Z→A when the cursor is clicked in a specific column). The narrow column in each field contains a number to designate the sorting order (1 or 2: Picture fields cannot be sorted). In the present example (Figure 105) the records are retrieved on the basis of intervallic sequence, where plus (ascending interval) precedes minus (descending) and lesser (smaller) precedes greater.

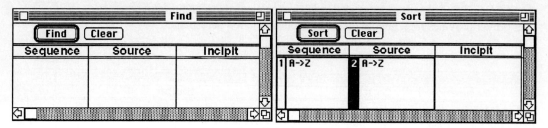

Figure 105. **Find...** and **Sort...** dialog boxes for retrieval and ordering of fields.

The **Report...** command displays a dialog box for designing the screen display or printout of the records. The dialog box is divided into three areas: Sort, Not Sorted and Not Shown. The program places the previously sorted fields (see Figure 105) in the Sort area and the Picture (Incipit) field in the Not Sorted column (Figure 106). If a field is dragged into the Not Shown column, its information will not appear on the report.

Sort	A->Z	A->Z	Not Sorted	Not Shown
Heading	Sequence	Source	Incipit	
Field	Interval Sequence	Source Melody	Incipit	

Figure 106. **Report...** dialog box, showing the Sort and Not Sorted fields.

When the **Preview** button is clicked, a new window is displayed to show how the sorted information will appear in printed form (Figure 107). Although the Incipit header is shown, the non-sorted (Picture) incipits are not included in the display, the report treats the common interval sequence as a single line of signed digits in the first column, and the related information—indicating possible thematic borrowings!—is displayed in the second column, in alphabetic order of sources. During the processing of the report the original list of records (see Figure 104) is likewise alphabetized: the incipits can then be printed with their related data by choosing **Print Records...** in the File menu.

100

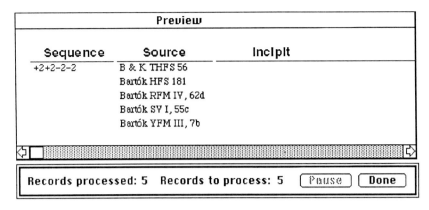

Figure 107. **Preview** display of diverse folk melodies with the same interval sequence.

THE CATALOGUE OF MUSICAL WORKS

The Catalogue of Musical Works datafile also is produced with *File,* since it is similar in construction to the Thematic Index. The following Tutorial, however, emulates more or less traditional practice in catalogue preparation, and the interval sequence field (see pp. 95–96, above) is therefore omitted. Begin with the notation of the Chopin themes shown in Figure 108, then scale them proportionately in a graphics program, such as *SuperPaint,* to a smaller size for field entry in the datafile.

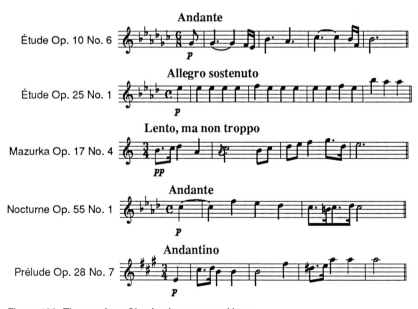

Figure 108. Themes from Chopin piano compositions.

Microsoft File

Construction of the Datafile.—Double-click the Microsoft *File* icon to display the Name for New Datafile dialog box, type **Catalogue**, and click the **New** button.

    1. The active Form window is displayed in front of the Datafile window, with a flashing insertion point in its default field box (see Figure 102).

    2. Type **Title** as the field name (a second field box is displayed during text entry).

    3. Press the Return key (the program automatically saves all entered data).

    •The Type (of data) dialog box is displayed, with the default **Text** button selected. Click the **OK** button.

    •The Title field name appears in the Catalogue window, and the insertion point flashes in the next field box in the Form window.

    4. Repeat Steps 2–3 and add the following fields:

    •**Op.** (Opus)

    •**No.**

    •**Composed**

    •**Published**

    •**Remarks**

    5. Repeat Steps 2–3 with **Theme** as the field name and **Picture** as the Type of data (Figure 109).

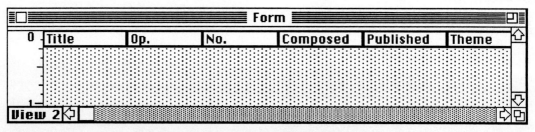

Figure 109. Field header entries in the Catalogue of Musical Works datafile Form window.

    Since the usual size of music fonts is 18 or 24 points, the default rectangular boundaries of the Theme field box will clip the notation. It will therefore be necessary to adjust the width and height of the box, after the first incipit has been pasted. Adjustment of the other field boxes depends on the number, style, and size of the characters entered in each field.

    Close the Form window to activate the Catalogue window. The text insertion point flashes in the Title field box of the New record.

    1. Type **Étude, Eb mi.**

    •Option-**e** followed by Shift-**e** produces É.

    2. Press the Return key to move the insertion point to the Op. field box.

    3. Type **10.**

    4. Repeat Step 2 and type **6** as the No. field, **1829–32** as the Composed

field, and **1833** as the Published field.

> •Type Option-hyphen to produce the dash in the Composed text field.
> •Press the Return key to skip the Theme field and move to Record 2.

5. Referring to Figure 110, enter the text data in the other records.

	Catalogue				
	Title	**Op.**	**No.**	**Composed**	**Published**
1	Étude, Ab ma.	25	1	1832-36	1837
2	Étude, Eb mi.	10	6	1829-32	1833
3	Mazurka, A mi.	17	4	1832-33	1834
4	Nocturne, F mi.	55	1	1843	1844
5	Prélude, A ma.	28	7	1836-39	1839
New					
5/5					

Figure 110. Catalogue window with completed text field data (default Chicago font), sorted alphabetically by Title.

In order to paste a theme or other Picture in the datafile, the field box must be selected prior to data insertion. When the I-beam (or Arrow pointer) cursor moves into that box, the shape changes to a selection cross. Then the box may be clicked, and its "fill" changes from white to black to verify the selection and enable the Paste command. In the case of pasting large graphics, such as music notation, the default field box "clips" the picture, that is, the box will not automatically adjust its size to display the theme. A successful paste, however, will revert the field box from black to white, and its sides can be manually adjusted to expose the theme.

1. **Copy** the first theme (Étude, Eb mi.) in the music application.

2. Return to the Catalogue window and select the Theme field box in Record 1.

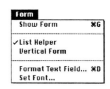

3. **Paste** (Command-**V**).

4. Choose **Show Form** in the Form menu to display the active Form window.

5. Position the multiple-arrow cursor on the bottom side of the Theme field box.

> •The cursor changes to a vertical double-arrowhead shape.
> •Click-drag down until the complete height of the muaic is displayed in the Catalogue window Theme box.

6. Position the cursor on the right side of the Theme field box.

> •The cursor changes to a horizontal double-arrowhead shape.
> •Click-drag to the right until the complete width of the music is displayed (Figure 111).

7. Paste the other themes in their respective records (see Figure 108).

> •If further adjustment of the Theme field box is necessary, return to the Form window and repeat Steps 5–6.

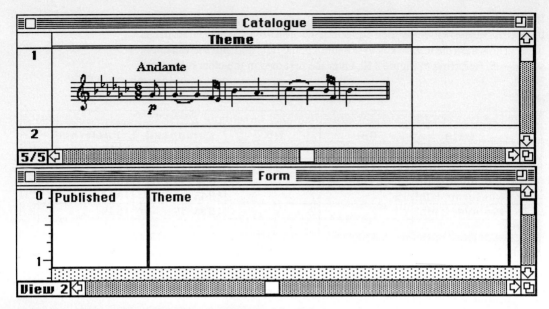

Figure 111. Display of the complete music notation in the Catalogue window, following vertical and horizontal adjustment of the Theme field box in the Form window.

In the event the datafile is destined for hard copy output, the text fields and headers should be changed from the default Chicago font to Times (or New York) and Helvetica (or Geneva), respectively.

    1. In Record 1 select the text in the Title field box with the I-beam.

      •Choose **Set Font...** in the Form menu, to display its dialog box (Figure 112). and select **Times** (or **New York**). The text in this field in Records 2–5 also reflects the font change.

      •Repeat the text font change in the other field boxes of Record 1.

    2. Select the Title header with the I-beam.

      •Choose **Set Font...** in the Form menu, to display its dialog box, and select **Helvetica** (or **Geneva**).

      •Repeat the font change in the other headers.

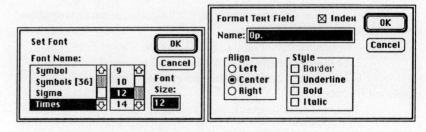

Figure 112. **Set Font** and **Format Text Field** dialog boxes.

Figure 113 is a screen dump of the completed Catalogue window. Rather than the default left alignment in the display, an optional enhancement would be the center alignment of the Op., No., Composed, and Published fields. The field selection procedure is the same as described above for setting the fonts, choosing **Format Text Field...** in the Form menu to display its dialog box (Figure 112), and clicking the **Center** radio button. The numerals in these fields in Records 2–5 also reflect the changed alignment.

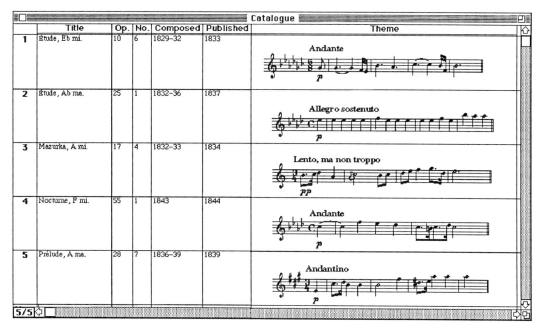

Figure 113. Completed Catalogue of Musical Works datafile. The distorted notation results from screen reduction of bitmapped music characters.

The final procedure is retrieval of information by use of commands in the Organize menu. The location of themes is implemented when **Find...** is selected and its dialog box (see Figure 105) is displayed for typing the information wanted ("Title", etc.), including symbolic operators such as the equal sign ("match exactly what is typed"). When the information is found, all the related records in the datafile are sequentially displayed. Theme fields cannot be searched, since they are non-retrievable Picture data.

The Catalogue text fields (opus numbers and dates are treated as text matter) can be listed according to alphanumeric order, from A→Z (or Z→A if the cursor is clicked in a specific column). When the **Sort...** command is selected, a dialog box is displayed for ordering the records (Figures 115–16), The narrow column in each field contains a number to designate the sorting order (1, 2... 5: Theme fields cannot be sorted).

The **Report...** command displays a dialog box for designing the screen display or printout of the records. The dialog box is divided into three areas: Sort, Not Sorted and Not Shown. The program places the previously sorted fields in the Sort area and the Picture (Theme) field in the Not Shown column (Figure 114).

Sort					Not Shown
Heading	Op.	No.	**Composed**	**Published**	
Field	Op.	No.	Composed	Published	Theme
Grand					

Figure 114. **Report...** dialog box, indicating the Sort fields and the "Not Shown" Theme field.

When the **Preview** button is clicked, a new window is displayed to show how the sorted information will appear in printed form (Figures 115–16).

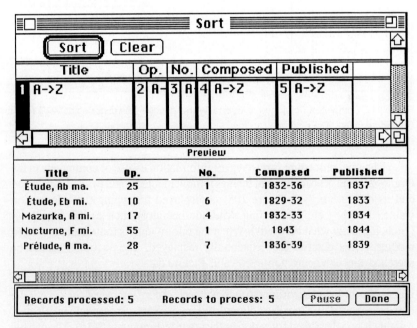

Title	Op.	No.	Composed	Published
Étude, Ab ma.	25	1	1832-36	1837
Étude, Eb mi.	10	6	1829-32	1833
Mazurka, A mi.	17	4	1832-33	1834
Nocturne, F mi.	55	1	1843	1844
Prélude, A ma.	28	7	1836-39	1839

Records processed: 5   Records to process: 5   Pause   Done

Figure 115. The **Sort...** dialog box with the Title field designated as the primary (**1**) alphanumeric (**A→Z**) field in the sorting order, and the resultant display when the **Preview** button is clicked in the **Report...** dialog box.

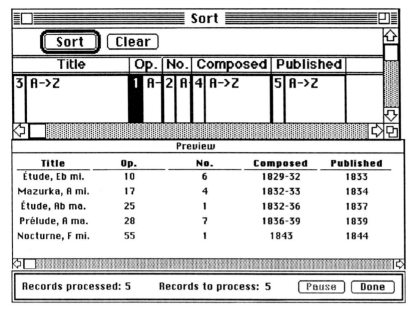

Figure 116. The **Sort...** dialog box with the Opus field designated as the primary field in the sorting order, and the resultant display when the **Preview** button is clicked.

The complete Catalogue of Musical Works can be printed in the format shown in Figure 113, according to the designated sorting order. An alternative, more flexible method of printing the Catalogue report is to export the file to a word processing program, such as Microsoft *Word*, for reformatting (Figure 117). When **Save As...** is selected in the File menu, a dialog box is displayed to name the exported file and click the **Text** radio button (the original Catalogue datafile is unaffected by this procedure). If the user intends to reformat the Catalogue in a word processing program, headers and text fields should be entered with the default Chicago font, to expedite construction of the datafile.

File	
New Datafile...	⌘N
Open Datafile...	⌘O
Close	⌘W
Save	
Save Records As...	
Page Setup...	
Print Records...	⌘P

Title	**Op.**	**No.**	**Composed**	**Published**
Étude, Eb mi.	10	6	1829–32	1833
Mazurka, A mi	17	4	1832–33	1834
Étude, Ab ma.	25	1	1832–36	1837
Prélude, A ma.	28	7	1836–39	1839
Nocturne, F mi.	55	1	1843	1844

Figure 117. The sorted Catalogue, exported to and reformatted in Microsoft *Word*.

The Tabulation of Folk Music Material

During the summer of 1938 Béla Bartók completed his assembly of 3,449 published and unpublished Yugoslav folk songs available till then. After his emigration to the United States in 1940 he transcribed seventy-five songs from the Parry Collection of Yugoslav folk music, reviewed the collections, and selected 3,503 melodies for classification purposes. He decided to group the material according to his own "grammatical" principles—rather than commonplace lexical (dictionary) indexing of themes—in order to describe the typical forms and structures. Bartók created a special instrument for this purpose, which he designated "Tabulation of Material," and completed its construction in July 1943.

Bartók's typological methodology and its format is particularly suitable as an approach to constructing datafiles of art-, folk-, or pop songs, since the analysis and organization of structural attributes enables the researcher to draw scientific conclusions about melodic types, transformations, and variant relationships. And it is certainly feasible to add the interval sequence as a supplementary field for additional, lexical indexing (see pp. 94–95, above).

The Tabulation of Material datafile, described and illustrated further below, is also processed with Microsoft *File*. General construction procedures replace specific, tutorial steps, since the latter are for the most part identical with those given in the preceding Thematic Index and Catalogue of Musical Works. The grammatical order of Tabulation headers and an explanation of each field are as follows:

1. *No.*— The numeric designation of records for printing purposes, corresponding to the numbers assigned by the program. If less than 100 records are constructed, single-digit record numbers must have a prefixal zero (01...09) in order to sort sequentially. In the case of 100 to 999 records: one or two prefixal zeros (001...009 and 010...099), and so on.

2. *Syllables.*—Western vocal melodies usually can be partitioned into two, three, or four melody sections, where each section corresponds to one text line. Isometric melodies have the same number of text syllables in each section, usually five or more. Heterometric melodies have one or several sections with a different number of syllables, such as this typical Slovak quaternary with alternating (07 06 07 06) lines: ‖: ♪♪♪♪ | ♪♪♩ | ♪♪♪♪ | ♩ ♩ :‖. Single-digit syllabic numbers also must have a prefixal zero (01...09) in order to sort sequentially.

3. *End-note 1.*—With the exception of the referential final note in the last melody section, the note considered to be the end note of the preceding sections is alphanumerically represented by a roman or arabic numeral and the suffixal letter b (= ♭), n (none) or s (= ♯) to indicate an accidental. When an end note is lower in pitch than the final note, it is designated by a roman numeral with a prefixal asterisk (the asterisk enables roman to precede arabic numerals during the sorting procedure).

Each end note is calculated as an interval related to the final note in terms of location and quality. If the final note is G and the first end note is F or F♯ below it, the field entry is *VIIn or *VIIs. If the end note is B♭ or B above G, the entry is 03b or 03n. Figure 118 is derived from Bartók's table of section end-note designations, where *I, 01, and 08 represent g, g¹ and g², respectively. It is noteworthy that Bartók transposed all melodies to g¹ as the final note, to minimize use of ledger notes as well as facilitate comparative analysis of his diverse materials. The researcher, however, need only base end-note designations on whatever note is considered to be the final one in transposed or untransposed melodies.

Notes:
Figures: *I   *II   *III   *IV   *V   *VI   *VII   01   02   03   04   05   06   07   08   09   10   11

Figure 118. Section end-note designations with prefixal * and 0 characters for sorting purposes.

3. *End-note 2.*—Same remarks as to *End-note 1*. This end note, which occurs at the midpoint of a quaternary, is considered to be the main caesura: it therefore takes precedence when sorting the three end-notes.

4. *End-note 3.*—Same remarks as to *End-note 1*. The third end-note follows *End-note 1* in the sorting order.

5. *Range.*—The same designations are used to indicate ambitus of the melody, from lowest to highest note. Non-principal notes of the melody (grace notes and other ornaments) are not included in the determination of range.

6. *Rhythm.*—Various types of indicators may be used, such as: skeletonized rhythm schemata, signed digits to mark syllabic subdivision (4+2, 3+4, etc.), and small letters to indicate isorhythmic (a a a a) and heterorhythmic sections (a a b b, a b a b, etc.).

7. *Structure.*—Similarity or difference in content of the sections, such as A A B A, A A B C, and A B C D in quaternary melodies.

8. *Type.*—Dance melodies, ceremonial-song designations, foreign variants, and other sortable remarks.

    The grammatical classification of autochthonous folk music material may require supplementation of the above-listed fields. During his study of Hungarian peasant songs, Bartók discovered that the melodies could be grouped into three styles: Old, New, and Mixed. He therefore had to include the determination of pentatonic scale structure and tempo, since pentatonicism and *parlando-rubato* (that is, free) rhythm are significant attributes of antiquity. Mixed-style Hungarian folk songs are close variants of Slovak melodies or contain certain foreign characteristics, such as the Ruthenian (Ukrainian) *kolomyjka* dance rhythm. Bartók's study of Slovak peasant songs disclosed the need to divide *parlando-rubato* and *Tempo giusto* (strict rhythm) melodies into separate groups. And he invariably used a Remarks "field" to indicate such peculiarities as the ending of Yugoslav melodies on a semi-cadence.

Figure 119 is a *File* Tabulation of Slovak Material which illustrates the headers and text fields listed above. The interested reader can replicate the datafile or substitute other fields (for instance, the interval sequence) for experimenting with different sorting procedures.

	Record	Syll.	Sec. 1	Sec. 2	Sec. 3	Range	Rhythm	Form	Type
1	01	6	*UII	3b	6b	*UIIn-6b	a a b c	A B C D	Hungarian
2	02	6	3	3n	5	1-6	a b c d	A B C D	Svadobná
3	03	6	1	4s	1	1-5	a b a b	A B A C	Zatevná
4	04	6	*UII	4n	*UII	*UIIn-5	a b a b	A B C D	Uspávanka
5	05	6	4	3b	*UII	*UIIn-7	a a a a	A B C D	Romanian
6	06	6	8	5	6b	1-9	a b a b	A B C D	Svadobná
7	07	6	5	5	3n	1-7s	a a a a	A A B C	Svadobná
8	08	6	4	3n	2	*UIIs-4	a a a a	A B C D	Hungarian
9	09	6	5	4n	2	1-7n	a a a a	A B C D	Gajdosská
10	10	6	7	1	5	1-9	a a b a	A B C D	Hungarian
11	11	6	4	5	3b	1-8	a a a b	A B C D	Hungarian
12	12	6	4	1	2	*UIIn-7	a b a b	A B C D	Svadobná
13	13	6	1	1	1	*UIIn-5	a a b c	A A B B	Hra
14	14	6	*U	2	1	*U-5	a a b c	A B C D	Hungarian
15	15	6	1	1	1	1-5	a b a b	A A B A	Zatevná
16	16	6	6	1	6n	1-9	a b a b	A B C D	Valaská
17	17	6	2	2	1	*UIIs-4	a b c c	A B C D	Uspávanka
18	18	6	3	2	5	*UIIs-5	a b c d	A B C D	Jarná
19	19	6	4	4n	1	1-5	a a b b	A A B C	Uspávanka
20	20	6	1	5	1	1-8	a b a c	A B A C	Valaská

20/20

Figure 119. Tabulation of Slovak Material datafile, constructed with the default Chicago font, text-field type, and left alignment. The records represent melodies published in Béla Bartók, *Slowakische Volkslieder*, vol. I (Bratislava: Slovenskej Akadémie Vied, 1959).

When datafiles contain a substantial number of records with sortable text fields, and the objective is classification of the data, the researcher will invariably rely on screen output rather than printed reports (exception: final copy for publication purposes). An important analytic procedure is the processing of data for frequence of occurrence, by means of the **Find...** dialog box. For example, how many melodies are related to the Hungarian material and where are they located in the Tabulation of Slovak Material? A click of the I-beam cursor in the Type field box places the insertion point for typing the full name or an appropriate abbreviation. When the **Find** button is clicked, only the located records are displayed and the total number found in the Tabulation (Figure 120).

110

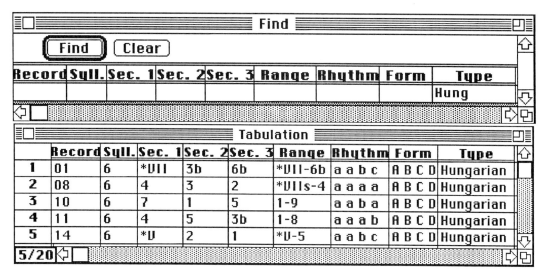

Figure 120. **Find...** dialog box, with abbreviated information in the Type field box, and the resultant screen display.

The Bartók-System grammatical classification of quaternary Slovak folk songs is based on the following sorting order (Figure 121):

(1) Syllabic structure.
(2) Section 2 end note (the main caesura).
(3) Section 1 end note.
(4) Section 3 end note.
(5) Range.
(6) Rhythm.
(7) Form.

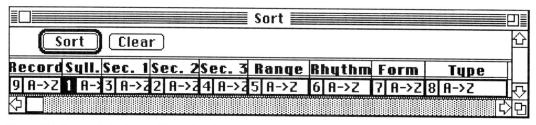

Figure 121. **Sort...** dialog box , with the Syll. field as the primary (1) alphanumeric (A→Z) field in the sorting order.

Figure 122 shows the the resultant classification. The Type of song is rarely considered in the grouping procedure, but is sorted for determining the relation between text and melody, generally in terms of ceremonial (religious events) and non-ceremonial songs.

	Record	Syll.	Sec. 1	Sec. 2	Sec. 3	Range	Rhythm	Form	Type
1	13	6	1	1	1	*VIIn-5	a a b c	A A B B	Hra
2	15	6	1	1	1	1-5	a b a b	A A B A	Zatevná
3	12	6	4	1	2	*VIIn-7	a b a b	A B C D	Svadobná
4	16	6	6	1	6n	1-9	a b a b	A B C D	Valaská
5	10	6	7	1	5	1-9	a a b a	A B C D	Hungarian
6	14	6	*V	2	1	*V-5	a a b c	A B C D	Hungarian
7	17	6	2	2	1	*VIIs-4	a b c c	A B C D	Uspávanka
8	18	6	3	2	5	*VIIs-5	a b c d	A B C D	Jarná
9	01	6	*VII	3b	6b	*VIIn-6	a a b c	A B C D	Hungarian
10	05	6	4	3b	*VII	*VIIn-7	a a a a	A B C D	Romanian
11	02	6	3	3n	5	1-6	a b c d	A B C D	Svadobná
12	08	6	4	3n	2	*VIIs-4	a a a a	A B C D	Hungarian
13	04	6	*VII	4n	*VII	*VIIn-5	a b a b	A B C D	Uspávanka
14	19	6	4	4n	1	1-5	a a b b	A A B C	Uspávanka
15	09	6	5	4n	2	1-7n	a a a a	A B C D	Gajdosská
16	03	6	1	4s	1	1-5	a b a b	A B A C	Zatevná
17	20	6	1	5	1	1-8	a b a c	A B A C	Valaská
18	11	6	4	5	3b	1-8	a a a b	A B C D	Hungarian
19	07	6	5	5	3n	1-7s	a a a a	A A B C	Svadobná
20	06	6	8	5	6b	1-9	a b a b	A B C D	Svadobná

20/20

Figure 122. Grammatical classification of the Tabulation of Slovak Material.

If the sorted datafile is to be published, it should be saved as a text file and exported to a word processor for reformatting. Figure 123 represents the kind of laser printer output that can serve as reproduction proofs. The title font is Helvetica italic 14, the headers are underlined Narrow Helvetica 12, and the text fields are *LaserFrench German Spanish* 12 (a Postscript Times font with special diacritical marks and overstrike accents). The asterisks are deleted, and music symbols replace letters for the accidentals.

Tabulation

The classified Tabulation can also serve as a datafile for compiling a thematic index. A copy of the file is opened and all data except the No. (melody designation) field are deleted. A new Interval Sequence header and its data fields are added (see pp. 94–96, above), followed by designation of the Interval Sequence as the primary (1) field in the Sort window.

An Index of First Lines is another useful datafile. If a separate index of text translations also is required, two fields—Texts, Translations—should be added to the previously sorted No. field. When the file is ready for display or printing, one or the other header is temporarily dragged to the Not Shown area in the Form window (see Figure 114, above), and the remaining one is designated as the primary sort field.

DATABASE CONSTRUCTION

TABULATION OF SLOVAK MATERIAL

No.	Syll.	Sec.1	Sec.2	Sec.3	Range	Rhythm	Form	Type
13.	6	1	1	1	VII-5	a a b c	A A B B	Hra
15.	6	1	1	1	1-5	a b a b	A A B A	Žatevná
12.	6	4	1	2	VII-7	a b a b	A B C D	Svadobá
16.	6	6	1	6	1-9	a b a b	A B C D	Valaska
10.	6	7	1	5	1-9	a a b a	A B C D	Hungarian
14.	6	V	2	1	V-5	a a b c	A B C D	Hungarian
17.	6	2	2	1	VII♯-4	a b c c	A B C D	Uspávanka
18.	6	3	2	5	VII♯-5	a b c d	A B C D	Jarná
1.	6	VII	3♭	6♭	VII-6♭	a a b c	A B C D	Hungarian
5.	6	4	3♭	VII	VII-7	a a a a	A B C D	Romanian
2.	6	3	3	5	1-6	a b c d	A B C D	Svadobná
8.	6	4	3	2	VII♯-4	a a a a	A B C D	Hungarian
4.	6	VII	4	VII	VII-5	a b a b	A B C D	Uspávanka
19.	6	4	4	1	1-5	a a b b	A A B C	Uspávanka
9.	6	5	4	2	1-7	a a a a	A B C D	Gajdošská
3.	6	1	4♯	1	1-5	a b a b	A B A C	Žatevná
20.	6	1	5	1	1-8	a b a c	A B A C	Valaská
11.	6	4	5	3♭	1-8	a a a b	A B C D	Hungarian
7.	6	5	5	3	1-7♯	a a a a	A A B C	Svadobná
6.	6	8	5	6♭	1-9	a b a b	A B C D	Svadobná

Figure 123. The sorted Tabulation, exported to and reformatted in Microsoft *Word*.

THE GRAPHIC BIBLIOGRAPHY

Scholarly research involves an exhaustive survey of primary and secondary sources, followed by mechanical or electronic listing and annotation of selected materials. In the latter case there is an unusual "hypervisual" approach to processing the data by means of the *Filevision IV* database program, where records can be linked to editable graphic "objects" which are displayed in a drawing window. And these objects include symbols, line art, music notations, imported graphics and, remarkably, text blocks or individual characters.

As a database application, *Filevision IV* can process a maximum number of 32,000 records and 16,000 characters per record (depending on memory and disk space). Moreover, the records may be placed in up to 32 individual, optionally-linked Types containing up to 255 fields. The extensive graphics capability is exclusively object-oriented (QuickDraw) drawing. Bitmapped MacPaint graphics, however, can be imported but are irreversibly converted to single (PICT format) objects.

The construction of a graphic bibliography is surprisingly uncomplicated, since the objects as well as the records are exclusively text-block entries. The following presentation of the author's *Filevision IV* database of Bartók sources, therefore, illustrates basic procedures rather than a stepwise tutorial.

Data Preparation.—The diverse sources consist of magazine articles, offprints, photocopied extracts from magazines and books, and annotated index cards and other handwritten material. Approximately 1,370 references were sorted alphabetically, according to the last name of the author or editor and the year of publication (including a suffixal letter where necessary), and placed in individual file folders. The collection was alphabetically subdivided into eighteen *Filevision IV* Types (that is, individual datafiles), with designations ranging from "Essays A" to "Essays Wi–Z." The largest Type, designated "Bartók Essays," contains 137 primary sources (that is, Records) and served as the model for design of the Drawing window. This window is displayed when the *Filevision IV* icon is opened or **New** is selected in the File menu (Figure 124).

Filevision

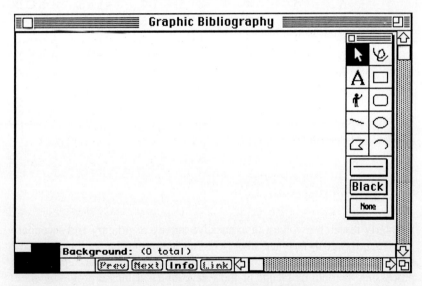

Figure 124. *Filevision IV* Drawing window with removable Toolbox.

Drawing Window Layout.—Figure 125 shows the completed layout of of the Bartók Essays Type, arranged in columns according to year of publication. Each date is a multi-functional object that serves as a pointer to the record and fields contained in the associated Info window. Datafile construction begins with

114

selecting **New** in the *Filevision IV* File menu: a dialog box is displayed for naming the file ("Graphic Bibliography"), and the **New** button is clicked to exit the dialog and open the Drawing window. Since the Bartók Essays are graphically represented by text blocks with four or five alphanumeric characters, their placement and alignment in the Drawing window is expedited when **Show Ruler**, **Grid**, **Guidelines** and **Snap to Grid are** selected in the Options menu. The Arrow pointer is placed in the horizontal or vertical Ruler and click-dragged to create and position the Guides.

Figure 125. The Drawing window for the complete Bartók Essays Type.

Creating Types, Records and Fields.— Choosing **Add Type...** in the Types menu opens a template (Figure 126) with Rulers, the Type-name box with the default **Type A,** and the Record box with **Name.** The Type-name box is activated by typing the user's datafile designation ("Bartók Essays"). Since the record names will consist of "Bartók" and a chronologically-oriented numbering of his essays, from 01 to 137, the default **Name** is accepted as the record designation.

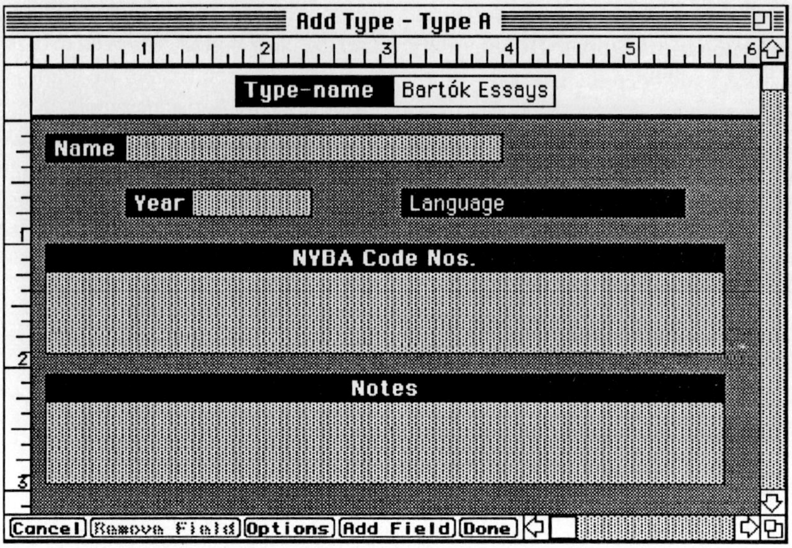

Figure 126. **Add Type...** Info template after entry of Type-name and data fields.

The next procedure is the addition and designation of the desired fields, such as **Year** (identical with the text blocks in the Drawing window), **Language** (Eng., Hung. etc.), **NYBA Code Nos.** (Numeric designations for Bartók's works as applied to the holdings of the New York Bartók Archive), and **Notes** (English titles, some with short annotations). When the **Add Field** button is clicked, a dialog box is displayed to choose the field type. The **Data Field** button is then clicked to position a field box in the template, which has an upper move handle (a dark square shape) and a lower resize handle. When the fields are positioned and resized, the **Done** button is clicked, the template window closes, and the newly designated Type-name appears in the Types menu and at the bottom of the re-activated Drawing window.

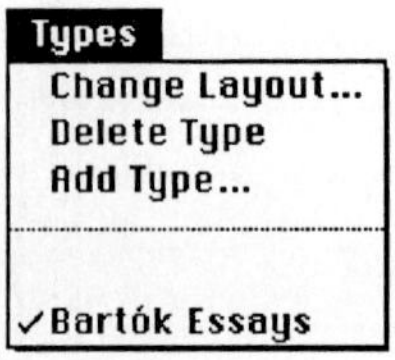

Creating Text-Block Objects and Their Info Displays.—The appropriate font for inserting substantial numbers of text blocks is Geneva 9 (the same font used for the icons in the Finder). When the Text tool (**A**) is selected, the cursor changes its shape to an I-beam—which is clicked in the Drawing window to display the flashing insertion point—and the first text-block (**1904**) is typed. The Arrow tool is then selected to click-drag the text block to its position as the first object in the Drawing window.

The text block or the Info button can be clicked to open the related Info window. Figure 127 shows the information entered for **1910b**: the record is the tenth in the series of Bartók Essays; the Date field, indicating that the essay is the second publication for **1910**, duplicates the Drawing window text-block; the Language field shows English as the source text; the numeral 8 in the NYBA Code No. field represents Bartók's *Rhapsody* for Piano and Orchestra, Op. 1;

116

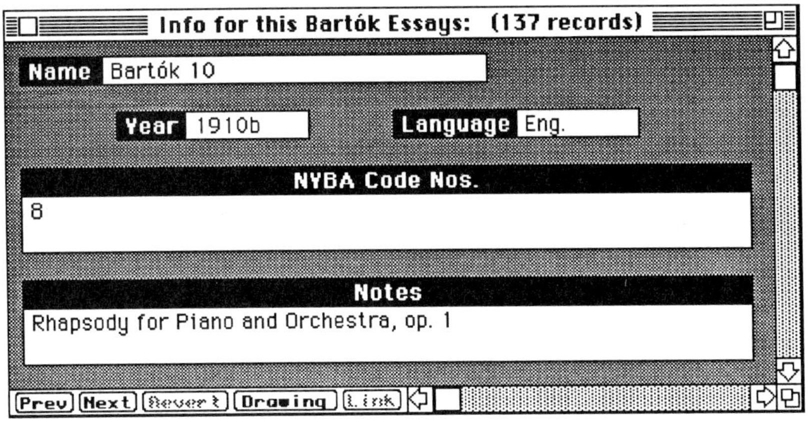

Figure 127. Info window for the **1910b** text block in the Drawing window.

and the Notes field indicates that the published essay in the collection has the same English title as the composition.

It is noteworthy that *Filevision IV* can also be used to construct a Thematic Index or a Catalogue of Musical Works. Figure 128 shows the **1910b** Info window with additional Interval Sequence and Music Example fields. Choosing **Change Layout...** in the Types menu returns the template for adding, deleting, or reformatting fields.

Figure 128. Info window with added Interval Sequence and Music Example fields.

Access

"Bartók Essays"s:
Sort By...
Find...   ⌘F
Find Same   ⇧⌘S
Highlight...   ⌘H
Highlight Selected   ⌘W
Highlight All   ⇧⌘A
Hide Selected   ⇧⌘H
Show Selected
Show Only These
Ignore

Show All Types
Cancel Highlighting   ⌘J

Information Retrieval.—Figure 129 illustrates the unique *Filevision IV* approach to selective viewing of the entire datafile, by highlighting each text-block object whose attached record contains requested data, and fading the other objects to gray.

Figure 129. Four highlighted Bartók essays, following a request for information about the composer's *Rhapsody* for Piano and Orchestra, Op. 1.

The highlighting procedure begins with the **Highlight...** command in the Access menu, to open its unusual dialog box which is partitioned into Comparator and Other Criteria areas (Figure 130). The uppermost selection box in the Comparator contains a scrolling list of all fields in the datafile, where NYBA Code Nos. is the chosen field. The other selections indicate the conditions to be met, which are simultaneously listed in the upper portion of the Other Criteria area. The symbolic representations can be interpreted as: **Highlight** all text blocks in the Drawing window whose records have (**is =**) the numeral **8** in the **NYBA Code Nos.** field. When the Done button is clicked, the dialog box closes and the Drawing window opens with a status message box which tracks the number of records remaining to be searched. While the four text-blocks highlighted in Figure 129 indicate that the related records have information concerning Bartók's *Rhapsody* for Piano and Orchestra, Op. 1, the 1910b Info window lists the *Rhapsody* in the Notes field as the title of an essay devoted to the work. The records attached to the other highlighted text-blocks, however, show that the work is one among others mentioned in Bartók autobiographies.

DATABASE CONSTRUCTION

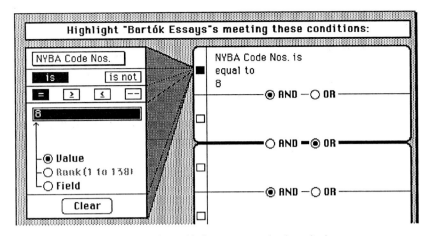

Figure 130. **Highlight**... dialog box with Comparator selection criteria.

Another equally abbreviated but more specific retrieval method would be **Notes is = to ..Op. 1..**, where the double period preceding and following the opus number would locate that character string and subsequently highlight only the 1910b text block. In addition the processing can be further narrowed by using the optional **and/or** criteria.

Constructing Symbols and Pop-up Displays.—Music examples can be added to the Drawing window as displays that temporarily pop into view when text blocks or their associated symbols are clicked. Since Info windows appear when text blocks are double-clicked, and pop-ups open with one click, a special symbol should be appended to the text block as a pop-up trigger (Figure 131).

1904	1913a	1920a	1921i	1930a	1933a	1937a	1941	1946
1905a	1913b	1920b	1921j	1930b	1933b	1937b	1942a	1951
1905b	1913c	1920c	1921k	1931a	1933c	1937c	1942b	1954
1906a	1914a	1920d	19211	1931b	1933d	1937d	1942c	1959
1906b	1914b							
1907	1917a							
1908	1917b							
1909	1917c							
1910a	1917d							
1910b	1918a							
1911a	1918b	1921a	1924a	1931i	1935e	1938e	1944c	
1911b	1918c	1921b	1924b	1931j	1936a	1938f	1945a	
1911c	1919	1921c	1927a	1932a	1936b	1938g	1945b	
1911d		1921d	1927b	1932b	1936c	1939	1945c	

Graphic Bibliography – Actual Size

Bartók, *Rhapsody for Piano and Orchestra* (Op. 1)

14

Vla.

Figure 131. Pop-up music example display with its ♪ symbol selected as the trigger.

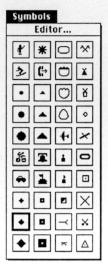

Although there are many shapes in the Symbol menu that could serve as a pop-up trigger, the mnemonic eighth-note is more appropriate. And the note can be quickly constructed with the Symbol Editor, by Fat Bits reshaping of the dark diamond tool (Figure 132).

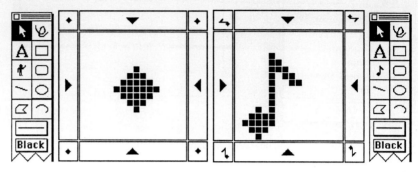

Figure 132. From left to right: the Tool window with its default symbol; the mid-size diamond tool in the Symbol Editor; the diamond transformed into eighth-note shape; and the Tool window with the newly-created eighth-note symbol.

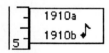

After the eighth-note symbol is selected in the Tool window, the cursor assumes that note shape for inserting the symbol in the Drawing window. A box encloses the inserted symbol, to indicate it is selected, and the Arrow tool is used to position the note next to the appropriate text block. (Since the symbol is a discrete object in the datafile, it can be clicked to open an Info window for creating a new record.)

When a symbol and its related music example are available, the procedure for constructing the pop-up can be undertaken (see Figure 128). In view of the number of commands involved the following explanation is given in the form of tutorial steps.

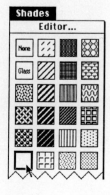

1. Click the eighth-note symbol to select it.
   •Choose **Send to Back** in the Edit menu.
2. Pull down the Shades menu to display the Shades palette.
   •Click the White Background Shade (that is, the box without a pattern).
3. Choose the **Rectangle** tool in the Tool window.
   •The cursor changes to cross hair shape.
4. Draw a rectangle approximately 5" wide by 2" high.
   •Nine handles are displayed to reshape or relocate the rectangle.
   •The text blocks are opaqued by the rectangular white background.
5. Copy the music example and paste it in the rectangle.
   •If necessary, use the Arrow tool to click-drag the music into position or reshape the rectangle.
6. Hold down the Shift key and click the eighth-note symbol, the music example, and the rectangle.

•All handles of the three objects are displayed.

7. With the Shift key still depressed, hold down the Command key and choose **Group** in the Edit menu.

8. Release the keys and click elsewhere in the Drawing window.

•The pop-up disappears.

9. Click the Eighth-note symbol to pop-up the music example.

Text matter, such as annotations, or other graphics can be be added to or replace the music prior to the Group command. If the pop-up requires editing at a later time, select it and choose **Ungroup** in the Edit window, then repeat Steps 5–9.

Creating Reports. When **Print Records...** is selected in the File window, the **Print Library** dialog box is displayed for creating New formats or editing earlier ones listed in the scroll box (Figure 133).

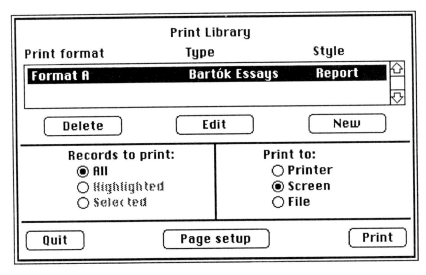

Figure 133. **Print Library** dialog box.

When the **New** button is clicked, a dialog box opens with a choice of three printing styles. Clicking the **Report** (or Form or Label) format button displays the Print Layout window with "Format A" and "Report Title" as the default Format-name and Header, respectively. The program also scans the datafile to determine the width of the fields in each record, and displays only those fields (and their headers) that will fit within printed page width. Moreover, the placement of fields (from left to right) is related their sequence in the Type Info window (Figure 134). A concurrent feature is the reconfigured menu bar: Format replaces Symbols; Types, Access, and Shades are grayed out; and certain File and Edit commands are likewise inactivated.

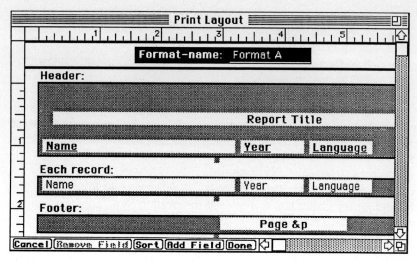

Figure 134. Print Layout default format for the Bartók Essays Type.

Figure 135 is a preview of the default layout when **Print to: Screen** is clicked in the **Print Library** dialog box. A click in the **Cancel** box restores the dialog box, where the **Edit** button may be selected to display the Print Layout window for reconfiguration.

View Print		
	Report Title	
Name	**Year**	**Language**
Bartók 01	1904	Eng.
Bartók 02	1905a	Eng.
Bartók 03	1905b	Eng.
Bartók 04	1906a	Eng.
Bartók 05	1906b	Eng.
Bartók 06	1907	Eng.
Bartók 07	1908	Eng
Bartók 08	1909	Hung.
Bartók 09	1910a	Eng.
Bartók 10	1910b	Eng.

Figure 135. View Print (screen preview) of Bartók Essays default layout.

The application has an exceptional approach to graphic control of editing layouts. The three dark rectangles in the Print Layout window have "window-shade" handles for control of leading (the distance between text lines), and their text blocks—Title, Headers, Fields, and Footer—also display move and resize handles when clicked (Figure 136).

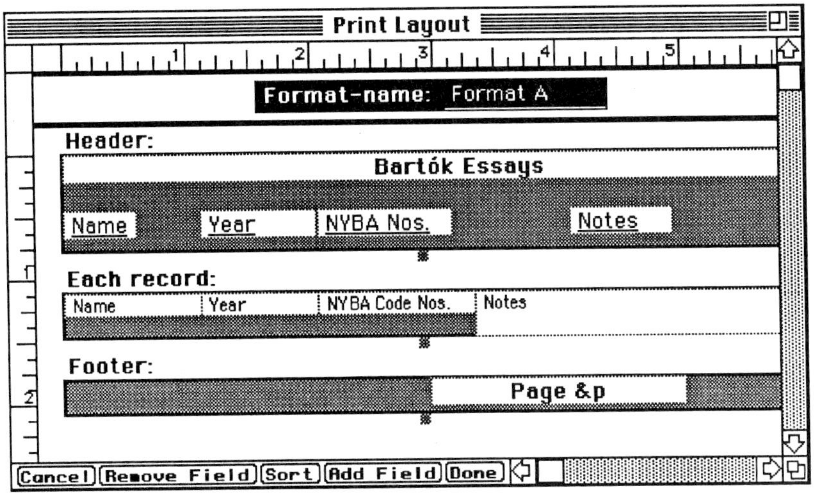

Figure 136. Print Layout window with reconfigured format.

After completion of the layout, the **Sort** button is clicked to display the default **Sort Printing as follows:** dialog box, with Name as the Primary sort field (Figure 137). The Secondary and Tertiary sort field boxes can be checked to activate two additional fields for hierarchical ordering in the report, such as NYBA Code Nos. and Year.

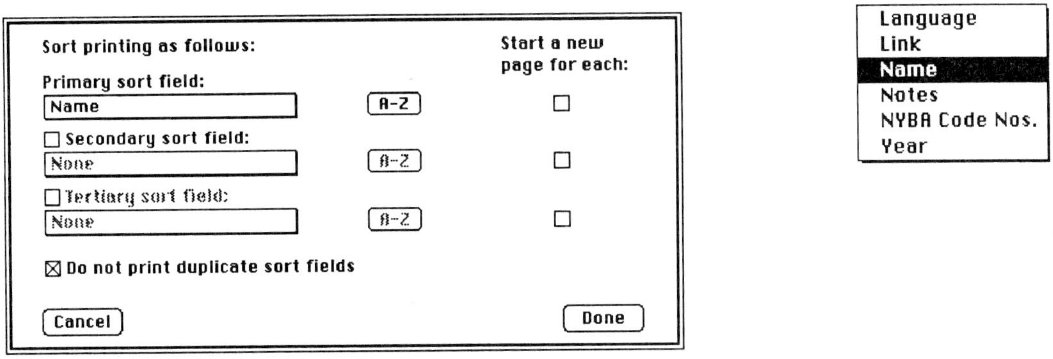

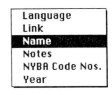

Figure 137. The default Sort Printing dialog box.

Figure 138 shows the completed, sorted report, with the title and headers in **Helvetica 12** font, and the text fields in **Times 10**. If NYBA Code Nos. had been designated as the Primary sort field, the report would stress the chronological sequence of works Bartók mentions or annotates in his literary publications.

Bartók Essays

Name	Year	NYBA Nos.	Notes
Bartók 01	1904	3	Kossuth Symphonic Poem
Bartók 02	1905a	88	Strauss: Sinfonia domestica, op. 53
Bartók 03	1905b	3, 10, 89	Autobiography
Bartók 04	1906a	13, 95	Appeal to the Hungarian Public (with Zoltán Kodály)
Bartók 05	1906b	13	Preface and Notes to Twenty Hungarian Folk Songs (with Zoltán Kodály)
Bartók 06	1907	88	Bach-Bartók: Preface and Notes to Well-Tempered Clavier
Bartók 07	1908	95	Székely Ballads
Bartók 08	1909	95	Transdanubian Ballads (music only)
Bartók 09	1910a	88	Strauss: Elektra
Bartók 10	1910b	8	Rhapsody for Piano and Orchestra, op. 1

Figure 138. The printed Bartók Essays report, sorted according to Name as Primary field, and Year and NYBA (Code) Nos. as Secondary and Tertiary sort fields, respectively.

SUMMARY

File is a versatile, user-friendly datafile manager, released in 1984 and upgraded to version 2.0a in 1988 by Microsoft, the world's largest manufacturer of software for the Apple Macintosh computer. The Thematic Index, Catalogue of Works, and Tabulation of Material tutorials presented above are specific exemplars of the design simplicity of the application and its power to store, retrieve, sort, and print text matter and related graphics for musicological and ethnomusicological purposes. The current street price is about $123.

Filevision, too, was vended in 1984 and upgraded in 1988 to its present version as *Filevision IV.* The program can effectively process the above-mentioned tutorial datafiles with equal friendliness. The program's unique visual approach to information retrieval, such as the Graphic Bibliography described above, is an invaluable contribution to computer-oriented research. The special discounted price for the academic community is $195.

CHAPTER 4

Electronic Publishing

The ongoing technological advances in word processing software significantly reduce the time factor involved in the production and editing of *typescript* manuscripts intended for publication and other purposes. Similar improvements in desktop publishing software, moreover, enable the production and editing of *typeset* copy, that is, reproduction proofs (repros) which are camera-ready for offset lithography by commercial printers. In either case the starting point is the "electronic manuscript"—a variable length essay (often with linked files) whose text is keyboarded with interplaced graphics or references to their location elsewhere, saved to disk for editing, printing, and export purposes. The tutorials in this chapter outline the procedures or specific steps to create an electronic manuscript and an "offprint" with Microsoft *Word,* and a book or manual with Aldus *PageMaker* (the reader may substitute other word processing and page makeup applications, if they have similar capabilities).

ELECTRONIC MANUSCRIPTS

The preparation of copy should follow the guidelines given in *The Chicago Manual of Style,* 13th ed. (The University of Chicago Press, 1982); *Writing about Music* (University of California Press, 1988); or the house rules of the prospective periodical or publisher. Since printed copy is invariably needed as preliminary output or usually required by a publisher, the following basic format is suggested.

   (1) Paper size: 8.5 by 11 inches, typed on one side.

   (2) Margins: one inch minimum.

   (3) Font: Courier (or New York) 12.

   (4) Text lines: double-spaced.

   (5) Title: centerhead, placed approximately two inches below the top of the page.

   •Subtitle (author's name): centerhead, two spaces after the title and three spaces before the opening paragraph.

   (6) Subheads:

   •Level 1: underlined centerhead, three spaces after the preceding paragraph and before the following one.

   •Level 2: underlined sidehead, flush left (that is, without indentation), same spacing as the Level 1 header.

•Level 3: underlined sidehead, with period and em dash (double-hyphen), to begin a paragraph.

(7) Illustration placeholder: underlined sidehead,such as <u>Example 1</u> [INSERT], flush left, same spacing as the Level 1 header.

(8) Paragraphs: The opening paragraph of a chapter and Level 1 and 2 headers are usually keyboarded flush left. Subsequent paragraphs are indented one-half inch, and quotation text blocks should be indented one inch..

Microsoft Word

Creating a Style Sheet.—When the Microsoft *Word* icon is double-clicked, the New window opens to Page 1, Normal style, with the flashing insertion point positioned at the top of the page, flush left.

1. Choose **Full Menus** in the Edit menu.

2. Choose **Show ¶** in the same menu.

•A gray paragraph marker appears next to the insertion point. Other important symbols are displayed as an aid to keyboarding, such as one or more dots to indicate the number of spaces between characters, tab marks, and so forth.

3. Choose **Show Ruler** in the Format menu (Figure 139).

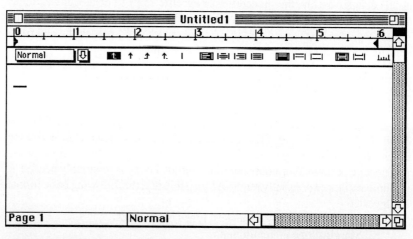

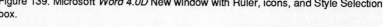

Figure 139. Microsoft *Word 4.0D* New window with Ruler, icons, and Style Selection box.

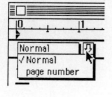

If the Down arrow in the scrolling Style Selection box is clicked, **Normal** appears as the default style selection. The program has a substantial number of preset document defaults, such as the New York 12 font and half-inch spacing of tab stops, that provide a typewriter-like environment for quick and easy text entry. While the casual user may find it useful to rely on default settings, there are obvious advantages in constructing a properly styled template for the preparation of electronic manuscripts.

Figure 140 shows the default dialog boxes that are respectively displayed when **Character...** and **Define Styles...** are chosen in the Format menu.

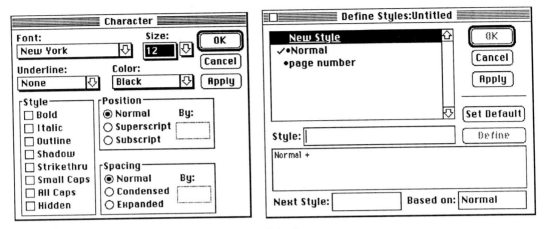

Figure 140. Default **Character...** and **Define Styles...** dialog boxes.

The following steps will create a style sheet with the suggested basic format.

1. When the default **Define Styles...** dialog box opens, **New Style** is highlighted in the list display, the insertion point flashes in the **Style:** box, and "Normal +" appears in the style description area.

2. Select **Normal.** "Font: New York 12 Point, Flush left" appears as the default style description.
   - If a laser printer will be used, choose **Courier** in the Font menu to replace **New York**.
   - Click the **Double space** icon in the Ruler.
   - Click the **Apply** button.

3. Select **New Style** and type **1st line indent**.
   - Drag the **First line indent marker** to the half-inch tick mark.
   - Click the **Apply** button.

4. Select **Normal** and click the **Apply** button. This will temporarily place **Normal** in the **Style:** box.
   - Select **New Style** (**Normal** moves to the **Based on:** box).

5. Type **Quotation indent** and drag the **Left indent marker** to the one-inch tick mark, then click the **Apply** button to define the new style.

6. Repeat Step 4 and type **Footnote text**.
   - Choose **10 Point** in the Font menu, then click **Apply**.

7. Repeat Step 4 and type **Footnote reference**.
   - Choose **9 Point** in the Font menu.
   - Choose **Character...** in the Format menu to display its dialog box (Figure 140).

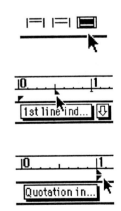

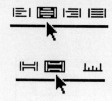

•Click the **Superscript** radio button, the **OK** button to exit the dialog box, and the **Apply** button.

    8. Repeat Step 4 and type **Centerhead**.

•In the Ruler click the **Centered** icon.

•Click the **Open Paragraph Space** icon.

•Choose **Paragraph...** in the Format menu, type **12 pt** in the **Before:** and **After:** boxes (Figure 141).

•Click the **OK** button to exit, then click **Apply**.

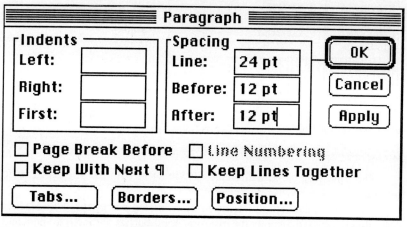

Figure 141. **Paragraph...** dialog box.

    9. Repeat Step 4 and type **Sidehead**.

•Choose **Paragraph...** in the Format menu, type **12 pt** in the **Before:** and **After:** boxes.

•Click the **OK** button to exit, then click **Apply**.

    10. Repeat Step 4 and type **Title**.

•In the Ruler click the **Centered** icon.

•Choose **Paragraph...** in the Format menu, type **72 pt** for **Before:**.

•Click the **OK** button to exit, then click **Apply**.

    11. Repeat Step 4 and type **Subtitle**.

•In the Ruler click the **Centered** icon.

•Choose **Paragraph...** in the Format menu, type **12 pt** for **After:**.

•Click the **OK** button to exit, then click **Apply**.

    Save the file and name it **MS Template**, but do not close until the following format adjustments in Section and Document layout are completed. Choose **Document...** in the Format menu and note the default settings in the dialog box. The default (checked) **Widow Control** box indicates that the program prevents the last line of a paragraph from appearing as the first line (the "Widow") of the next page. The default margins are acceptable but may be

128

changed to one inch on all sides. Since publishers invariably require endnotes rather than footnotes, **Footnotes position** should be changed (in the scroll box) from **End of Page** to **End of Document** (Figure 142). Click the **Set Default** button, to save the current settings, and exit the dialog box.

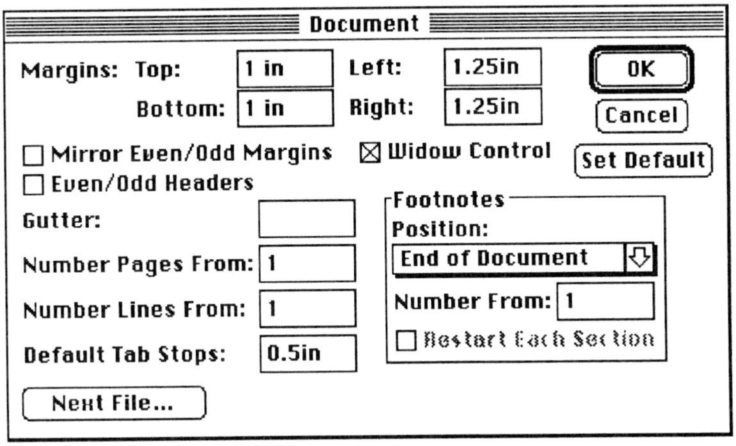

Figure 142. **Document...** dialog box.

Choose **Section...** in the Format menu to display the dialog box. Check the the **Page Number Auto** and **First Page Special** boxes, and change **From Right:** to **4.25in** (the default is 0.5 inches). All pages except New Page (= First Page) will be automatically numbered, with the numbers centered at the top of the page and in accordance with the default margin specifications (Figure 143).

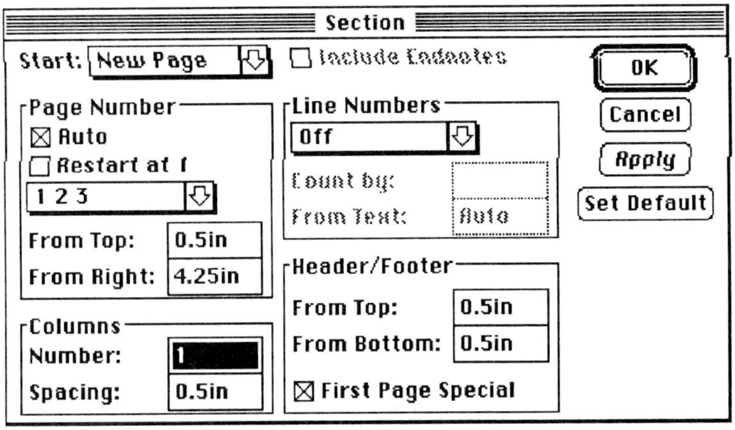

Figure 143. **Section...** dialog box.

World of Music

Click the **Apply, Set Default,** and **OK** buttons, and be sure to save the completed file. Whenever an electronic manuscript is to be prepared, work with a *copy* of the **MS Template** file (click its icon in the Finder, type Command-**D,** then rename the new document). Figure 144 illustrates the use of the electronic manuscript format for a journal article.

---

(4) Ruthenian Sources

The Ruthenians, a tribe of Ukrainian people, inhabit former Hungarian territory (now part of the Soviet Union) that borders Czechoslovakia to the east and Transylvanian Rumania to the north. Bartók collected Rumanian folk music in that area in 1909 and, two years later, about a hundred instrumental and vocal Ruthenian melodies.

Rhythm Structure

The kolomyjka is the most characteristic Ruthenian dance music, and its infectious four-bar rhythm schema was taken over by Hungarian and Rumanian peasants for vocal and instrumental melodies. The following folk song melody is transcribed as No. 10 ("Ruthenian Song") in Forty-four Duos for Two Violins (1931):[28]

Example 7 [INSERT]

The essential difference between the transcription and the folk song is the former's use of characteristic Hungarian

---

Figure 144. Extract from Benjamin Suchoff, "Ethnomusicological Roots of Béla Bartók's Musical Language," *The World of Music,* 1987, no. 1:56.

If the article contains music examples and other illustrations, it is often useful to provide the future publisher with an offprint, that is, a "typeset" approximation of the printed text and graphics, in addition to the electronic manuscript. The offprint provides an editor with important details concerning pagination and the proper placement of graphics. After the published article appears, moreover, the offprint can be corrected and photocopied for special distribution purposes. It should be noted, moreover, that the visual effect and quality of the offprint graphics may induce the editor to accept them without further processing.

Figure 145 shows a page from the author's offprint of his article which appeared in *The World of Music,* a publication of Florian Noetzel Verlag, Wilhelmshaven. The trimmed paper size of the journal is approximately 5.75 by 8.25 inches, and its printed page, including the drop folio (that is, the page number at the bottom), approximately 4.75 by 6.625 inches (experienced users may prefer the pica as the unit of measurement). There are no headers or footers; sans serif font, similar to Helvetica, is used throughout; and all titles and headings are flush with the left margin.

The following changes were made in the *Word* **Define Styles...** dialog box, in a renamed copy of the electronic manuscript (see pp. 127–28, above, for the original format specifications).

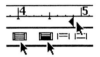

1. **Normal.** Font: **Helvetica, 10** point, Indent: Right **1.125in,** Justified, Line Spacing: **12 pt.**
   •The single-space and justified-text icons are selected.
   •The Right indent creates the printed page width of the journal.
   •Line Spacing (that is, "Leading") is typed in the **Paragraph...** dialog box (Format menu). It should be noted that the **Apply** button must be clicked in the various dialog boxes to modify the preset format.

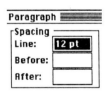

2. **1st line indent.** Normal + Indent: First **0.125in.**
3. **Quotation indent.** Normal + indent: Left **0.375in.**
4. **Footnote text.** Normal + Font: 8 point.
   •The font size is changed and applied in the **Character...** dialog box.

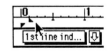

5. **Footnote reference.** Normal + Font: **7** point, Superscript: **3** Point.
6. In the **Style** box change the former **Centerhead** designation to **Sidehead 1.**
   •Normal + Font: **Helvetica, Bold,** Flush left, Space Before: **24 pt,** Space After: **12 pt.**
   •Space Before and Space After are typed and applied in the **Paragraph...** dialog box.

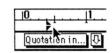

7. In the **Style** box change the former **Sidehead** designation to **Sidehead 2.**
   •Normal + Font: **Helvetica Oblique,** Before: **24 pt,** After: **12 pt.**
8. **Title.** Normal + Font: **Helvetica, Bold,** 12 Point, Flush left, Space After: **36 pt.**
9. **Subtitle** (Author's name). Normal + Font: **12** Point, Flush left, Space After: **12 pt.**

10. **Page No.** Normal + Centered.

The next procedure is copying the music example to the clipboard, pasting it in the page, and reducing it proportionately.

1. Click the notation inside its dotted-line frame, to display the sizing handles.

2. Hold down the Shift key, place the Arrow pointer on the corner handle, and click-drag diagonally upward until the example is centered in the print page, with approximately half-inch margins.

---

played A-E as a double-stop, the result was the fifth-chord D-A-E. It is precisely this chord and in the same *ostinato* rhythm pattern which serves as the accompaniment to the bagpipe motifs in the fifth movement of the *Concerto for Orchestra*, all providing the means for re–creating the color and spirit of rural Transylvanian dance style.

(4) Ruthenian Sources

The Ruthenians, a tribe of Ukrainian people, inhabit former Hungarian territory (now part of the Soviet Union) that borders Czechoslovakia to the east and Transylvanian Rumania to the north. Bartók collected Rumanian folk music in that area in 1909 and, two years later, about a hundred instrumental and vocal Ruthenian melodies.

Rhythm Structure

The *kolomyjka* is the most characteristic Ruthenian dance music, and its infectious four-bar rhythm schema was taken over by Hungarian and Rumanian peasants for vocal and instrumental melodies. The following folk song melody is transcribed as No. 10 ("Ruthenian Song") in *Forty-four Duos for Two Violins* (1931):[28]

Poco rubato

Example 7

The essential difference between the transcription and the folk song is the former's use of characteristic Hungarian dotted-rhythm in variable *tempo giusto*.[29] In the first movement of the *Dance Suite for Orchestra* (1923), an ori-

56

Figure 145. Redefined electronic manuscript in *The World of Music* format. Copyright © 1987 by Florial Noetzel Verlag.

The difference between the publication and the offprint is the latter's use of centered page numbers, in order to simplify the layout for xerographic self-publication by the user. If a professionally printed and bound offprint is the objective, *Word* supports the placement of page numbers flush with the left and right margins, respectively, on facing pages of the master copy.

Finally, the offprint file can be duplicated, renamed, and easily redefined for producing an offprint with a different style sheet. As a case in point *Ethnomusicology,* the journal of the Society for Ethnomusicology, shares a number of stylistic similarities with *The World of Music.* The major differences are type page measurements, use of the Times font, and footnotes instead of endnotes.

CREATING A BOOK

A Musician's Guide to Desktop Computing is one of those recent publications which exemplify a new relationship between author and publisher. Instead of submitting an electronic manuscript for supplementary keyboarding by the publisher's typesetter, the author cum compositor provides the publisher with laser-printed reproduction proofs, that is, camera-ready copy for offset printing. The advantages in this kind of relationship are considerable: reduction in production time and expense for both parties, and the opportunity for the author to play a leading role with regard to style and layout.

Although word processors like *Word* are more effective in creating scholarly electronic manuscripts, particularly where there are numerous footnotes, they cannot match the typesetting and formatting attributes of page layout applications, which are specifically designed to work with high-resolution laser printers and PostScript imagesetters. In the case of profusely annotated files, therefore, the style sheet and text should be prepared with a word processor and imported into a page layout application which has a filter for importing the files intact. On the other hand, *A Musician's Guide to Desktop Computing* and similar graphics-oriented publications are best created directly with a page layout application, such as Aldus *PageMaker,* which also has a sophisticated word processor as an integral part of the program.

Preparing a Prospectus.—Book contracts invariably contain language which grants the publisher the right to edit and publish the work in a style suitable as to paper, printing, and binding. In order to minimize the possibility of later misunderstandings or requests for substantial revisions, the author should draft a prospectus with the following suggested inclusions:

1. Introduction: title, general description of the proposed work, need for the publication, and intended audience.

2. Table of Contents: a brief description of the proposed chapters and appendices.

3. Provisional chapter: the content and format sample.

4. Graphic style sheet: see Figure 146.

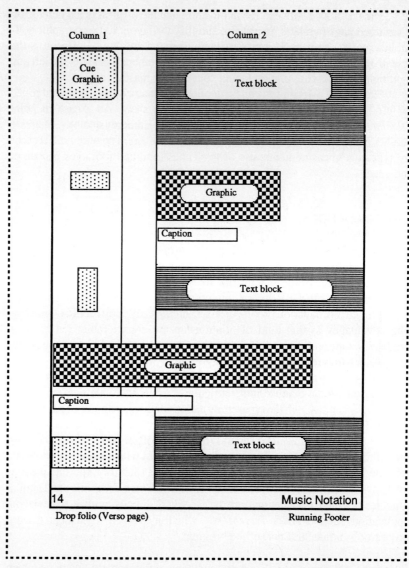

Figure 146. Preliminary two-column layout for *A Musician's Guide to Desktop Computing*.

Constructing a Layout.—The preliminary layout illustrated in Figure 146, a non-proportional modification of a *PageMaker* template (*Manual 2*), shows horizontal and vertical non-printing guide lines which define the the print page and its columnar divisions. The print page and the suggested 7 by 9.25 inch trim page (the dashed rectangle) approximate the specifications of a single-column book published by Prentice Hall (Fred T. Hofstetter, *Computer Literacy for Musicians*, 1988).

134

In the case of a single-column layout by the same publisher, the graphic style sheet differs considerably. The typography, however, is similar: a contrasting non-serif font for the heads and captions and a serif font for the body text (Figure 147).

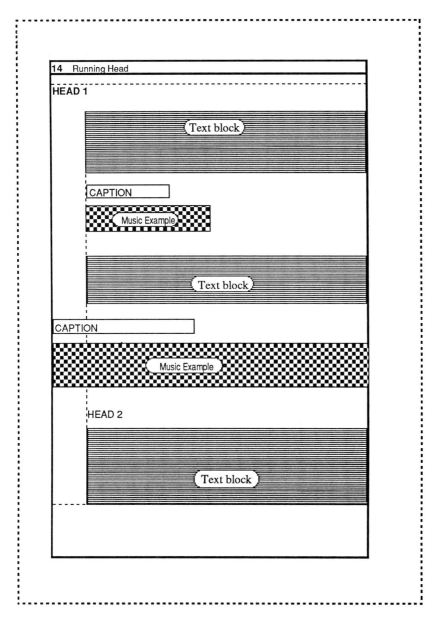

Figure 147. Prentice Hall layout for Stefan Kostka, *Materials and Techniques of Twentieth-Century Music*, 1990.

PageMaker

Returning to the *Guide* format, the following Tutorial emulates the steps taken to construct its two-column layout with the *PageMaker* application.

1. Double-click the *PageMaker* icon to display the **Page setup** default dialog box, and type the following changes (Figure 148):

•Page dimensions: **7** by **9.25** inches.

•Margin in inches: Inside= **1.0**, Top= **0.563**, Outside = **0.375**, Bottom= **0.688**. These figures yield a print page of **5-5/8** by **7-7/16** inches, which in turn is an approximation of the publisher's request for **34** by **48** picas.

Page setup   OK

Page: [Letter]   Cancel

Page dimensions: [8.5] by [11] inches   Numbers...

Orientation: ◉ Tall ○ Wide

Start page #: [1]   # of pages: [■]

Options: ☒ Double-sided ☒ Facing pages
        ☐ Restart page numbering

Margin in inches: Inside [1]   Outside [0.75]
            Top [0.75]   Bottom [0.75]

Page setup   OK

Page: [Custom]   Cancel

Page dimensions: [7] by [9.25] inches   Numbers...

Orientation: ◉ Tall ○ Wide

Start page #: [1]   # of pages: 1

Options: ☒ Double-sided ☒ Facing pages
        ☐ Restart page numbering

Margin in inches: Inside [■]   Outside [0.375]
            Top [0.563]   Bottom [0.688]

Figure 148. *PageMaker* default and custom **Page setup** dialog boxes.

---

2. Click the **OK** button to exit the dialog box and display the untitled New window and movable Toolbox window (Figure 149).

•The shadow box represents an empty page (the trim page) based on the changed page measurements but reduced to **Fit in Window** view.

•The dashed rectangle (the print page) is positioned within the shadow box, in accordance with the new margin specifications. The empty page and the default inch Rulers are positioned on the "pasteboard," that is, the total length and width of the window. Since the pasteboard area outside the empty page is non-printing, text and graphics can be placed there as reference matter or for use elsewhere.

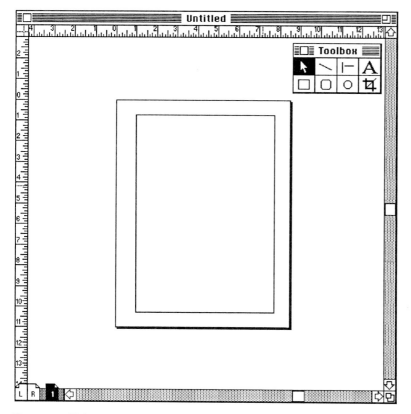

Figure 149. **Fit in window** view of empty page centered on the pasteboard.

The layout is completed when guides and drop folios have been placed in the facing master pages. Master pages are template-like constructions, represented by the two-page (**L|R**) document icon at the lower left corner of the window, which automatically display the facing drop folios (page numbers in the footer area).and master guides (the non-printing vertical and horizontal alignment lines) whenever new pages are added to the document.

1. Click the Arrow pointer on the two-page icon to display the facing master pages.

2. Choose **Column Guides...** in the Options menu to display the dialog box (Figure 150)..

•Type **2** for the number of columns.

•Type **0.25** for the space between columns, and exit the dialog box.

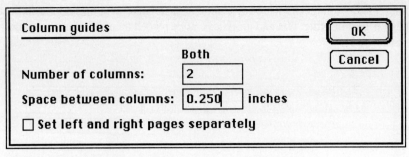

Figure 150. **Column guides...** dialog box with two-column settings..

3. In order to precisely align the two-column guides on each page with the ruler tick marks, choose **200% size** in the Page menu.

•Click-drag each two-column guide (the cursor changes to a two-head arrow) to the 5-5/16ths- and 5-9/16ths-inch tick marks.

4. Any number of individual vertical and horizontal guides can be created by dragging them out of their respective rulers. Place the Arrow pointer in the horizontal ruler and click-drag a guide down to align with the 8-3/8ths-inch tick mark on the vertical ruler.

•On small-size monitors: release the guide, use the vertical scroll bar to reposition the window, then continue dragging the guide into position.

•This (non-printing) guide forms the upper line of the drop folio/ footer rectangle. Other than the footer, no text matter (or graphics) may be inserted into this area.

5. Automatic pagination is enabled by inserting a page-number marker in the footer area of each master page.

•Press and hold down the Option key, click in the window (the cursor changes to a hand), and drag until the dashed borderlines forming the lower leftmost corner of the left page come into view.

•Select the Text tool (**A**) in the Toolbox and click the cross bar of the I-beam at the intersection of the borderlines.

6. Press Command+Option+P to insert the page-number marker (**LM**).

•Choose **Alignment** in the Type menu, to display its submenu, slide the Arrow pointer to the right and select **Align left**.

7. Repeat Step 5 at the rightmost corner of the right page.

•Press Command+Option+P to insert the page-number marker (**RM**).

•Choose **Alignment** in the Type menu, to display its submenu, slide the Arrow pointer to the right and select **Align right**.

8. Choose **Save as...** in the File menu, name the file "Book Template," click the **Template** radio button, and exit the dialog box.

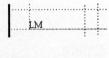

Creating a Style Sheet.—Although the *PageMaker* package includes filters for importing style sheets and text formats from Microsoft *Word*, there may be instances where the user will compose and format text matter directly in

PageMaker. In addition there are certain specifications in the *Manual 2* template which were adapted for use in this book. The Tutorial that follows below, however, is developed from *PageMaker* default styles—Body text, Caption, Headline, Subhead 1 and Subhead 2—and includes other styles created specifically for the *Guide*.

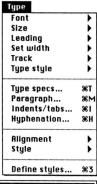

1. Referring to Figure 151, choose **Define styles...** in the Type menu to display the default dialog box.

•Click the **New...** button to open the default **Edit style** sub-dialog box.

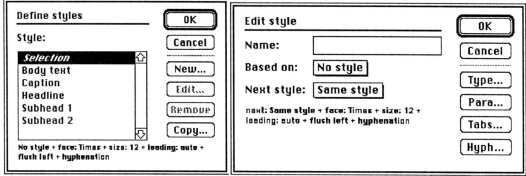

Figure 151. *PageMaker* default **Define Styles...** dialog box and its **Edit style** sub-dialog box.

2. In the Name box type **Musician's Guide**.

•Click the **Type...** button to open the next default sub-dialog box (Figure 152).

3. In the Size box type **10** as the number of points.

•Click the **OK** button to return to the **Edit style** sub-dialog box.

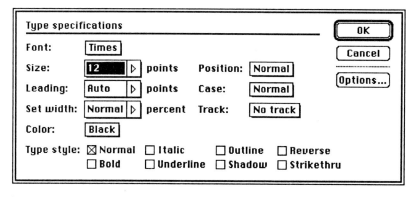

Figure 152, **Type specifications** default sub-dialog box.

4. Click the **Para...** button to open its default sub-dialog box (Figure 153).

5. In the Alignment box click and hold on **Left** (to display the options), and drag down to select **Justify**.

•Click the **OK** button to return to the **Edit style** sub-dialog box.

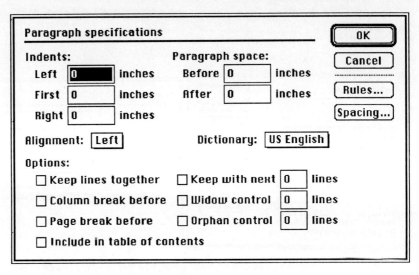

Figure 153. **Paragraph specifications** default sub-dialog box.

In summary this procedure creates the new typography (Times 10) and paragraph format (justified text lines), retains the default automatic leading (12 points) and hyphenation, and assigns all to "Musician's Guide" as the basic style. During the definition of styles, moreover, the various names appear in the Style palette in alphabetic order (exception: prefixal numbers and special characters precede letters). The next procedure defines some of the other styles used in the *Guide*.

1. In the **Define styles** dialog box click **Body text**, then the **Edit...** button to open the **Edit style** sub-dialog box.

•The default **Body text** name and assigned attributes are displayed.

2. Click the **Type...** button to open the next default sub-dialog box.

•In the Size box type **10** as the number of points.

•Click the **OK** button to return to the **Edit style** sub-dialog box.

3. Click the **Para...** button to open its default sub-dialog box.

• In the Alignment box click and hold on **Left** (to display the options) and drag down to select **Justify**.

•In the **first Indent** box select **0.313** and type **0** (that is, no indent) as the replacement.

•Click the **OK** buttons to return to the **Define styles** sub-dialog box.

4. In the **Define styles** dialog box click **Caption**, then the **Edit...** button to open the **Edit style** sub-dialog box.

•The default **Caption**.name and assigned attributes are displayed.

5. Click the **Type...** button to open the next default sub-dialog box.

•In the Font box click-drag the Arrow pointer upward until **Helvetica** is selected.

•In the Size box type **8** as the number of points.

•Click the **OK** button to return to the **Edit style** sub-dialog box.

6. Click the **Para...** button to open its default sub-dialog box.

•In the Alignment box click and hold on **Left** (to display the options) and drag down to select **Justify**.

•Click the **OK** button to return to the **Edit style** sub-dialog box.

7. Click the **Hyph...** button to open its default sub-dialog box.

•Click the **On** radio button.

•Click the **OK** buttons to return to the **Define styles** sub-dialog box.

In order to avoid repetition of procedural steps the following list specifies the format changes for the remaining default styles.

Headline: Name, **Title**; Font and Size, **Helvetica 30**; Case, **All caps**; Alignment, **Right**; **Include in table of contents** box checked.

Subhead 1: Name, **Head 1**; Font and Size, **Helvetica 18**; Leading, **24**; Case, **Normal**; Alignment, **Justify**; Space before, **0.333**; **Include in table of contents** box checked.

Subhead 2: Name, **Head 2**; Font and Size, **Helvetica Oblique 14**; Case, **All caps**; Leading, **24**; Alignment, **Justify**; Space befoe, **0.25**; Space after, **0.175**; **Include in table of contents** box checked.

Working with Graphics.—Music examples and other illustrations can be pasted as independent graphics, after they have been cut or copied to the Clipboard. If they have been stored as disk files, they can be inserted by choosing **Place...** in the File menu and selecting the name of the document when it is displayed in the dialog box (Figure 154)

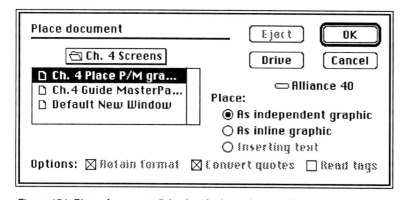

Figure 154. **Place document** dialog box for importing graphics.

With regard to spacing between text blocks and graphics or from a caption to the following text block: three-eighths inch, unless an occasional page layout problem requires minor adjustments; between graphics and their captions: one-eighth inch. The use of guides for uniform and precise placement of graphics and their captions is invariably necessary. To proportionately resize a graphic, position it flush with a column guide, hold down the Shift key, and click-drag (the cursor changes to an angular two-head arrow) one of the corner handles.

The Cropping tool enables the user to hide unwanted portions of an illustration.

1. Select the tool and click the graphic to display the handles.

2. Center the tool cross hair on one of the handles (the Shift key is not used) and click-drag in the desired direction.

3. Click-drag the tool in the center of the newly-created rectangular frame (the tool changes to a grabber hand) and drag the graphic into position.

•Cropped graphics are only temporarily hidden from view: reversing the procedure restores the original size.

Figure 155 shows the Line and Fill submenus of the Elements menu, which enable the drawing tools (see Figure 149) to create variable-width solid or dashed lines and rectangular or circular shapes with different fills.

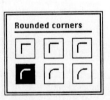

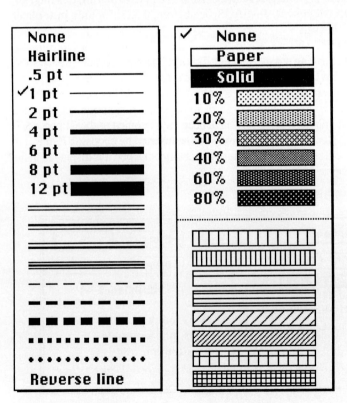

Figure 155. Selection options in the Line and Fill submenus.

Working with Text.—As mentioned further above (p. 138) text created with a word processor can be imported, including the style definitions, by choosing the **Place...** command in the File menu to open the **Place document** dialog box (Figure 156).

Place document

⬜ Guide Front Matter

▢ GUIDE Intro

[Eject]   [OK]

[Drive]   [Cancel]

▭ Alliance 40

Place:
- ⦿ As new story
- ○ Replacing entire story
- ○ Inserting text

Options: ☒ Retain format   ☒ Convert quotes   ☐ Read tags

Figure 156. **Place document** dialog box for importing text.

Alternatively, choosing **Edit story** in the Edit menu opens a Story window with a flashing insertion point for entering text. The untitled window, automatically designated with the opening words of the text, may be moved, resized, closed or hidden behind the main window. The **Preferences...** dialog box has pop-up menus for selecting the story font and size (Figure 157).

Preferences   [OK]

Layout view:
Measurement system: [Inches]   [Cancel]
Vertical ruler: [Inches]   [   ] points
Greek text below: [9] pixels

Guides: Detailed graphics: Show layout problems:
⦿ Front   ○ Gray out   ☐ Loose/tight lines
○ Back   ⦿ Normal   ☐ "Keeps" violations
                 ○ High resolution

Story view:
Size: [12   ▷] points   Font: [Geneva]

Save option: ⦿ Faster   ○ Smaller

Figure 157. **Preferences...** dialog box with default settings.

Edit

Cannot undo   ⌘Z

Cut   ⌘X
Copy   ⌘C
Paste   ⌘V
Clear
Select all   ⌘A

Find...   ⌘8
Find next   ⌘,
Change...   ⌘9
Spelling...   ⌘L

Show clipboard
Preferences...

Edit story   ⌘E

The ingenious two-column layout features the automatic listing of styles in the left column, in accordance with whatever selection has been made in the Style palette (Figure 158). When a change of style is needed, the insertion point is clicked in the paragraph and the applicable style is selected in the Style palette.

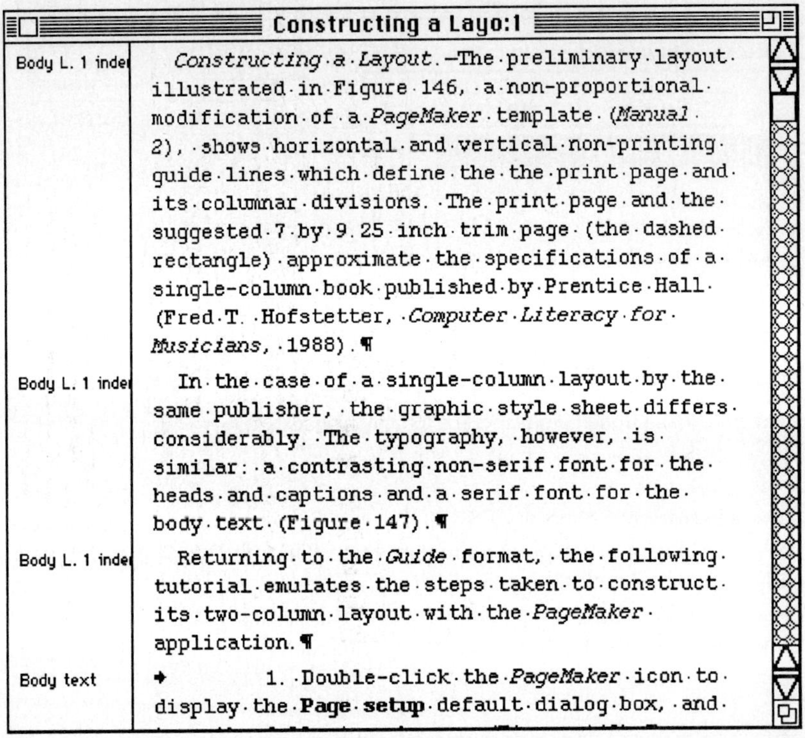

```
╔═══════════════ Constructing a Layo:1 ═══════════╗
║ Body L. 1 inde│ Constructing·a·Layout.—The·preliminary·layout·
║               │ illustrated·in·Figure·146,·a·non-proportional·
║               │ modification·of·a·PageMaker·template·(Manual·
║               │ 2),·shows·horizontal·and·vertical·non-printing·
║               │ guide·lines·which·define·the·the·print·page·and·
║               │ its·columnar·divisions.·The·print·page·and·the·
║               │ suggested·7·by·9.25·inch·trim·page·(the·dashed·
║               │ rectangle)·approximate·the·specifications·of·a·
║               │ single-column·book·published·by·Prentice·Hall·
║               │ (Fred·T.·Hofstetter,·Computer·Literacy·for·
║               │ Musicians,·1988).¶
║ Body L. 1 inde│    In·the·case·of·a·single-column·layout·by·the·
║               │ same·publisher,·the·graphic·style·sheet·differs·
║               │ considerably.·The·typography,·however,·is·
║               │ similar:·a·contrasting·non-serif·font·for·the·
║               │ heads·and·captions·and·a·serif·font·for·the·
║               │ body·text·(Figure·147).¶
║ Body L. 1 inde│    Returning·to·the·Guide·format,·the·following·
║               │ tutorial·emulates·the·steps·taken·to·construct·
║               │ its·two-column·layout·with·the·PageMaker·
║               │ application.¶
║ Body text     │  ➜       1.·Double-click·the·PageMaker·icon·to·
║               │ display·the·Page·setup·default·dialog·box,·and·
╚═════════════════════════════════════════════════╝
```

Figure 158. The Story window with Courier as the preferred font.

Summary

Microsoft *Word* 5.0 and Aldus *PageMaker* 4.2 are the latest upgrades (which arrived after completion of this chapter), and the current street price is about $295 and $494, respectively. To a certain extent, both applications can be used as a word processor or a page layout program, for creating electronic manuscripts and printing offprints that compare favorably with professional publications. The chapter begins with the procedures for constructing an offprint from an electronic manuscript, and ends with a description of the specific steps for creating a book with the *PageMaker* program, namely, *A Musician's Guide to Desktop Computing*.

CHAPTER 5

Music and Scanning

In 1991 Apple Computer introduced the *OneScanner* flatbed scanner with its specially developed Light Source *Ofoto* scanning software. The Preface to the Owner's Guide states that the *OneScanner* "represents a revolution in scanning," and so it does! Place a sheet of music—manuscript or published copy—on the scanner glass surface, click the **Autoscan** button in the Scan Controls window, and—lo and behold!—a high-quality image is captured (Figure 159). The program provides such MacPaint tools as the Pencil and Eraser, controls for editing the image, and EPS, Paint, PICT and TIFF file formats for export to page layout, word processing, and graphics programs.

Figure 159. Extract from Béla Bartók's holographic transcription of a Serbian instrumental folk tune, collected in 1912 and used as the source melody for "Serbian Dance" in his *Forty-four Duos* for Two Violins (1931). The image was scanned from a photostat of the printed version of the manuscript.

The first inexpensive scanner for Macintosh computers was—and still is—the digitizing cartridge, *ThunderScan,* manufactured by Thunderware. The company later produced the medium-priced, hand-held *LightningScan 400* and its remarkable *ThunderWorks* scanning software. The tutorials in this chapter explain the procedures and the specific steps for scanning Line Art and Grayscale images with the *OneScanner* and *LightningScan 400* scanners and their respective software. The chapter concludes with an illustrated discussion of *ThunderScan,* for comparative purposes.

ONESCANNER

 Ofoto

When the *Ofoto* icon is double-clicked, the New and Scan Controls windows are simultaneously displayed (Figure 160).

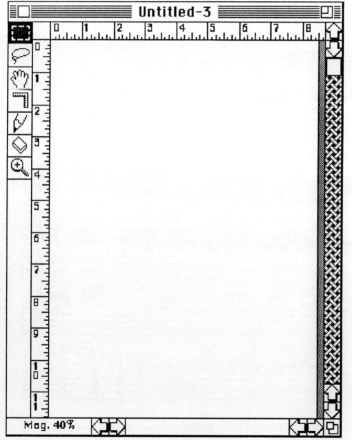

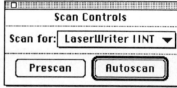

Figure 160. *Ofoto* New and Scan Control windows.

Unless the user has the LaserWriter IIN printer—the *Ofoto* default selection—it will be necessary to choose the applicable one from the **Scan for:** pop-up menu in the Scan Controls menu. Each printer among the many listed brands in the pop-up menu has a predefined calibration, to ensure matching the printed copy with the scanned original, and unlisted printers can be calibrated with the **Customize…** procedure. Figure 161 shows LaserWriter Plus output of *Ofoto*-scanned printed music.

Figure 161. *Ofoto* high-resolution Line Art scan of a page from *Investigating Music* (*New Dimensions in Music,* vol. 4. New York: The American Book Company, 1970). Copyright © 1969 by Benjamin Suchoff.

Figure 162 is an edited version of the scanned document shown in Figure 161, intended to illustrate the capability of *Ofoto* to produce a thematic excerpt.

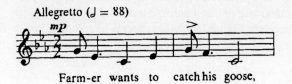

Figure 162. Thematic excerpt from Figure 161.

The following Tutorial demonstrates the ease with which printed music can be scanned and edited, to yield a high-quality image for various purposes. The reader should work with an original document or high-quality photocopy, preferably less than 8 inches in width.

1. Place the music document face down on the scanner glass, with its upper right hand corner close to and aligned with the two rulers.

•If the edges are not precisely aligned with the rulers, the program will trigger an automatic straightening procedure.

2. Click the **Autoscan** button in the Scan Controls window. A status box, consisting of five grayed icons appears, highlights the applicable icons and their pop-up captions in this sequence: **Prescanning...**, **Scanning Line Art...**, **Resizing...**, **Straightening...**,and **Cropping...**

•In most cases the procedure will be limited to Prescan and Scan functions.

3. **Save** the scan as a PICT file (the default selection) and give it a name.

4. Choose the **Selection Rectangle** in the Tools palette and click-drag to select the desired area.

•Use the variable-shape pointer to move or resize the rectangle.

5. Choose **Crop** in the Edit menu.

•If unnecessary white space remains, choose **Suggest Crop** (the program encloses the image with a precisely-positioned selection rectangle), then the **Crop** command.

6. Choose the Magnifier tool or **Zoom In** (Command-=) in the Windows menu, and enlarge the image to the desired size for editing.

•The Grabber (hand) tool can be used to freely position the enlarged image.

•Reduce the image by holding down the Option key while the Magnifier is clicked or by choosing **Zoom Out** (Command-hyphen).

7. Choose the Eraser or Pencil to delete unwanted music, stray pixels, and so forth.

8. In the event the image is too large for publication or other purposes, choose **Resize...** in the Image menu to display the dialog box (Figure 163).

9. In the **Width:** box select (that is, highlight) the given dimension and

type the new width only.

- The program calculates the Height and Scale.
- The default units of measure are inches. Other units can be selected by choosing **Units...** in the Options menu to display the dialog box and its submenus (Figure 163).

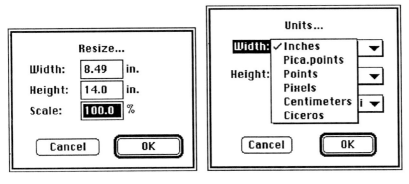

Figure 163. Default **Resize...** and **Units...** dialog boxes.

An exceptional feature of the *Ofoto* program is its ability to reproduce the tones (that is, the brightness and contrast) of photographic images, including holographic music manuscripts in ink or pencil. When a photographic reproduction of the original manuscript is scanned, the image will also include extraneous halftones (Figure 164).

Figure 164. Cropped scan of Bartók, *Rumanian Dance* No. 1 for Piano, Op. 8a (1909). Facsimile Edition published by Editio Musica, Budapest, 1974, p. 8.

These halftones, which are by-products of a method of printing photographs, should be (temporarily) suppressed by adjustment of the brightness and contrast tone controls or, when necessary, eliminated with the Eraser or Pencil. And during this toning procedure the music can be clarified to approximate the the appearance of the original autograph (Figure 165).

Figure 165. Enlarged view of Figure 164, with **Brightness** at -20 and **Contrast** at +60.

Another remarkable aspect of *Ofoto* editorial treatment is restoration of an autograph to reveal the composer's original concept. After the image is clarified, it is enlarged to Fat Bits or other mode to enable precise removal of strike outs, ink blots, stains, and stray pixels (Figure 166).

Figure 166. The same image as shown in Figure 165, with the last bar restored to its original content.

Sharp focus black and white photos are ideal documents for the production of high-quality images. Figure 168 is a high-resolution (300 dots per inch) scan of an 8 by 10 inch glossy original. Since the landscape-view photo was too wide to fit the scanner glass, it had to be oriented as a tall document. The reader interested in scanning similar documents should follow this procedure:

1. Choose **Expert Controls On** in the Options menu to display the extended Scan Controls dialog box (Figure 167).
2. Click the default **Autodetect** box to uncheck it.
   •The default **Photo** radio button should be on.
3. Click the **Manual** radio button to activate its selection boxes.
   •Scan Bits: **8.**
   •Scan dpi: **300.**
   •Print Bits: **8.**
   •Print dpi: **300.**

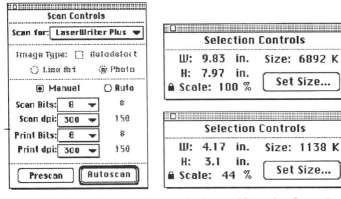

Figure 167. **Expert Scan Controls** dialog box and **Selection Controls** dialog boxes (before and after resizing the image).

4. Click the **Autoscan** button.

5. **Resize** the image menu (see Figure 163), and enter a reduction size in width, height, *or* scale (Figure 167).

6. **Rotate** the image **90 Degrees** to Landscape view.

7. **Crop** (if needed).

Figure 168. The author with the Hungarian composer, Zoltán Kodály, at the Bartók Archive, New York, 16 September 1966.

In addition to the basic (default) PICT format, which can be used by many graphics and page layout programs, *Ofoto* provides saving as EPS (Encapsulated PostScript), Paint, TIFF (Tag Image File Format) and TIFF LZW Compression file formats. Certain applications, such as *PageMaker*, prefer TIFF documents (the size of the compressed image in Figure 168 is 684K).

Figure 169 demonstrates the capability of *Ofoto* to scan a 5 by 7 inch color photograph for conversion to a grayscale image. The procedure is the same as described for Figure 168, except that the rotation step is eliminated. The file size of the cropped, reduced, and compressed TIFF image is 1100K.

Figure 169. Kir Ismail, a Turkish village singer, performing with his *cura irizva*. Cf. Béla Bartók, *Turkish Folk Music from Asia Minor,* edited by Benjamin Suchoff. Princeton and London: The Princeton University Press, 1976, p. 57.

Figure 170 is a high-resolution scan of a life-sized negative photostat of a printed (positive) drawing.

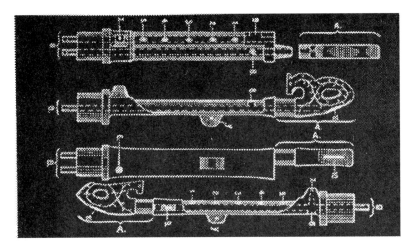

Figure 170. *Ofoto* scan of a negative photostat of the Hungarian bagpipe illustrated in *Zenei Lexikon* [Music Encyclopedia], edited by Bence Szabolcsi and Aladár Tóth, Budapest, 1931.

The following steps comprise the preliminary procedure for scanning a negative drawing similar to the image in Figure 170.

1. Choose **Expert Controls On** in the Options menu to display the extended Scan Controls dialog box.

2. Click the default **Autodetect** box to uncheck it.

3. The default **Photo** radio button should be on.

•A negative drawing should be treated as a Photo for scanning purposes, not as Line Art.

4. Click the **Manual** radio button to activate its selection boxes.

•Scan Bits: **8**.

•Scan dpi: **300**.

•Print Bits: **8**.

•Print dpi: **300**.

5. Click the **Autoscan** button.

6. Choose **Sharpen** in the Image menu.

•This command adds definition to a printed image.

The next procedure involves Brightness and Contrast, since scanned negative images usually require adjustment of the Tone Controls.

1. Choose **Apply Scan Controls** in the Windows menu to display the dialog box.

•Brightness: **66**.

•Contrast: **93**.

2. Choose **Save As** in the File menu to display the dialog box.

•Name the file and choose **PICT** (42K file) or **TIFF LZW Compression** (24K) as the format (Figure 171).

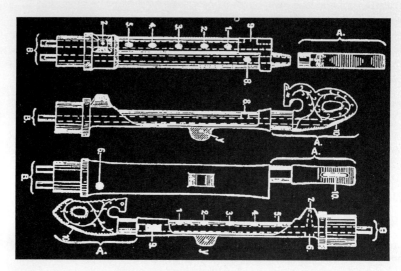

Figure 171. Tonal modification of the bagpipe image shown in Figure 170.

The negative image is easily converted to a positive one by choosing **Invert** in the Image window. The inverted image may require further adjustment of tonal quality: Figure 172 was improved by setting the Brightness to **3** and the Contrast to **-5**.

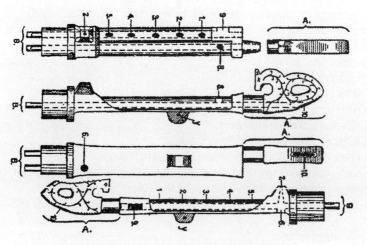

Figure 172. Reduced view of the inverted bagpipe image.

154

The same drawing was printed in larger size, with German captions, in another publication. In later reprints the drawing appears with English captions. Figure 173 is a high-resolution (300 dpi) scan of the German version, in which the captions were erased; the image was cropped, resized, and saved in PICT format; and the file was opened in the *SuperPaint* Draw layer, where English captions were entered and grouped with the drawing.

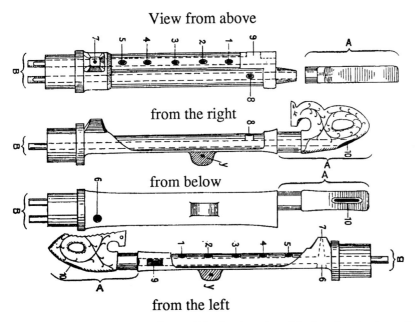

View from above

from the right

from below

from the left

Figure 173. Edited scan of the first (1923) printed version of the bagpipe drawing, with English instead of German captions. Cf. Béla Bartók, *Rumanian Folk Music,* vol. 5, edited by Benjamin Suchoff. The Hague: Martinus Nijhoff, 1975, p. 33.

LIGHTNINGSCAN 400

This hand-held, flat surface scanner has a scan width of 4.2 inches. Wider documents will therefore require a second scan and subsequent joining of the two halves. Scanner calibration of the scanner is essential for creating better grayscale images, and the procedure is fully explained in the *LightningScan 400* manual and the *ThunderWorks* User's Guide. Readers interested in producing such images should consult those excellent sources, since it is beyond the scope of this chapter to discuss the various steps involved, which include preliminary adjustment of scanner switches. The bundled software consists of the *Lightning-Scan* desk accessory, which can be opened within other applications, and the more sophisticated *ThunderWorks* program.

LightningScan

Scanner	
New Scan...	⌘L
Open...	⌘O
Save As...	⌘S
Select All	⌘A
1-Bit Rendering	⌘G
Re-Size	▶
Rotate 90° Left	
Rotate 90° Right	
Flip Horizontal	
Flip Vertical	
About...	
Calibrate...	
Quit	⌘Q

LIGHTNINGSCAN DA

The desk accessory is installed in the System Folder with the Font/DA Mover or a utility such as *Suitcase* (see Chapter 9).

1. Set the scanner switches.
   •Dither: **Line Art.**
   •Resolution (dots per inch) according to the printer: ImageWriter to position **2** (144 dpi), LaserWriter **3** (300 dpi) and StyleWriter **4** (400 dpi).
   •Light/Dark (Brightness dial): **midpoint.**
2. Install the *SnapGuide* on the scanner.
   •Place a page of sheet music or music manuscript on a flat surface.
3. Choose **LightningScan** in the Apple menu to display its menu bar.
4. Choose **New Scan...** in the Scanner menu to open the scan window (Figure 174).

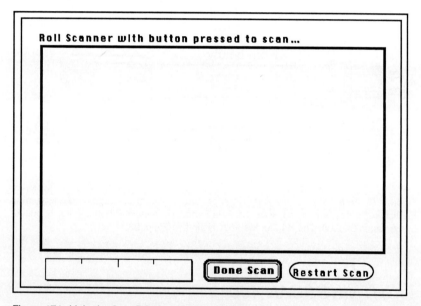

Figure 174. *LightningScan* DA **New Scan...** window.

5. Place the 13-inch plastic guide on the document, hold down the start button and slowly drag the scanner across the page.
6. Click the **Done Scan** button.
7. **Save** the file in PICT or compressed TIFF format.
   •PICT files can be opened by most programs; Compressed TIFF files are usually placed in page layout programs. Although these files are economic with regard to kilobyte size, they cannot be enhanced or otherwise fully edited in graphics and page layout programs.

It should be noted that the **Re-Size** options are temporary commands for screen display purposes and will not be saved when the file is closed. In order to enlarge or reduce the image, the file must be exported to another application. Figure 175, for example is a Line Art scan of the upper half of a music manuscript photocopy, 4.1 by 7.9 inches, placed in *PageMaker* and resized to its present dimensions.

Actual Size	⌘1
Fit To Window	⌘2
✓Full Size	⌘3
Zoom In	⌘=
Zoom Out	⌘-

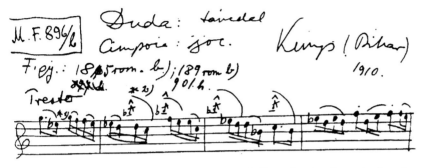

Figure 175. High-resolution (300 dpi) Line Art scan of a Transylvanian-Rumanian bagpipe melody collected and transcribed by Béla Bartók. The file was saved in Compressed TIFF (102K) format.

THUNDERWORKS

In addition to Line Art *ThunderWorks* scans and edits grayscale images produced with *LightningScan 400* and other Thunderware scanners.

    1. Set the scanner Dither switch to the smallest dot in the **Photo** diagram. The other settings are the same as for the *LightningScan* DA.

    2. Double-click the *ThunderWorks* icon.

      • The menu bar and the Tools and Gray Shades palettes are displayed.

    3. Choose **New...** in the File menu to display the default settings in the New File Options dialog box (Figure 176).

ThunderWorks

File	
New...	⌘N
Open...	⌘O
Close	⌘W
Join Files...	⌘J
Create Gray...	⌘G

New File Options

Height: `10.00` in   Image Type: `1-bit ▼`

Width: `8.00` in   Resolution: `72` `▼` dpi

Needed Memory - 50 K bytes.
Available Memory - 1030 K bytes.   `Cancel`   `OK`

Figure 176. **New File Options** dialog box.

Scanner

New Scan... ⌘L
Scan & Join...
Apply Calibration
Calibrate...

Setup...

4. Choose **8-bit** in the Image Type scroll box.

5. Click the **OK** button to open the scan window.

•Except for icon buttons to specify scan direction, the window is similar to the one shown in Figure 174.

6. Choose **New Scan...** in the Scanner menu.

7. Place a photograph on a flat surface and scan from top to bottom (the default scan direction).

8. Choose **Create Grays...** in the File menu to display the Create Gray Options dialog box—the default options are 6 x 6 Dither and Double Size—and click the **OK** button (Figure 177).

9. **Save** the file in the (default) Compressed TIFF format.

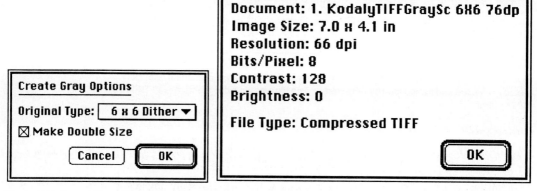

Create Gray Options

Original Type: [6 x 6 Dither ▼]

☒ Make Double Size

[Cancel] [OK]

Document: 1. KodalyTIFFGraySc 6X6 76dp
Image Size: 7.0 x 4.1 in
Resolution: 66 dpi
Bits/Pixel: 8
Contrast: 128
Brightness: 0

File Type: Compressed TIFF

[OK]

Figure 177. **Create Gray Options** and **Document Info...** dialog boxes.

Figure 177 also shows the Document Info... dialog box (File menu) which specifies the dimensions and settings of the scanned image which appears in two versions in Figure 178. The original document is the same black and white, Landscape View photograph which was scanned, resized and placed as Figure 168 in the *OneScanner/Ofoto* tutorial further above. Since the *LightningScan 400* scanner has a maximum scan width of 4.1 inches, the right half of the photograph was scanned vertically 7 inches and saved in Compressed TIFF format (file size: 45K). *ThunderWorks*, too, cannot export a cropped or resized image, the file was therefore placed and duplicated for editing in *PageMaker*. As Figure 178 shows, the full-sized, cropped image is paired with its uncropped but resized version.

The original document can be reproduced by carefully scanning the left half (Steps 6–9, above) and naming the file as such when it is saved. When the **Join Files...** command is chosen in the File menu, the program loads the halves by way of standard dialog boxes for opening files, and the two images are displayed in a new (untitled) window. The Join Tool palette simultaneously appears with two special alignment tools—the Skoogy and the Tack—in

158

addition to the Grabber and Magnifying Glass. The ingenious procedure for matching the halves and its parts is clearly explained and illustrated in a special tutorial in the *ThunderWorks* User's Guide.

Figure 177. *LightningScan 400* full-sized scan of the black and white photograph of Zoltán Kodály (at the Bartók Archive, New York, 16 September 1966), placed and edited in *PageMaker* as cropped and resized versions. Cf. Figure 168.

Black and white photographs are usually reproduced in commercial publications by a process of screening to simulate gray shades. The simulations are called halftones, that is, dots of black ink and the surrounding white space, which form areas that are perceived as different shades of gray. When published photographs are scanned, including black and white reproductions of color prints, the intensified background halftones may be distracting, sometimes to the degree where parts of the foreground image are obscured. In such cases the intrusive background halftones can be "opaqued" by increasing brightness. Since this adjustment also affects the black and gray tones of the foreground image, a balanced increase in contrast will also be necessary.

Figure 179 demonstrates the outcome when a scan is made of a published black and white photograph. The image is the lid of a decorated mirror-box, constructed of wood and painted by a peasant artisan in a Transdanubian village (Hungary, about 1840). The same photograph was used by a commercial artist, as the basis for illustrating the cover of a transcription for symphonic band (see the scan in Figure 187, below).

Figure 179. **Create Grays...** scan of a published black and white photograph from *L'Art populaire en Hongrie* [Folk Art in Hungary], edited by Edit Fél, Tamás Hofer and Klára K.-Csilléry. Budapest: Corvina, 1958, plate no. 169. The image, 4.1 by 6.6 inches, was saved as a Compressed TIFF file (65K).

The same nine steps given above for the scan in Figure 177 are followed here. Then **Show Gray Map Editor** is selected in the View menu to display the default dialog box (Figure 180).

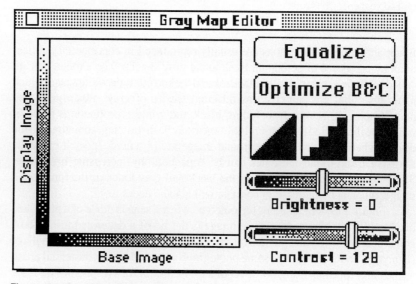

Figure 180. **Gray Map Editor** default dialog box.

The image is then enhanced by adjusting the Brightness and Contrast sliders until the background is opaqued and tonal balance is achieved in the foreground (Figure 181).

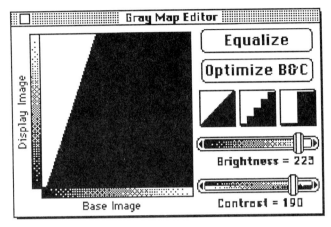

Figure 181. Gray Map Editor with adjusted Brightness and Contrast sliders.

It is important to note that Gray Map Editor changes are not permanent unless they are applied to the image.
    1. Choose **Select All** in the Edit menu.
    2. Choose **Apply Gray Map** in the Effects menu.
    3. **Save as...** Compressed TIFF to reduce file size (Figure 182).

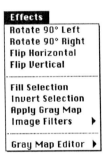

Figure 182. Enhanced image after setting Brightness slider to 233 and Contrast slider to 190 in the Gray Map Editor. The applied changes further reduce the file size to 31K.

The last step is editing the lid outline, hinges, and remaining wood-grain halftones until only the decorative art remains for additional tonal adjustment (Figure 183).

Figure 183. Editorial treatment of the scanned image to clarify the decorative art.

When a document is Line Art in color, it can be scanned and enhanced by following the same procedures described above. Figure 184 shows the scan of a professionally-designed emulation of Hungarian decorative art, that needed adjustment of Brightness (33) and Contrast (70) settings, without further editing.

Figure 184. Cover design for Béla Bartók, *Pieces and Suites* for Piano Duet, transcribed by Benjamin Suchoff. Copyright © 1962 by Sam Fox Publishing Company.

MUSIC AND SCANNING

THUNDERSCAN

The *ThunderScan* digitizing cartridge originally had the *ThunderScan* program, its User's Guide, and a manual for installing the scanner cartridge in place of the ribbon cartridge on ImageWriter printers. This low-cost device, now bundled with the *ThunderWorks* program, was the first scanner used by the author and with excellent results. The following *ThunderScan* images are provided for comparative purposes and, to avoid redundancy, without listing the previously described *ThunderWorks* procedures.

Figure 185 shows the scan of a positive photostat of a page of music manuscript. The need for cropping was avoided by positioning the scanner above the desired notation, beginning the scan, and clicking the **Quit Scan** button after the selection appeared in the Image Pane. Some editing was necessary to erase stray pixels and other extraneous matter.

Figure 185. Scan of a Transylvanian Rumanian Christmas carol, collected and transcribed by Béla Bartók. The file was saved in Compressed TIFF (22K) format.

Figure 186 is a scan of examples from Bartók's collection of Rumanian choreography. The PICT file was opened in *SuperPaint* for insertion of captions.

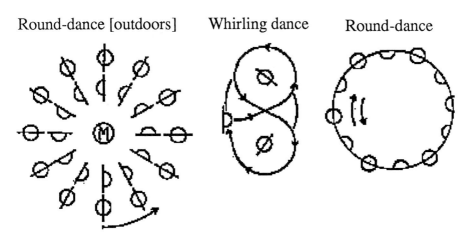

Figure 186. Scan of choreography from Bartók's collection of Rumanian folk dances.

The same photograph scanned as Figure 179 was transformed by a commercial artist as part of a cover design in color (Figure 187). Figure 188 shows the complete design, where the scanned transformations of Hungarian decorative art are combined with different typography.

Figure 187. Scan of transformed Hungarian decorative art. Cf. Figure 179.

FOUR PIECES
for BAND

By

Béla Bartók

Transcribed for Band
By
BENJAMIN SUCHOFF

SAM FOX MUSIC PUBLISHING COMPANY, INC.
170 N.E. 33rd ST. • FT. LAUDERDALE, FL 33334

Figure 188. *SuperPaint* reconstruction of a cover design for Béla Bartók, *Four Pieces for Band.* Copyright © 1962 by Sam Fox Music Publishing Company.

Summary

The flatbed Apple *OneScanner* and its bundled LightSource *Ofoto* scanning software is available from authorized dealers for the discounted price of approximately $950. Version 1.1 (the first upgrade) of the *Ofoto* software appeared in January 1992, and also as a stand-alone program for use with a number of other scanners (list price: $395).

As the designation of the scanner implies—thanks to the truly unique software—the user need only place a Line Art or Grayscale image on the scanner glass and click a dialog-box button in the monitor window, to duplicate the kind of results that are illustrated in the first part of this chapter. In addition to the aspects of automation discussed further above, Version 1.1 includes Auto-Sharpening, that is, adjusting contrast to delineate adjacent objects. Another important attribute of the upgrade is reduction of file size without loss in image quality.

The hand-held *LightningScan 400* and its bundled *ThunderWorks* software can be purchased for the discounted price of about $385. The package includes a desk accessory which can be activated for scanning while the user is working in other applications. The scanner is capable of producing high-quality Line Art and Grayscale images, as demonstrated in the second part of this chapter.

Precision scanning requires manual setting of scanner switches, use of the supplied *SnapGuide* and its rule, and a controlled scanning speed to avoid distortion of the image. While *ThunderWorks* provides the saving of edited, rotated and flipped images, resizing is limited to screen adjustments. The files must therefore be exported to applications which can open them for resizing purposes. And the treatment of Grayscale images may involve rather sophisticated procedures to optimize printed ouput.

The *ThunderScan* package-available from vendors for the discounted price of approximately $199—includes a digitizing cartridge (the scanner) which replaces the ribbon cartridge on ImageWriter printers; the *ThunderWorks* software; and the Power Port, for those Macintosh computers which have non-powered serial ports. The Macintosh II, however, requires the Power Accessory ($49). The four illustrations which close this chapter show the capability of this inexpensive scanner to produce high-resolution Line Art and Grayscale images.

Since the scanner travels bi-directionally, at the same speed as the printer head, its input is quite slow, especially if large areas are scanned or high-resolution scans are involved. There are, too, a number of problems that sometimes occur when documents are irregularly shaped, not precisely inserted in the printer, or shift as they advance during scanning.

CHAPTER 6

Music and *HyperCard 2*

HyperCard

HyperCard 2 is such a versatile application for the management of information that only a few of its features can be presented in this chapter. The most widespread uses are browsing information and retrieving typed data in stacks created by commercial vendors, educators, and other developers. A higher level is database construction of biographical matter, thematic indexes, and catalogues of works, which also include the performance of incipits or longer melodies. Among the more recent developments are the the application as the front end for accessing information on CD-ROM discs and scanning images. In the event the reader is unfamiliar with *HyperCard 2* the following tutorial should be helpful.

Home

Navigating.—Double-click the *HyperCard 2* icon to open the Home stack to its first card (Figure 189).

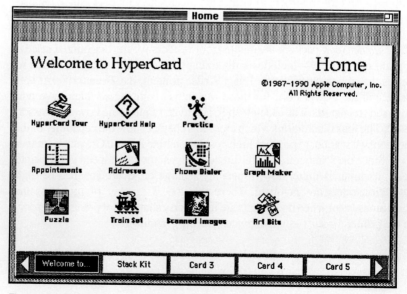

Figure 189. First card of the *HyperCard 2* Home stack.

1. The Arrow pointer changes to the Browse tool inside the card window.

2. Choose **Message** in the Go menu to display the Message box with its flashing insertion point.

3. Type **nav** and press **Return** to display the Navigator Palette (Figure 190).

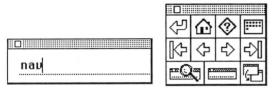

Figure 190. Message box and Navigator Palette.

The Message box can be used to type commands or as an electronic calculator. The Navigator Palette serves as the graphic equivalent of Go menu commands.

1. Choose **Last** in the Go menu (or click the right-arrow/bar button in the Navigator Palette) to display the Preferences card.

•The default user level is set to Typing (Figure 191).

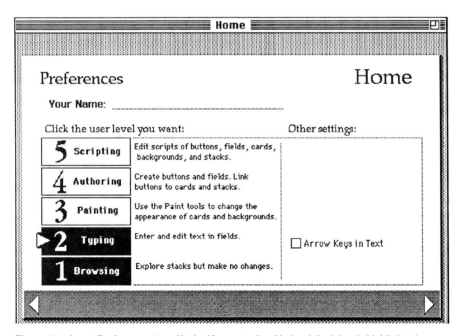

Figure 191. **Last** (Preferences) card in the Home stack, with the default levels highlighted.

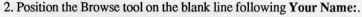

2. Position the Browse tool on the blank line following **Your Name:**.
  •The tool changes to the I-beam for text entry.
3. Click the I-beam and type the name at the flashing insertion point.
4. Click the **5 Scripting** level to select it.
5. Click the Browse tool on the arrow head at the lower right-hand corner of the window (or click the left-arrow/bar button in the Navigator Palette) to return to the first card.

Music Notation and Performance.—A limited number of music symbols are available for performance purposes in *HyperCard 2*, and they are represented by alphanumeric characters which describe pitch class, pitch modifier, octave register, and duration (Figure 192).

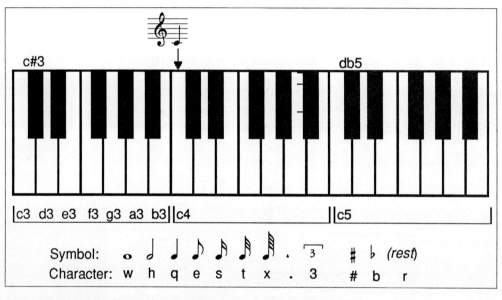

Figure 192. Alphanumeric representation of music symbols in *HyperCard 2*.

As a case in point, Figure 193 illustrates a simple message that will instruct the application to play the C melodic minor scale at tempo *96*, using the built-in *harpsichord* sound resource.

play "harpsichord" tempo 96 "c4q3 d eb f g a b c5 bb4 ab g f eb d c"

Figure 193. Message box character string for the C melodic minor scale (cf. Figure 197, below)..

The **Play** command syntax and explanatory remarks are given in Figure 194. There are many interesting sound resources which can be purchased from commercial vendors or downloaded from CompuServe (see the music stacks described further below), Berkeley BMUG, and Boston BCS Macintosh user groups, and other information services.

Command syntax: **play** [*voice*] **tempo** [*200±*] [*notation*]

Voice: "harpsichord" (non-legato), "flute" (legato, *8va*) or "boing"

Notation: [a b c d e f g] [# b] [3, 4, 5] [w h q e s t x] [.] [3]

Rests: [r] [w h q e st x] [.] [3]

Remarks: (1) Voice designation and note sequence are placed in quotes
         (2) Notes are separated by spaces
         (3) Duration, octave register and triplet sign are effective until changed
         (4) Accidentals do not carry over in the note sequence and must be
            reentered (natural signs are therefore unnecessary)
         (5) If the sequence contains letters only, the defaults are octave 4 register
            and quarter-note duration (the default tempo is 200)

Figure 194. Play command syntax for messages and scripts.

Creating a Play Button.—The user Preferences level (see Last Card in the Home stack) should be set to **5**, since the preparation of a Play script will follow the creation of the Play button.

    1. Click the **Card 3** button to display the practice card.

    •Click the Browse tool in the Tools palette and drag downward to detach the palette and place it in the card (Figure 195).

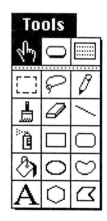

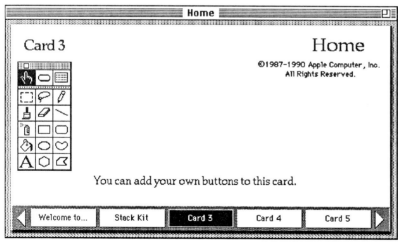

Figure 195. Card 3 in the Home stack, with the repositioned Tools palette

Objects

Button Info...
Field Info...
Card Info...
Bkgnd Info...
Stack Info...

Bring Closer ⌘·
Send Farther ⌘-

New Button
New Field
New Background

New Button

2. Choose **New Button** in the Objects menu.

•A button named "New Button" is displayed in the center of the card, with a flashing marquee to indicate it is selected.

•The Arrow pointer can be used to reposition or resize the button.

3. Choose **Button Info...** to display the dialog box (Figure 196).

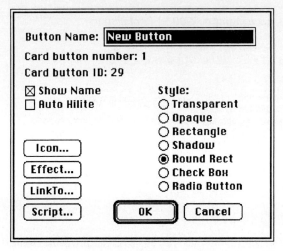

Figure 196. **New Button**...dialog box.

4. Type **Play Music** in the Button Name box.

5. Click the Auto Hilite box.

•The button will highlight (that is, temporarily revert to white on black) when it is clicked with the Browse tool.

•Do not exit the dialog box.

Creating a Button Script.——The Play character-string shown in Figure 193 is a Message box script: a temporary instruction that is valid until replaced by another message. Button scripts, however, are attached to specific objects, such as the Play Music button created on Card 3, and they are effective until edited.

1. Click the **Script...** button to display the dialog box (Figure 197).

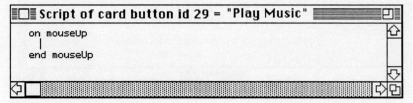

Figure 197. **Script...** window with insertion point in position for text entry.

2. The indented flashing insertion point indicates where text entry is to begin.

•Type the following script (make sure to observe the quote marks and the space between each letter of the melody): **play "harpsichord" tempo 144 "d4e e e e d e b a g dq. eh"** (Figure 198).

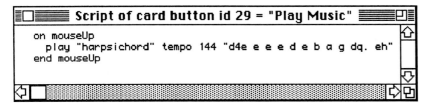

Figure 198. Completed script for "Play Music" (card button identification no. 29).

3. Close the window to return to Card 3.

•Select the Browse tool and click the Play Music button to test highlighting and performance (Figure 199).

•If the music cannot be heard or is too soft, reset the Speaker Volume in the Control Panel **General** dialog box.

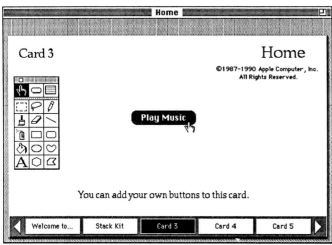

Figure 199. The Play Music button when highlighted with the Browse tool.

If a notated music incipit and its caption are added to the card, the audio-visual components of a multimedia thematic index or other music database are in place (Figure 200).

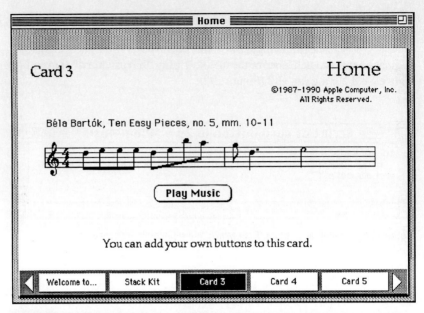

Figure 200. The Play Music button and its related music incipit. Although the melody was notated in *Deluxe Music Construction Set* (*Sonata* font) and saved as a PICT file, *HyperCard 2* converts this format into a bitmap (PAINT file).

 Maestro

THE *MAESTRO* MUSIC STACK

Maestro is a mouse-driven stack that features a piano score containing a quarter rest and a six-octave C scale of whole notes as the graphic interface for creating music scripts (Figure 201). Each note is encompassed by an invisible rectangular button whose stereotyped script changes in accordance with pitch class and octave register. The visible rectangular buttons contain radio buttons or check boxes for entering sound resources, accidentals, durations, octave transpositions, and triplet and dot modifiers. Tempo is changed by selecting the numbers in the Tempo box and typing new ones (the quarter note is a fixed unit of measurement). A set of command buttons appears above the scrolling windoid which displays the words or characters when the note buttons are clicked.

 Maestro always enters the **Play** command on a new line whenever a note button is clicked. The user should set the tempo first (the default is ♩ = 100) and thereafter follow *HyperCard 2* syntax (see Figure 194, above) by the sequential clicking of the desired sound resource, optional accidental, duration, optional rest, dot, triplet, and optional octave change (intended primarily for scripting the non-notated highest and lowest registers). Accidentals and dots do not carry over from note to note, and the triplet will automatically turn off when three notes have been entered. The cursor changes to an I-beam in the **other:** area of the sound resource box, for typing **Flute** (*HyperCard 2* built-in resource) or the name of some other available sound resource.

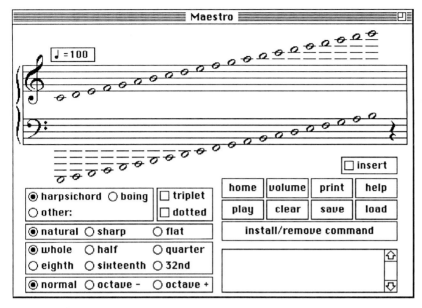

Figure 201. The *Maestro* music stack main screen.

The following Tutorial outlines the procedures for using the *Maestro* graphic interface as an alternative method for creating a music script and pasting it in a Play Music button in Home stack Card 4.

    1. Construct a C melodic minor scale, and compare the script to the Message-box character string in Figure 189. The text should match the windoid entries in Figure 202.

```
play "harpsichord" tempo 96 c4q
play "harpsichord" tempo 96 d4q
play "harpsichord" tempo 96 eb4q
play "harpsichord" tempo 96 f4q

play "harpsichord" tempo 96 g4q
play "harpsichord" tempo 96 a4q
play "harpsichord" tempo 96 b4q
play "harpsichord" tempo 96 c5q

play "harpsichord" tempo 96 bb4q
play "harpsichord" tempo 96 ab4q
play "harpsichord" tempo 96 g4q
play "harpsichord" tempo 96 f4q

play "harpsichord" tempo 96 eb4q
play "harpsichord" tempo 96 d4q
play "harpsichord" tempo 96 c4q
```

Figure 202. Composite windoids of the scale script.

play

save

2. Click the **Play** button to audio-proof the script. Errors can be corrected with the keyboard.
•The Browse tool changes to an I-beam in the windoid.
3. Click the **Save** button to display the dialog box (Figure 203).

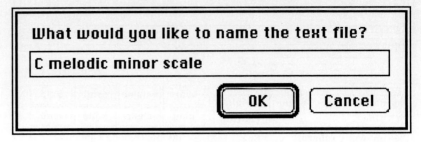

Figure 203. **Save** (file designation) dialog box.

C melodic minor scale

home

load

4. Type **C melodic minor scale** and click **OK** to exit.
•The file is automatically placed in the *HyperCard 2* application folder, and it can be loaded in the *Maestro* windoid or opened in Microsoft *Word* or other word processors for editing purposes.
5. Click the **home** button to close the *Maestro* stack and transfer to the *HyperCard* Home stack.
The next procedure is creation of a Play Button in Card 4 of the Home stack. The reader may wish to follow the steps in the *Creating a Play Music Button* and *Creating a Button Script* sections (pp. 169-71, above) or alternatively, copy the Play Button (Command-C) in Card 3 and paste it (Command-V) in Card 4. In the latter case it will be necessary to delete the current Play script (see Figure 198), but make sure that the flashing insertion point is positioned on a blank line between the **On mouseUp** and **end mouseUp** commands, before pasting the new script (cf. Figure 197).
1. After creating the new Play button on Card 4, open the *Maestro* stack and click the **load** button to display the dialog box (Figure 204).

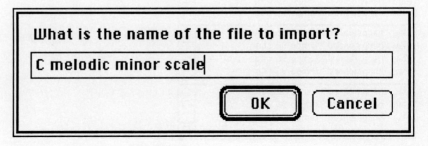

Figure 204. **Load** (file import) dialog box.

174

2. Type **C melodic minor scale** and click **OK**.

•The script is displayed in the windoid.

3. Position the I-beam at the beginning of the text and click-drag downward until the complete script is selected.

4. Copy the selected script and click the **home** button to return to the Home stack.

5. Go to Card 4 and paste the script in the new Play Music button.

•Click the Play Music button to test highlighting and performance. Figure 205 shows the button and its related music notation.

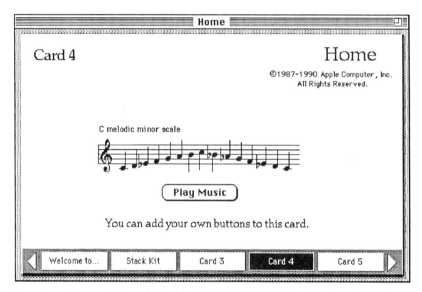

Figure 205. Home stack Card 4 with Play Music button and its related music notation.

THE *SOUND SCRIPTER* STACK

When *Sound Scripter* is opened, the first card displays a piano keyboard as the graphic interface for the creation of music scripts (Figure 206). Each piano key is a Play button: whenever the black keys are clicked, the respective pitch classes are always scripted as C# Eb F# Ab and Bb. Exception: when **Chromatic Scale...** is chosen in the Script menu, the program enters each pitch class according to its optional *HyperCard 2* numeric equivalent (Middle C = 60 or C4, C# = 61 or C#4, etc.). Since scripts may be freely edited, the user may type Db to replace C or its numeric equivalent (the Browse tool changes to an I-beam in the scripting windoid.

Although pitch class and octave register are automatically entered, the user must follow *HyperCard 2* syntax: any change in duration, modification, tempo or voice must be selected before a button key is clicked. Tempo changes are

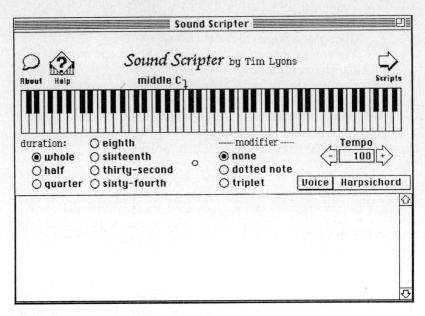

Figure 206. The *Sound Scripter* main screen.

made in increments of 10 when the Browse tool clicks the left or right arrow, or increments of 1 when the Shift key is held down while clicking. Alternatively, clicking the number box displays a dialog box for changing tempo (Figure 207).

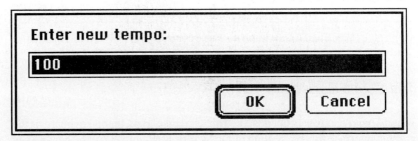

Figure 207. **Enter new tempo:** dialog box.

When the Voice box is clicked, a pop-up menu is displayed for choosing Silence (that is, a rest), two sound resources (the default is Harpsichord) and Customize menu. Selecting Customize menu displays a Debug/Script dialog box with a seemingly unrelated message. In any event if the Cancel button is clicked a large dialog box appears for adding the *HyperCard 2* Flute and external sound resources (Figure 208). When the dialog box is exited, the added resource appears at the bottom of the pop-up menu.

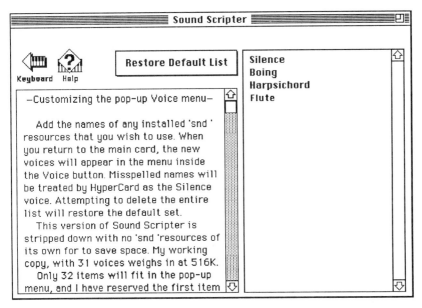

Figure 208. Dialog box for customizing the pop-up Voice menu.

The following Tutorial outlines the procedure for scripting and saving a *Sound Scripter* file:

      1. Referring to the them in Figure 209,   click the proper   *Sound Scripter* keyboard buttons and duration radio buttons to transform the music into its *HyperCard 2* script (use the default Tempo and Voice).

Figure 209. W.A. Mozart, Variations in C, K. 265 (*"Ah! vous dirai-je, maman"*).

      2. If the keyboarded script matches the windoid text in Figure 210, choose **Save to file...** in the Script menu. A dialog box will appear for entering the name of the script.

      •If necessary, click the I-beam in the windoid to edit the script.

Figure 210. Windoid display of the scripted Mozart theme.

3. Type **Mozart theme** and exit the dialog box.

 •The script is saved as a designated card in the *Sound Scripter* stack of card scripts, where it can be freely edited with the I-beam or played when the Play Script button is clicked with the Browse tool.(Figure 211).

Scripts

Figure 211. *Sound Scripter* card with Mozart theme script.

Help

More Help

Keyboard

 4. Go to the first card, click the Help icon to display Help Card #1, and then click the More Help button until Help Card #7 appears (Figure 212).

 5. Click the Install Stack Icon button to automatically paste it in the first card of the Home stack.

 •*Sound Scripter* can thereafter be opened by clicking its icon in the Home stack.

 6. Click the Keyboard arrow to return to the first card.

 •Note that the script will be displayed in the windoid until it is deleted.

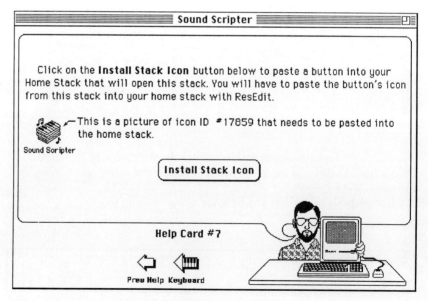

Figure 212. Help Card #7 with its Install Stack Icon button.

The next procedure is creating a Play Script button which will play the Mozart theme, and pasting the button in Home stack card 5 (if necessary, review the *Creating a Play Music Button* and *Creating a Button Script* sections on pp. 169-71, above),

1. Click the Scripts button until the Mozart theme card appears, select the Button tool in the Tools menu and click the Play Script button.

2. Type, in order, Command-C.and Command-V. A duplicate Play Script button is placed on top of the original one: click-drag it to the center of the card.

3. Follow the procedure for opening a button script, and select and delete the text matter between **on mouseUp** and **end mouseUp** (Figure 213).

Scripts

Play Script

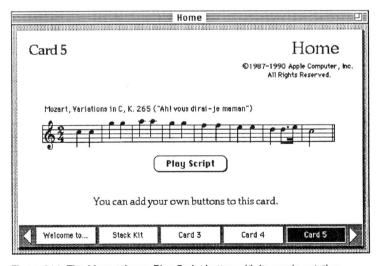

Figure 213. Selected text of the *Sound Scripter* button script.

4. Copy the Mozart theme script and paste it at the flashing insertion point in the Script window and verify the music performance. Finally, copy the edited Play Script button and paste it in Card 5 of the Home stack (Figure 214).

Figure 214. The Mozart theme Play Script button with its music notation.

Canary

Canary

The *Canary* Stack

This unusual music stack provides the means for constructing Play button scripts with a MIDI instrument, an ingenious mouse-driven graphic editor, a graphic piano keyboard, or the computer keyboard. Whenever the stack is opened, a dialog box is displayed for the optional installation of the *Canary* Open Stack button among the other buttons in the first card of the Home stack (Figure 215).

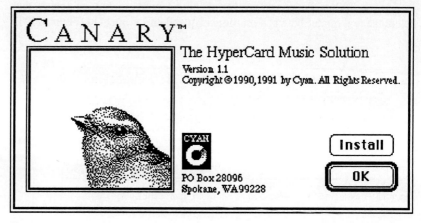

Figure 215. *Canary* stack opening dialog box.

When the dialog box is exited, another is presented for choosing the basic mode of script construction and playback (Figure 216). If the **No** button is clicked, the Control card appears with the grayed-out (inoperative) MIDI Control; Play, Edit, Tempo and pop-up Instrument buttons; and the active HyperTalk Control windoid. Figure 217 shows the Control card with the default Flute Up button script, when the Canary stack is opened for the first time.

Figure 216. Dialog box for choosing the basic mode of Play script construction.

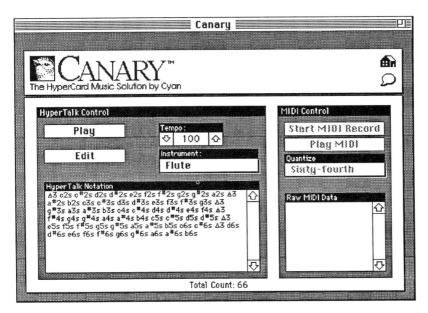

Flute Up

Figure 217. Control card with the Flute Up button script.

The pop-up Instruments menu contains thirty sound resources, including the standard Boing, Harpsichord, and Flute. Any sound can be deleted and exported or imported, but the menu is limited to a maximum of forty-nine sound resources. The instrumental timbres can be sampled by choosing **Keyboard** in the Go menu, to display the graphic piano keyboard (Figure 218), selecting the desired instrument and clicking the keys with the Arrow pointer. The inclusion of major and minor chord patches adds an interesting quasi-polyphonic dimension to otherwise strictly monophonic *HyperCard 2* Play scripts.

Figure 218. The *Canary* stack graphic piano keyboard.

When the Edit button is clicked or **Editor** is chosen in the Go menu, the Control card is replaced by the gridded Edit card (Figure 219). At first view this graphic representation of the Flute Up button script appears to be a complicated approach to script editing. However, a brief study of the *Canary* Users Guide, together with comparison of the button script and a little practice, should quickly lead users toward mastery of the few, relatively simple editing procedures.

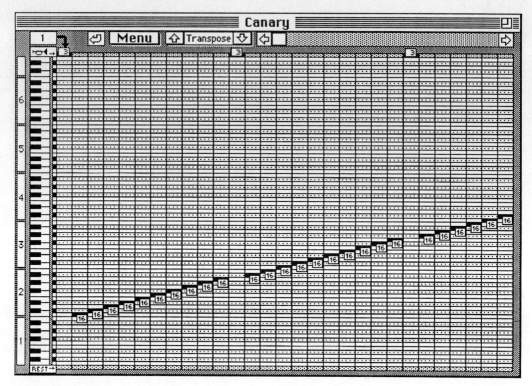

Figure 219. The Edit card, showing the graphic representation of the beginning of the Flute Up button script.

Each horizontal bar on the Edit card grid represents a pitch class which corresponds to the respective key in the fixed, vertical piano keyboard. The bars and the keys are Play buttons which produce Harpsichord sounds when clicked with the browse tool. Each bar, moreover, displays an arrow icon with the pitch class designation, which points to the corresponding key, and the bar can be dragged vertically to alter pitch or horizontally to change duration. Moreover, if a bar column is selected with the Browse tool, the movable piano keyboard can be displayed to alter the pitch (also limited to Harpsichord sounds). The selection process also activates the Transpose menu.

The outstanding feature of the *Canary* stack is its straightforward approach to MIDI-controlled creation of Play button scripts, as can be seen in the following Tutorial.

1. Turn on the MIDI instrument.
    •The output should be connected to headphones or an amplifier. See also Appendix A (Connecting MIDI) in the *Canary* Users Guide, p. 21.
2. Open the *Canary* stack and click the **Yes** button in the MIDI option dialog box (see Figure 216, above).
3. The application provides a Metronome sound resource to mark tempo during recording, However, the ticking sound is fixed at approximately

THE *CANARY* STACK

Tempo = 235± and continues throughout the recording session. The user can click the default **Metronome** command (MIDI menu) to disable the sound.

    4. Click the Start MIDI Record button and play a melody.

    5. Click the Play MIDI button

    •The Start MIDI Record button name changes to Converting MIDI, numeric strings appear in the Raw MIDI Data windoid, and the related Hyper-Talk script is displayed in the HyperTalk Notation windoid.

    6. Click the Play MIDI button again to play the recorded melody with the MIDI instrument, according to the user's preselected patch.

    •The patch can be changed at any time before, during or after playback.

    7. Click the Play button in the HyperTalk Control section.

    •The melody will be played with the computer speaker, according to the currently displayed Tempo and Instrument.

    8. When the desired Tempo and Instrument are satisfactory, choose **Save as Button...** in the File menu.

    •The **Name this new button...** dialog box appears, with New Tune as the default designation.

    9. Name the button and click **OK** to exit.

    •The application creates the new *Canary* icon button with its Play script, the Button card appears (Figure 220), and the new button is displayed for placement in the card.

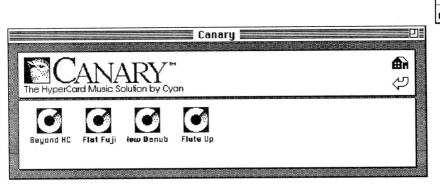

Figure 220. *Canary* stack Button card.

    10. Click the button at the desired location.

    •When the cursor to changes to the Browse tool, click the button again to audio-proof the script.

Whenever the Buttons card is accessed, a special Buttons menu appears with commands for deleting or re-editing buttons. When the **Re-edit Button...** command is chosen, whichever button is clicked has its script displayed in the HyperTalk Control windoid, where it can be edited with the computer keyboard, and in graphic form in the Edit card, for editing with the mouse or the graphic piano keyboard. A third editing method was used by the author, based on *HyperCard 2* procedures for creating a Play script (see pp. 170-71), as follows:

1. The MIDI option was selected, the Metronome enabled in the MIDI menu, and the Start MIDI Record button clicked. The music (Figure 221) was then played on a Casio *CZ-101* synthesizer, using its Flute Preset, No. 07.

Adagio

Figure 221. Béla Bartók, *For Children* for Piano, (1908), vol. 1, no. 17

2. The Play MIDI button in the MIDI Control section was clicked, to convert the data into its HyperTalk script, and clicked again to audio-proof the music. The melody was audio-proofed again, this time by clicking the Play button in the HyperTalk Notation section, at Tempo 100 and with the Flute sound resource (Figure 222).

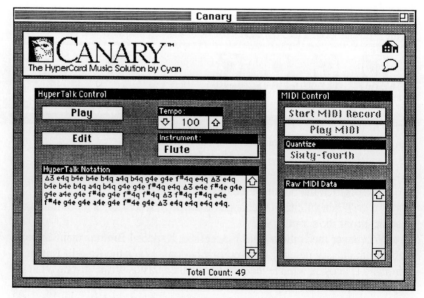

Figure 222. The Control card with the Bartók music example converted into HyperTalk.

3. The script was saved as a **Bartók** button (File menu) and, when the Button card appeared, the newly-designated *Canary* button icon was clicked to place it in the card.

Bartók

4. **HyperCard Menubar** was chosen in the Edit menu, to change the Canary menus to the standard *HyperCard 2* menus, and the Button tool was clicked in the Tools palette.

5. The Bartók button was clicked with the Browse tool to select it, then **Button Info...** was chosen in the Objects menu to display the dialog box.

6. When the **Scripts...** button was clicked, the Bartók HyperTalk script was displayed in *HyperCard 2* format, for evaluation or editing purposes (Figure 223).

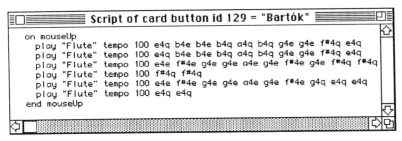

Figure 223. *HyperCard* script notation of the Bartók button (cf. Figure 217).

HYPERSCAN 2

HyperScan 2.0

This program works with the Apple *One-Scanner* and its bundled *Ofoto* software to produce and store black and white bit-mapped images at a resolution of 72 dots per inch, for pasting in *HyperCard 2* stacks or other applications. Since *HyperScan 2* is limited to low-resolution scanning, it is therefore economical for constructing an image-intensive stack, such as a large music database or an educational application. If high-resolution images are preferred, such as gray-scale Photographs or 300 dpi Line Art, the reader should refer to the *Ofoto* tutorial (pp. 146-55, above).

The following presentation briefly explores *HyperScan 2* and its use in developing a music stack as a project for classroom or individual purposes. The program can be opened in the *HyperCard 2* Home stack or by double-clicking the *HyperScan 2* icon. In either event the *HyperScan 2* menu is added to the *HyperCard 2* menu bar, with commands to open (or close) the Navigation Palette, Scan Control Palette, and HyperScan Help. When the choice is Hyper-Scan Help, the menu changes to List of Topics (including a "Walk through" tutorial) and List of Tips. Since a manual is not provided with the application, the user can work with the lists on screen or printouts of their cards.

Figure 224 shows the composite window display when the card size is set to normal and an image is to be scanned at life size (100%). The rectangle in the fixed scan window, which marks the scan area, flashes to indicate that the Scan Control Palette is active. The scan window and the Scan Control Palette are somewhat similar in appearance to those in the *Ofoto* program (cf. Figure 160, above), and the Navigation Palette resembles the pop-up *Ofoto* status-box icons. It should be noted that *HyperScan 2* sets the User level to 4 (Authoring).

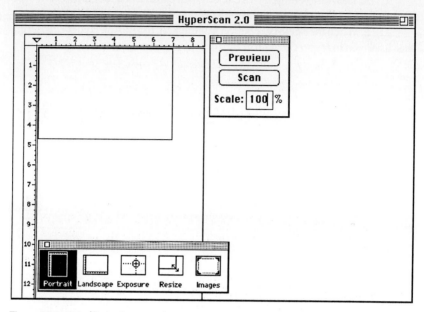

Figure 224. *HyperScan 2* composite window display.

     1. Click the Portrait or the Landscape icon in the Navigation Palette.
       •Choose a card-size image (preferably 4 by 6 inches or less).
     2. Align the image with the ruled margins of the scanner glass.
       •*HyperScan 2* does not have an automatic straightening procedure.
     3. In the Scan Control Palette type **100** as the Scale setting and click the Preview button.
     4. If the Browse tool is clicked inside the the flashing rectangle, the shape can be repositioned elsewhere on the image; if it is clicked at one of the four corners, the rectangle can be resized.
       •If the rectangle is reduced in size, the image will be proportionately enlarged (as indicated in the Scale box) after it is scanned.
       •Conversely, if the rectangle is enlarged, the image will be reduced proportionately.
     5. Click the Scan button in the Scan Control Palette.
       •After the image is scanned, the program transfers it to the Exposure card and displays the Exposure Palette for the individual or simultaneous adjustment of Brightness and Contrast (Figure 225).

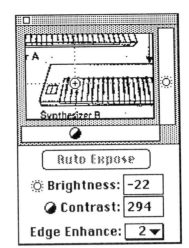

Figure 225. Exposure Palette, showing the scanned image ready for adjustment of settings.

Auto Expose

☼ **Brightness:** -22

◖ **Contrast:** 294

Edge Enhance: 2 ▼

6. It will generally be necessary to choose one or more tools in the Tool Palette, to clean up stray pixels or enhance the image.

7. Choose **Save Image** in the HyperScan menu.

• The program transfers the saved image to a card in the *HyperScan 2* stack (Figure 226), where it may be copied to another stack or application.

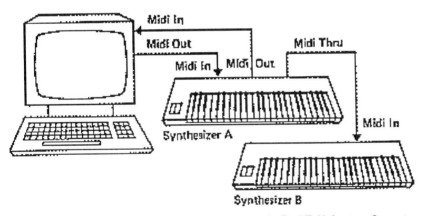

Figure 226. Illustration of "A typical MIDI configuration" in Fred T. Hofstetter, *Computer Literacy for Musicians.* Copyright © 1988 by Prentice Hall Inc., p. 79.

The quality of bitmapped images, such as photographs and musical scores, suffers in comparison with *Ofoto* high-resolution scanned output. On the positive side, however, is that *HyperScan 2* images are significantly smaller with regard to kilobyte size. When these images are converted to PICT format in *HyperCard 2* or a graphics program, they can be reduced or enlarged without distortion or loss in legibility. Thus, *HyperCard 2* databases of the multimedia kind—combined music, graphics, sound, and scanned images—become economically feasible with regard to file size.

Figure 227 illustrates a sample card for a "Keyboard Composers" stack, which can serve as a prototype for a similar individual or classroom project, thematic index, catalogue of musical works, and other multimedia music stacks. The modified background and its navigation buttons were copied from the Practice stack in the *HyperCard 2* folder; the text waa typed with the Text tool; composer, instrument, and music images were scanned with *HyperScan 2*; and the "Fugue Subject" Play script was typed in *HyperCard 2* and linked to a button.

Figure 227. First card in the "Keyboard Composers" stack. The scanned bitmapped images are reductions of illustrations and music in *Early Keyboard Music* (New York: G. Schirmer, 1904), vol. 2, p. 138. Card size: 36 kilobytes.

The Play buttons in Figure 228 were constructed in the *Canary* stack, using the MIDI-controlled procedures for creating scripts. These buttons and the scanned music provide an audiovisual approach to comparative analysis of an art-music theme and its folk music source.

Figure 228. Card 2 in the "Keyboard Composers" stack, based on Bartok's *For Children* for Piano (1908).

SUMMARY

In this chapter the *HyperCard 2* application is sampled with regard to the creation of Play buttons and their scripts, for use in multimedia stacks such as music indexes and catalogues. Tutorials are also given for using the *Maestro*, *Sound Scripter*, and *Canary* stacks, which respectively provide music notation, a graphic piano keyboard, and an optional MIDI keyboard as an alternative to typing Play scripts.

    Next follows the simple procedures involved in scanning images with the Apple *OneScanner* and its bundled, stack-oriented *HyperScan 2* software, for the production of bit-mapped graphics. The minimal kilobyte size of *HyperScan 2* output allows the development of large, graphics-intensive database stacks, particularly by music educators and students for classroom or individual projects, as represented by the "Keyboard Composers" stack which closes the chapter.

CHAPTER 7

CD-ROM: *The Orchestra*

THE_ORCHESTRA

Compact Disc-Read Only Memory (CD-ROM) is based on the same technology as CD audio discs, except that text, scores, graphics, images, animation, and sound resources can be included with music performance. In other words CD-ROM allows the construction of sophisticated multimedia databases. Macintosh owners are fortunate that *HyperCard* has been adopted as the interface for accessing CD-ROM data, and that certain CD-ROM discs, such as *The Orchestra* (Warner New Media *Audio Notes* CD-ROM series), also include an upgrade (version 2.1) of the program.

The Orchestra, based on Benjamin Britten's *The Young Person's Guide to the Orchestra* (1946), is a unique, interactive form of multimedia production, with additional features such as narration and challenging quizzes, that combines information and entertainment for music education or appreciation in classroom and home environments. The disc contains *HyperCard* (version 2.1) and Orchestra folders, and the Tour application. The *HyperCard* application is disabled (that is, locked) except for the Quit command, and the Orchestra folder has a Notebook stack and five program stacks. The folders and the Tour application must be copied to a hard disk in order to run the program (exception: if *HyperCard 2* and the Home stack are already installed).

The disc includes the complete digital recording of the work by the London Philharmonic Orchestra, conducted by Benjamin Britten (1913–1963). Britten was commissioned by the Ministry of Education in England to compose the music for an educational film about orchestral instruments. *The Young Person's Guide to the Orchestra,* an acknowledged masterpiece of variation form, is a standard work in the concert repertory and has been adapted for ballet accompaniment.

When the first stack is double-clicked, the complete performance can be heard without interruption, unless the user interrupts the music by clicking a button or dragging the Music Slider in the simultaneously-displayed Program Map (Figure 229). Thus, the music can be enjoyed solely as a listening experience, as if the disc had been intended for a CD player.

If, on the other hand, the user begins by opening the Tour application, the Program Map is displayed without musical accompaniment. Pop-up instructions concerning button function appear, followed by an animated cursor which activates the display of a related example. Since the program contains a

STACK1

TOUR

substantial amount of rapidly changing information and is not interactive, the Tour is automatically repeated until the Quit the Tour button is clicked. The following presentation, therefore, is intended to serve the music educator and student as a structured approach to the Program Map and its components, including areas not covered in the Tour.

Figure 229. *The Orchestra* Program Map, showing the position of the Music Slider during the performance of the Theme.

About the Help Buttons.—When the Help button at the bottom of the Program Map is clicked, a dialog box appears with instructions concerning the Music Slider, the four numbered channels, and the eight boxes which branch to related topics. A General Help button is provided to access the interactive General Help window (Figure 230). Whenever this window is opened, the music stops until such time as the user clicks the Return to Orchestra button. The third type of Help button is an inverted-style question mark: when the symbol is gray, help is unavailable for that specific screen or section.

Channel 1 • Exploring the Music.—The first channel is represented by an extraordinary window which displays related pop-up instrumental designations and boxed annotations during the performance (Figure 231). When specific instruments or instrumental choirs are featured, they appear on the screen with

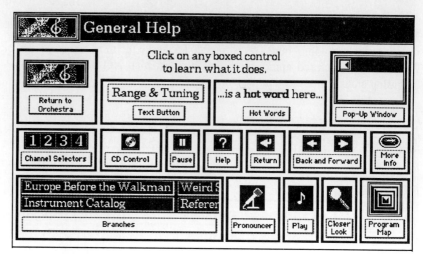

Figure 230. Interactive General Help window.

small, prefixal white circles; if the function changes from foreground to background, the circles are grayed in synchronization with the music.

At the bottom of the window are the temporary branch boxes linked to the current display, which change topic or disappear and return as the music progresses. If a box is selected for reference purposes, the music pauses until the Return to Orchestra button is clicked. The boxed annotations frequently include

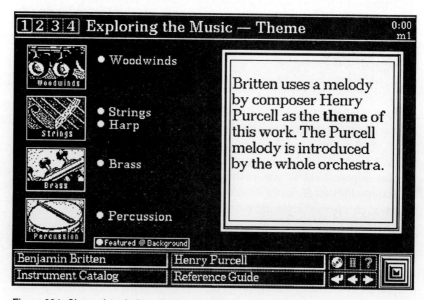

Figure 231. Channel 1 window display at the beginning of the performance.

CD-ROM: *The Orchestra*

boldface "hot words" (that is, hypertext) like **theme**, which may be clicked to immediately access information contained in the glossary and indices (Figure 232). Note, too, the several *HyperCard* navigation buttons for moving around the channel during the performance.

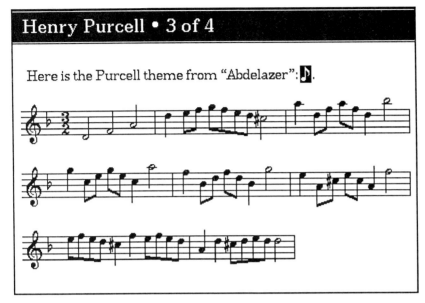

Here is the Purcell theme from "Abdelazer":

Figure 232. Notation display when **theme** is clicked in the annotation box shown in Figure 225 (the theme can also be retrieved by way of the Henry Purcell branch box). The Play button triggers a piano rendition of the notation.

Channel 2 • Theme and Variations.—The second channel emphasizes analysis of the theme, its variations, and the closing fugue. The window design maximizes the use of explanatory text, including hypertext words, and the button at the upper right-hand corner serves as an animated signpost for the synchronized display of instrumental designations during the performance (Figure 233). This in-depth examination of Britten's compositional technique is linked to a large number of excerpts from the published score. A case in point is Britten's adaptation of Henry Purcell's source melody (see Figure 232, above). When the two versions are compared, Britten's edition ostensibly differs only in the addition of expression marks (Figure 234).

Here is interesting grist for the musicologist's mill! Further research discloses that Christopher Harwood, the noted English conductor, published a scholarly performing edition of Purcell's incidental music for strings (Violins I and II, Viola, Bass) to the tragedy, *Abdelazer or the Moor's Revenge* (London: Faber Music, Ltd., 1985). The Purcell theme appears in the second piece, *Rondeau* (Vn. I, mm. 1–16), in Harwood's annotated score. The notation,

Figure 233. Channel 2 window display at the beginning of the performance.

limited to key, meter, and accidentals, and derived from comparative analysis of publications (ca. 1697–1705) and manuscripts in the London Royal College of Music, is concordant with the given Purcell and Britten music examples.

Figure 234. Britten's edited version of the Purcell theme (cf. Figure 232). Copyright © 1946 by Hawkes & Son, Ltd. (London). Copyright Renewed. Reprinted by permission of Boosey & Hawkes, Inc.

Variation
Flute

The flute excerpts are the first among many notations which demonstrate the composer's genius in creating interesting variations. Play buttons are also provided, to enhance the listening experience with a piano rendition of the theme and its variations, together with an unaccompanied flute performance of the variations from the recording. And the same audiovisual procedure is followed in the closing fugue section.

194

Channel 3 • Music Guide.—This channel is particularly appropriate while reading the published full score. The section boxes, arrow buttons, or branch boxes can be clicked for different navigating purposes (Figure 235).

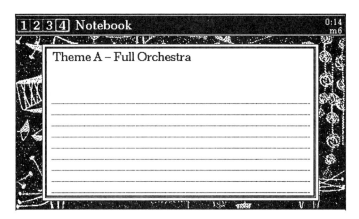

Figure 235. Channel 3 window display at the beginning of the performance.

Channel 4 • Notebook.—The fourth channel consists of cards, synchronized to the music, for typing comments in the ruled text field (Figure 236). The Pause button must be clicked to stop the music and emplace the insertion point, the right arrow may be used to display a continuation blank card, and the basic *HyperCard* text editing commands are available.

Figure 236. Channel 4 window display at the beginning of the performance.

Instrument Catalog and Related Branches—Figure 237 shows the five components of the Instrument Catalog. Each of the interactive units devoted to the Woodwinds, Brass, or Strings is further partitioned into family, individual instruments, and special effects cards; the Percussion unit consists of the family and its instruments of definite and indefinite pitch.

Figure 237. The components and branches of the Instrument Catalog window.

The Acoustics unit consists of five cards, some with Play buttons and graphics to illustrate the explanatory text, which discuss principles of vocal and instrumental sound production (Figure 238).

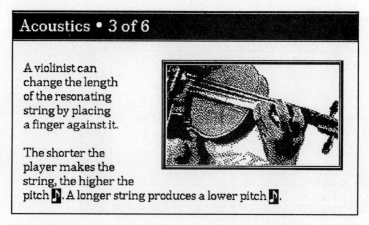

Figure 238. Acoustics unit card for tone production on the violin.

CD-ROM: *THE ORCHESTRA*

The Strings unit is characteristic of the scope and content of the orchestral families that constitute the Instrument Catalog. Figure 239 shows the concise text presentation, music notations, and related Play buttons in the third card of the String Family group.

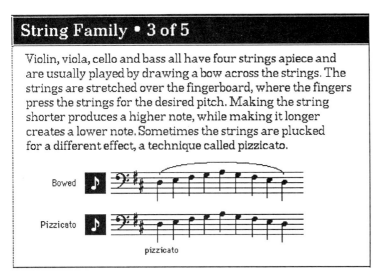

Figure 239. String Family card 3.

The Violin group includes a Play button to demonstrate a bowed tone; a sound clip of the Violin 1 performance of the opening bars from the Mozart Symphony No. 40; a graphics-oriented description of parts of the instrument; and a Range & Tuning button, that displays an unusual card with Play buttons for sampling the actual sounds (Figure 240).

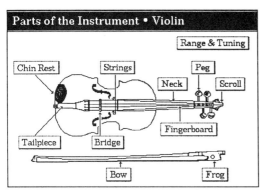

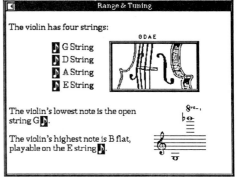

Figure 240. From the Violin group: Parts of the Instrument card and its related Range & Tuning display.

Special Effects is an important set of seven cards, which include Play and Pronunciation buttons. Among the topics are bowings (Figure 241), chord playing, and harmonics. The last card is devoted to the harp.

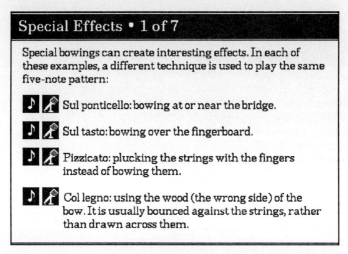

Figure 241. Special Effects card 1 with Play and Pronunciation buttons.

When the innovative Orchestration Lab box is clicked (see Figure 231, above), a card appears with a dozen check boxes and a Play button for selection and playback of instrumental combinations (Figure 242).

Orchestration Lab

Click on an instrument to play the melody and another to play the accompaniment.

Melody	Select	Accompaniment	Select
♪ Flute	☐	♪ Bassoon	☐
♪ Violin	☐	♪ Cello	☐
♪ Tuba	☐	♪ Oboe	☐
♪ Xylophone	☐	♪ Trombone	☐
♪ Harp	☐	♪ Horn	☐
♪ Cymbals	☐	♪ Bass Drum	☐

♪ Play Selected Melody & Accompaniment Together

Figure 236. Orchestration Lab card display.

CD-ROM: *The Orchestra*

Simultaneously, a box with Play and Show Notation buttons is displayed on the card, suggesting that the user listen to the piano version of *Greensleeves* (Figure 243) and choose different instrumental combinations for performance of the melody and its accompaniment. When the Play button is clicked, the combination is performed, and a box appears with an evaluation of the selection.

Figure 243. Two-part notation of the old English tune, *Greensleeves*.

The Orchestration Lab is also listed as the last subdivision of the five sets of cards in The Orchestra branch. The first listing, Evolution of the Orchestra, contains fourteen frames which begin with a discussion of fifteenth-century viols and gambas. Hypertext, graphics, and sound clips—from Bach to Bruckner—enhance the presentation. The next listing is Sounds of the Orchestra, an interesting collection of annotated sound clips, which includes masterpieces of the twentieth century by Bartók, Debussy, and Stravinsky (Figure 244).

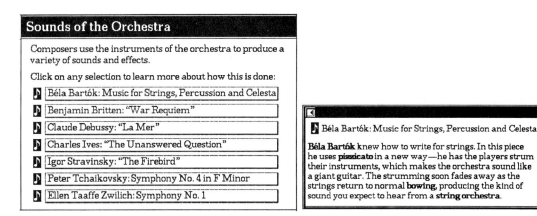

Figure 244. Sounds of the Orchestra display and its related annotation for the Bartók sound clip.

The third listing in The Orchestra branch traces the growing role of women as instrumentalists and conductors. And the fourth subdivision, "Weird Sounds from the Orchestra," offers a humorous contrast to the other topics (Figure 245).

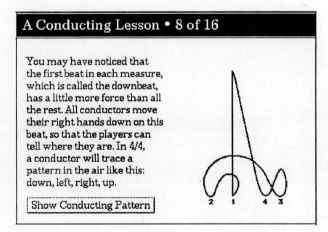

Figure 245. Interactive Weird Sounds from the Orchestra card.

The Conducting branch has three areas of exploration: The Conductor, A Brief History of the Baton, and A Conducting Lesson.A particularly instructive inclusion is the comparison of two performances of the Beethoven Symphony No. 7, with regard to the difference in tempo. Sixteen cards explore the conductor's role in establishing tempo and style, and graphically demonstrate conducting techniques. Figure 246 shows the conducting pattern which is traced by an animated drawing of a hand-held baton.

A Conducting Lesson • 8 of 16

You may have noticed that the first beat in each measure, which is called the downbeat, has a little more force than all the rest. All conductors move their right hands down on this beat, so that the players can tell where they are. In 4/4, a conductor will trace a pattern in the air like this: down, left, right, up.

Show Conducting Pattern

Figure 246. Conducting pattern for animated baton technique.

Europe Before the Walkman is a fascinating mini-tour of some noteworthy inventions and musical events, from "In the beginning…" to "The Age of Solitude." The path features pop-up captions and boxes, images and amusing line drawings, early music notation, hypertext, and sound clips from Chant to New Music (Figure 247).

Figure 247. Music Before the Walkman window, showing the New Music pop-up caption, and part of the related information box.

Britten & Company is perhaps an understated title for a branch consisting of heterogeneous subdivisions, such as Variation Technique, Fugal Process, Tempo Guide, and Dynamics, in addition to biographical information about Britten and Purcell. It is interesting that mention is made of Britten's early introduction to the music of Bartók and Schoenberg by Frank Bridge. his composition teacher, since the Variation Technique subdivision highlights several variations which are based on the arpeggiated chord of the major seventh. The first appearance of this configuration—D F-sharp A C-sharp— as a pervasive motive will be found in Bartók's piano music, beginning in 1908. Britten's adaptation—in the same key!— is played by the viola (Figure 248).

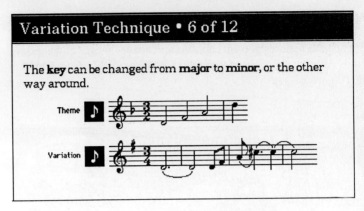

Figure 248. Viola transformation of the D-minor head motive.

The Fugal Process subdivision contains eight cards, which compares the construction of the more or less standard exposition–episode construction of the Baroque era (1600–1750) with Britten's unusual design: a large exposition, containing four smaller ones without episodic material, where additive texture serves as the partitioning means (Figure 249).

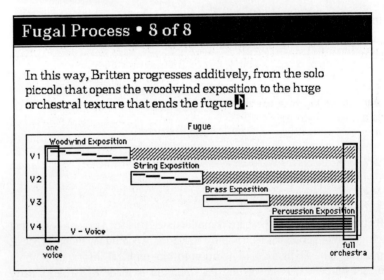

Figure 249. Additive-texture layout in Britten's fugal process.

Another noteworthy inclusion is the Tempo Guide, a pronouncing glossary of eleven terms, with Play buttons to access portions of the related music as conducted by the composer himself (Figure 250).

Figure 250. Tempo Guide with terms and related Pronunciation and Play buttons.

The second card of the two comprising the Dynamics subdivision is a glossary of symbols, ranging from *ppp* to *fff,* which also includes Play and Pronunciation buttons. When the Tempo Guide or Dynamics cards appear, a Rhythm branch is also displayed, with examples of different schemata, syncopation, and the contrast between strict and free rhythm.

The Reference Guide branch consist of four subdivisions: Glossary, Index, Pronouncer Index, and Sound Clip Index. The clickable Glossary entries display small boxes containing definitions or descriptions, frequently with Play and Pronunciation buttons.Certain boxes include More Information and Closer Look buttons, which display related cards (Figure 251). The Index entries, on the other hand, are only linked to cards. The Sound Clip Index consists of Play buttons and complete publication data about the recordings used in the disc, including the special clips created by Warner New Media.

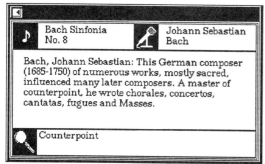

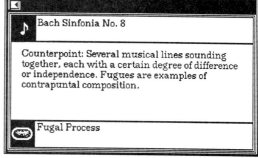

Figure 251. Hierarchical information boxes for the Glossary entry, Johann Sebastian Bach. Note the Closer Look button for "Counterpoint" and the More Infomation button for "Fugal Process."

When the Arcade window opens, three game-oriented, graphic subdivisions are displayed: Name that Instrument, Keep it in the Family, and Music Trivia. The first two games evaluate the ability of the user to identify individual and grouped instruments, respectively. The timed Music Trivia selections are followed by replacement of number boxes with icons and display of appropriate information boxes (Figure 252). At the conclusion of each game a How Did You Rate? window appears, with an animated display of the level of competency: Flunked Out, Summer School, Passing Grade, "B" Student, or Honor Roll!

Figure 252. Music trivia window with number and icon boxes.

SUMMARY

The Orchestra, a CD-ROM disc based on Benjamin Britten's *A Young Person's Guide to the Orchestra*, is the fourth production in the Warner New Media *Audio Notes* series. The discounted price is under $80, and the orchestral pocket score is available from the publisher, Boosey & Hawkes, Inc.

Perhaps the best description of the disc is that it represents a tour de force in the application of multimedia technology to music appreciation and education in the home or the classroom. The educational levels addressed range from upper elementary school grades to higher education courses in music analysis, composition, and orchestration.

The *HyperCard*-based technology features a variety of buttons for the retrieval of information, and striking examples of interactivity throughout the program. In the final analysis, *The Orchestra* CD-ROM disc is a remarkable fusion of technological ingenuity and great literature within a musicological environment, and a major contribution to computer-assisted instruction.

CHAPTER 8

MIDI-Keyboard Notation

Nowadays, MIDI (Musical Instrument Digital Interface) is a familiar acronym to most musicians, particularly composers and performers of electronic music. While the word may have become commonplace, the technological aspects of this new, internationally-widespread field is indeed complex. In fact, a substantial number of articles and books have been published about MIDI hardware and software, and information networks (CompuServe and GEnie, among others) and Macintosh users groups (Berkeley, Boston, etc.) provide MIDI shareware and freeware for their subscribers. More recently, the Association for Technology in Music Instruction (ATMI) was formed, to meet the needs of musicians interested in sharing information about the use of computers, MIDI keyboards, and music applications in the classroom.

Another recent event was the publication of *The Book of MIDI,* an interactive *HyperCard* stack developed by Opcode Systems, which addresses the concerns of beginners and advanced users. Since the stack also includes an illustrated discussion of MIDI keyboards in a computer environment, an annotated overview of the related cards follows below, as an introduction to this chapter.

THE BOOK OF MIDI

The program features an unusual, vertical-arrow navigation button, called the DEEPER icon, which enables the interested user to further investigate or return from a specific subject. In addition to the navigation buttons are branch icons which access Chapters (that is, the Table of Contents), Glossary, Index, Print (current card or entire book), Quit, and Help (Figure 253). Five chapters and three appendices are listed in The Table of Contents, each one preceded by a "Go" icon button:

The Book of MIDI

- •1. What is MIDI?
- •2. Setting Up Your MIDI Studio
- •3. MIDI Hardware
- •4. MIDI Software
- •5. MIDI Messages
- •The MIDI Game
- •MIDI Implementation Chart
- •Bibliography

Figure 253. *The Book of MIDI* title page.

Figure 254 is a display of the Glossary and its information box, when "Keyboard" is clicked. The definition is particularly appropriate, since it reflects the objective of Chapter 8.

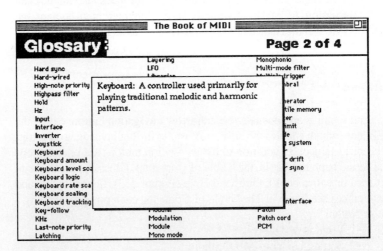

Figure 254. Second card of the Glossary with superimposed information box.

The Index entries may be clicked to access stack cards. If "Controllers, General" is selected, the related card has a Book icon to display an information box with published sources (Figure 255).

MIDI-KEYBOARD NOTATION

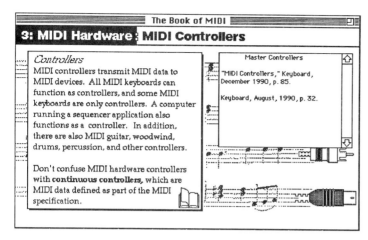

Figure 255. Stack card display, with a Book icon and its information box.

The second chapter, "Setting Up your MIDI Studio," begins with basic information, such as the difference between Audio and MIDI signals, and an illustrated description of their different paths in terms of amplifier and sound-module configurations. respectively. Next follows an animated display of the cable connections and the suggested hardware for a "Modest Studio." The chapter concludes with a similar approach to setting up a "Complex Studio," where a computer, patchbay, and drum machine are included in the configuration (Figure 256).

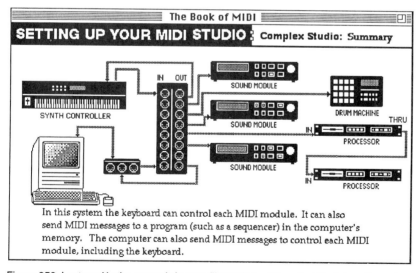

Figure 256. Last card in the second chapter, illustrating a "Complex Studio' configuration.

Although *The Book of MIDI* is almost biblical in extent, its studio approach to hardware configurations is beyond the needs and probably the means of most desktop musicians. The MIDI objectives of this *Guide* and chapter are basically defined by title: a desktop computing environment where a MIDI-keyboard controller serves as a tool for expediting data input in notation-oriented music programs (Figure 257. Cf. Figure 226).

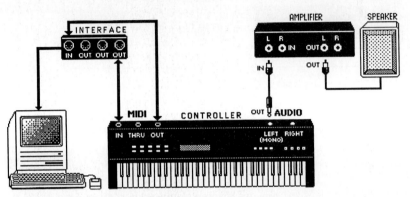

Figure 257. Suggested desktop configuration for MIDI-keyboard data input and playback. Headphones and MIDI keyboards with built-in speakers are practical options.

MIDI-keyboard input, furthermore, consists of two discrete methods, Step-time and Real-time. Step-time requires the user to select each note or rest value, with the mouse or computer keyboard, before a MIDI controller-key is played, and it is the method treated in this chapter. Real-time, where the controller is freely played, invariably requires user quantizing, that is, the preliminary selection of a quarter note, eighth note, or other value as the location where a beat or subdivision of a beat falls. Inaccuracies in rhythm during the performance are then corrected by the program, so that notes are moved forward or backward to the specified location. The variables—proper quantizing, keyboard proficiency, and above all, the degree of data complexity (see Figure 1, above!)—are such that most users will find Step-time entry to be the most efficient method of input for notating complicated scores.

Turning next to MIDI-keyboard selection, and in view of data input as the prime objective, any MIDI-capable instrument will be satisfactory. The preferred choice is an inexpensive ($100 and up), preprogrammed "Pop" keyboard, which is not only simple to operate but has many presets (that is, instrumental patches) that should be useful for audio-proofing instrumental compositions and orchestrations, or for other playback purposes. There usually is a secondary market in discontinued synthesizers, such as the mini-keyboard Casio *CZ-101* and Yamaha *X-100*, which are also equipped with a number of presets.

Mention should be made of the required MIDI interface, such as Opcode's MIDI *Translator* (1 IN, 3 OUT; a power supply is not required), and a minimum of two MIDI Input/Output cables to connect the interface with the keyboard. In addition the reader should note that MIDI keyboards have sixteen discrete channels, numbered from 1 to 16, for communicating with computers. The channels to be selected for sending or receiving information are generally described in the respective hardware and software user manuals. A good approach for the uncertain beginner is to use the manufacturer's default settings or other suggestions.

Finally, be sure all equipment is turned off, then connect the MIDI interface cable to the computer modem port (the jack with the telephone icon above it), and connect the interface to the keyboard with the MIDI Input/Output cables (see the diagram in Figure 257, above).

CONCERTWARE+MIDI

Open the *Music Writer* program, choose **New** in the File menu, and create the desired page layout, including staves, clefs, key and time signatures, and playback tempo—the default is ♩ = 100—for audio-proofing the score (if it is necessary, review the Tutorial in pp. 4–7, above).

Music Writer

1. Choose **MIDI** in the Sound menu, to enable data entry from the MIDI keyboard.

2. Choose **Step Time Entry** in the Sound menu.

•Step Time Entry enables input of single pitches or chords (if the **Chords** box has been checked in advance of entry), according to the preselected (that is, highlighted) value in the row of boxed notes at the top of the *Music Writer* window.

3. Click the desired Voice (the default is Voice 1) where the notation is to be inserted.

Figure 258 shows the Macintosh-keyboard input equivalents—durations, accidentals, rests, and triplet sign—which are available for use in tandem with MIDI keyboards. Although the mouse can be used as an alternative selection

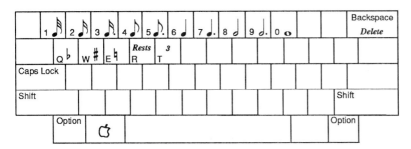

Figure 258. Macintosh-keyboard input equivalents, for use with MIDI keyboards.

device, the quickest and most reliable method of notation is the interaction of computer and MIDI keyboards.

It should be noted that when the score shows a signature with sharps, or is without a key signature, the program inserts a prefixal sharp sign to the respective note while each MIDI-keyboard black key is played. If a signature with flats has been selected, a prefixal flat sign will be inserted. Any default insertion can be replaced by selecting the desired accident al (Q, W, or E on the computer keyboard) prior to performance. T he triplet sign is also available (T), and when the Rest key (R) is selected, its value is the same as the previously-selected (highlighted) boxed note.

Figure 259 shows the *Music Writer* default window, with added key and time signatures, where the G scale was notated with a Casio *CZ-101* synthesizer and the sixteenth note and rest values were selected with the computer keyboard.

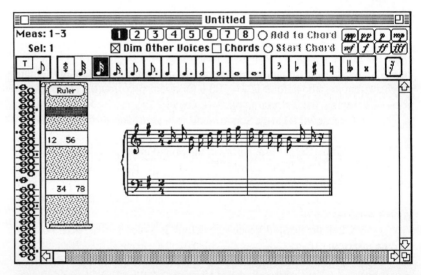

Figure 259. *Music Writer* scalar notation from interacting MIDI and computer keyboards.

Deluxe Music v.2.5

DELUXE MUSIC CONSTRUCTION SET

If the MIDI interface is not connected to the computer, turn off all equipment and then connect the MIDI interface cable to the computer modem port (the jack with the telephone icon above it), and connect the interface to the keyboard with the MIDI Input/Output cables (see the diagram in Figure 257, above).

Open the *Deluxe Music Construction Set* program, choose **New** in the File menu, and create the desired page layout: staves, clefs, key and time signatures, and playback tempo—the default is ♩=90—for audio-proofing the score (if it is necessary, review the tutorial in pp. 14–20, above).

MIDI-Keyboard Notation

1. Choose **Show MIDI Channel** in the Sound menu, to replace it with the MIDI menu.

2. Choose **MIDI Active** and **MIDI Input Enabled** in the MIDI menu.

•**MIDI Active** activates the Modem Port to which the Interface.

•**MIDI INPUT ENABLED** allows the MIDI keyboard to enter notes in the Score window (Figure 260).

Sounds			**MIDI**		
✓:Instruments:Keyboards:Pianic			Set Basic Channel... 1	⌘M	
			Set MIDI Instrument...	⌘N	
			MIDI Setup...		
Show MIDI Channel	⌘M		✓MIDI Active		
			✓MIDI Input Enabled		
Remove Instrument					
Load Instrument ...					
Keyboard Play Style			Show Mac Sounds	⌘A	

Figure 260. Sounds and MIDI menus (note the selected commands in the MIDI menu).

3. If the default piano score is used, the insertion point will flash in the first measure of Staff Number **1**.

Figure 261 shows the Macintosh-keyboard input equivalents—durations, accidentals, triplet signs, Clear Mods, and the Arrow pointer—which are available for use in tandem with MIDI keyboards.

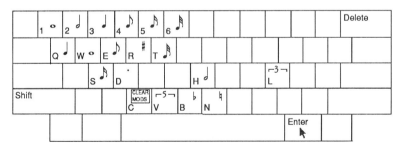

Figure 261. Macintosh-keyboard input equivalents, for use with MIDI keyboards.

Since the MIDI keyboard and the *DMCS* graphic piano keyboard are not programmed to input rests, the mouse or the computer keyboard must be used (see Figure 14, above). Note, too, that the Delete key only erases previously-selected (shown in outline shape) notation. While the Enter key may be used to display the Arrow pointer for selection purposes, the mouse is nevertheless required to position and click the notation to be deleted.

It should be noted that when the score shows a signature with sharps, or is without a key signature, the program inserts a prefixal sharp sign to the respective note while each MIDI-keyboard black key is played. If a signature with flats has been selected, a prefixal flat sign will be inserted. Any default insertion can be replaced by selecting the desired accidental (R, B, or N) on the computer keyboard—after the performance—and clicking the mouse on the note to be altered. The tuplet signs (L or V), however, can be applied during the performance.

Figure 262 shows the *DMCS* default screen, where the Score window has added key and time signatures, the F scale notated with a Casio *CZ-101* synthesizer, and the sixteenth note values selected with the computer keyboard. The sixteenth rest, however, had to be inserted with the MIDI-mouse.

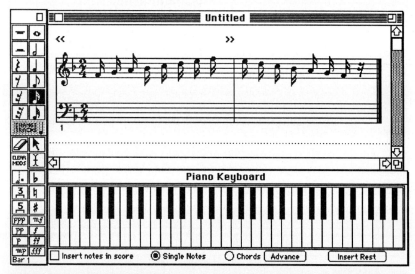

Figure 262. *DMCS* scalar notation from interacting MIDI and computer keyboards. The insertion of rests is not available from the MIDI keyboard or the Piano Keyboard.

MusicProse™2.1

MUSICPROSE

If the MIDI interface is not connected to the computer, turn off all equipment and then connect the MIDI interface cable to the computer modem port (the jack with the telephone icon above it), and connect the interface to the keyboard with the MIDI Input/Output cables (see the diagram in Figure 257, above).

Open the *MusicProse* program, choose **New** in the File menu, and create the desired page layout: staves, clefs, key and time signatures, and playback tempo—the default is ♩ = 120—for audio-proofing the score (if it is necessary, review the Tutorial in pp. 24–27, above).

1. Click the Entry icon in the Main Tool Palette, to replace the Staff menu with the Entry menu.

2. Choose **MIDI Playback** and **MIDI Configuration...** in the Play menu.

•In the default dialog box, if both **Modem Port** radio buttons (MIDI In, MIDI Out) are selected, click the **OK** button to exit (Figure 263).

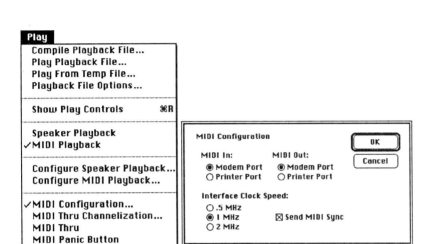

Figure 263. *MusicProse* Play menu and its related **MIDI Configuration** dialog box.

3. Choose **Speedy Entry** and **Speedy Entry Options...** in the Entry menu.

•Choose **Enable MIDI** in the default dialog box. (Figure 264).

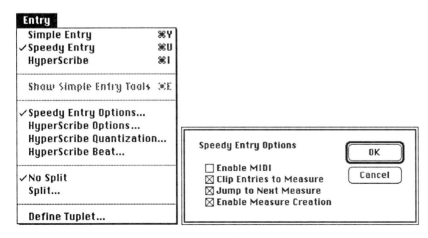

Figure 264. Entry menu and its related **Speedy Entry Options** dialog box.

4. Click the first measure in Staff **1**.

•The Speedy Entry window appears, with the Pitch Insertion Bar
ready for MIDI-keyboard input of Voice **1**.

The Speedy Entry input method is designed to work with an extended
Macintosh keyboard, particularly when a MIDI instrument is used for note entry.
Thus, a substantial number of music symbols and computer commands are for
the most part assigned to the Keypad and Arrow keys, and the *MusicProse* User
Manual and Quick Reference Guide provide helpful diagrams to assist the user.
The reader is advised, however, that to a certain extent the standard Macintosh
keyboard can also be used (Figure 265).

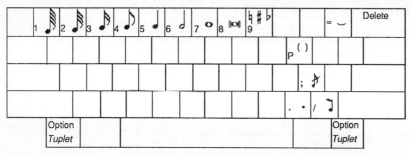

Figure 265. Standard Macintosh keyboard equivalents for MIDI-keyboard Speedy Entry.

Figure 266 shows the *MusicProse* default screen, with added key and time
signatures, the G scale notated with a Casio *CZ-101* synthesizer, and the
automatically beamed sixteenth-note values selected with the computer keyboard. The sixteenth rest, however, had to be inserted with the computer
keyboard. It should be noted that optional flagged notes, grace notes, ties, and
accidentals can be typed during the MIDI-keyboard performance

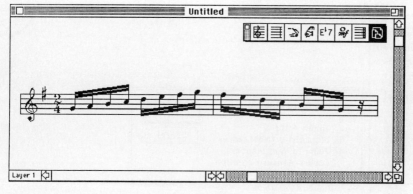

Figure 266. *MusicProse* scalar notation from interacting MIDI and Macintosh keyboards.

214

FINALE

If the MIDI interface is not connected to the computer, turn off all equipment and then connect the MIDI interface cable to the computer modem port (the jack with the telephone icon above it), and connect the interface to the keyboard with the MIDI Input/Output cables (see the diagram in Figure 257, above).

Open the *Finale* program and create the desired page layout: staves, clefs, key and time signatures, and playback tempo—the default is $\downarrow$ = 96—for audio-proofing the score (if it is necessary, review the Tutorial in pp. 38–46, above).

1. Click the **Speedy Note Entry** icon in the Tool Palette, to add the default Speedy menu to the menu bar.

　•Verify that the **Use MIDI Keyboard** command is checked.

2. Choose **MIDI Setup…** in the Special menu, to display the default dialog box..

　•If both **Modem Port** radio buttons (MIDI In, MIDI Out) are selected, click the **OK** button to exit (Figure 267).

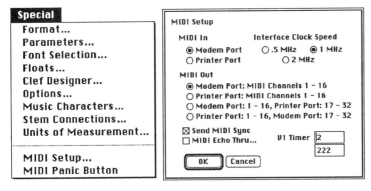

Figure 267. *Finale* Special menu and its related **MIDI Setup** dialog box.

3. Click the first measure in Staff **1**.

　•The Speedy Note Entry window appears, with the Pitch Insertion Bar ready for MIDI-keyboard input of Voice **1**.

The *Finale* Speedy Note Entry input method is virtually the same as the procedure used in the later *MusicProse* application: designed to work with an extended Macintosh keyboard, particularly when a MIDI instrument is used for note entry. Thus, a substantial number of music symbols and computer commands are for the most part assigned to the Keypad and Arrow keys. The reader is advised, however, that to a certain extent the standard Macintosh keyboard can also be used (See Figure 265, above).

Figure 268 shows the Finale default screen, with added key and time signatures, the F scale notated with a Casio *CZ-101* synthesizer, and the

automatically beamed sixteenth-note values selected with the computer keyboard. The sixteenth rest, however, had to be inserted with the computer keyboard. It should be noted that optional flagged notes, grace notes, ties, and accidentals can be typed during the MIDI-keyboard performance

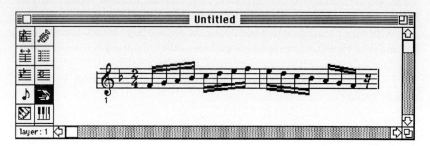

Figure 268. *Finale* scalar notation from interacting MIDI and Macintosh keyboards.

Encore™ v2.5.1

ENCORE

If the MIDI interface is not connected to the computer, turn off all equipment and then connect the MIDI interface cable to the computer modem port (the jack with the telephone icon above it), and connect the interface to the keyboard with the MIDI Input/Output cables (see the diagram in Figure 257, above).

Open the *Encore* program and create the desired page layout: staves, clefs, key and time signatures, and playback tempo—the default is ♩ = 100—for audio-proofing the score (if it is necessary, review the Tutorial in pp. 58–60, above).

    1. Choose **MIDI Setup...** in the Goodies menu, to display the default dialog box.

      •The display and its selected radio buttons should match those shown in Figure 262.

      •Click the **OK** button to exit the dialog box.

    2. If the default piano score is used, the insertion point will flash in the first measure of the topmost staff.

MIDI-keyboard note entry may begin whenever a note value is selected from among the Macintosh number keys (1–8). The Pencil icon is also highlighted, to indicate that input is enabled (including mouse selections). It should be noted, when the black keys are played, that the program intermixes sharps and flats in the following key signatures:

    C: C-sharp, E-flat, F-sharp, G-sharp, B-flat;

    F: C-sharp, E-flat, F-sharp, A-flat, B-flat;

    G: B-flat, the other black keys are sharps;

    B-flat: F-sharp, the other black keys are flats;

enharmonic changes, however, cannot be made with the MIDI keyboard, only by way of the mouse alone or with the computer keyboard (see Figure 77, above).

216   MIDI-KEYBOARD NOTATION

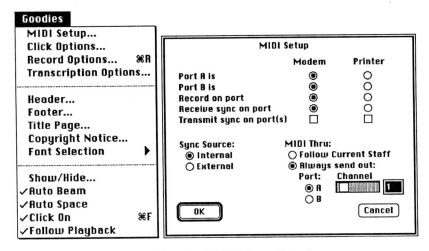

Figure 269. Goodies menu and its related **MIDI Setup...** dialog box.

Figure 270 shows Macintosh-keyboard input equivalents—durations, rests (R), triplet sign (T), and tie (Shift-T)—which can be entered with the standard keyboard during MIDI-keyboard performance. In the case of an extended Macintosh keyboard, the number keys (1–8) are also available for entering values, and the left and right arrow keys can be used, instead of the respective nudge keys, to move the insertion point for selecting the preceding and following notes or rests.

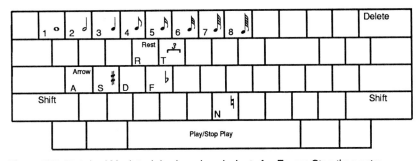

Figure 270. Standard Macintosh keyboard equivalents for *Encore* Step time entry.

Figure 271 shows the *Encore* default window, which includes the time signature, with the added key signature. The G scale was notated with a Casio *CZ-101* synthesizer, and the sixteenth-note values and the sixteenth rest were selected with the computer keyboard during the MIDI-keyboard performance. Mention should also be made of the additional Play/Stop Play commands, which are activated by pressing the Space bar.

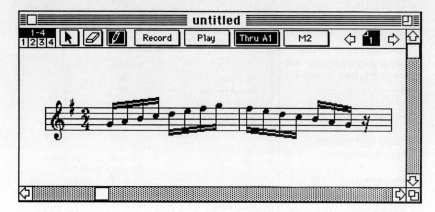

Figure 271. *Encore* scalar notation from interacting MIDI and Macintosh keyboards.

Summary

The Book of MIDI overview, which opens this chapter, is intended to provide the reader with a brief introduction to those aspects of MIDI technology that are related to the use of MIDI instruments with Macintosh computers. The complete *Hypercard* stack, created in 1990 by Opcode Systems, is an invaluable resource for teachers, students, and performers, and is available at the discounted price of $29.

So far as this book is concerned, the application of MIDI technology for musicians is defined by its titular "desktop" metaphor, that is, a workspace where hardware proximity allows the user to simultaneously type and play or rapidly alternate the two discrete activities. Such hardware interaction obviously calls for a MIDI keyboard as the performance tool for optimizing data entry.

The five music applications explored in Chapter 1—*ConcertWare+MIDI, Deluxe Music Construction Set, MusicProse, Finale*, and *Encore*—are then reexamined with regard to their MIDI capability, and each one is provided with a brief Tutorial for Step-time note entry as the preferred MIDI-keyboard method.

CHAPTER 9

A Toolbox for Musicians

The designation "Toolbox" as a caption made its first appearance in the *PageMaker* application, as a special window containing eight drawing tools. In this chapter Toolbox is used as a metaphor for a small collection of literally indispensable programs, commonly referred to as "utilities," which are recommended for musicians interested in expediting desktop computing.

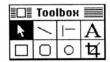

System Folder

These tools consist of CDEVs (Control Panel DEVices), DAs (Desk Accessories), INITs (Startup documents), and other small programs which are installed in the System Folder. The eight utilities presented below are listed in alphabetical order and, for the most part, given in tutorial format: *DiskDoubler, DiskTop, Norton Utilities (Disk Doctor), Now Utilities (WYSIWIG Menus), PopChar, QuicKeys 2, Retrospect,* and *Suitcase II.*

DISKDOUBLER

The utility is a package of three files which are automatically installed in the System Folder as an INIT, a Data document, and an application. The menu is listed as "DD" in the Finder menu bar, and its default **Settings...** dialog box should apply to most requirements for compressing files (Figure 272).

DiskDoubler™ INIT

DiskDoublerData(3.7)

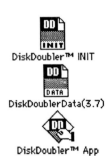

DiskDoubler™ App

DD	
Compress	
Expand	
Combine	
Split	
File Info	
Help...	
Settings...	
About DD™...	

How To Compress: [Method A ▼]
Recompress Files: [Automatically ▼]
Show Progress: [Immediately ▼]
Update Disk Info: [After Every File (slower) ▼]
Size (in K) For Split Files: [760]
☒ Delete Combined Files After Expanding
☒ Quit Immediately When Done
☒ Verify Files After Writing (slower)
☐ Expand Related Application Files
☐ Can Switch To Background
(Find Applications)   (Cancel)   (OK)

Figure 272. *DiskDoubler* menu and its related **Settings...** dial box.

In addition to individual files *DiskDoubler* compresses folders and disks.

1. Select the file, folder, or disk to be compressed
2. Choose **Compress** in the DD menu.

•A temporary box appears with an animated document icon and changing kilobyte numbers, to indicate the processing status (Figure 266).

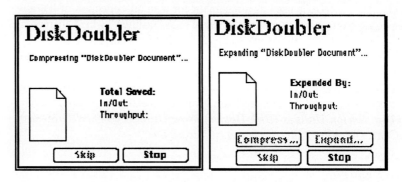

•Individual files and those in folders or disks are converted into *DiskDoubler* documents. Folders and disks, on the other hand, retain their original icon form.

3. Files are expanded by double-clicking or choosing **Expand** in the DD menu.

•Another temporary status box appears (Figure 273).

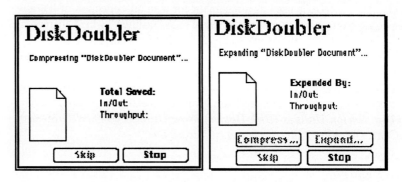

Figure 273. Animated status-box displays during Compressing and Expanding.

Groupings of files and folders can be compressed into a Combined File.

1. Select the items to be compressed and choose **Combine** in the menu.

•The program creates a duplicate, compressed set of the selected items. The orginal files and folders are not processed.

2. The combined file is expanded by double-clicking or choosing **Expand** in the DD menu.

•The program separates and expands the combined file, and places them in an Expand folder

Although an individual item or group of items can be duplicated in the Finder and then compressed, an alternative method is to create a Self-Expanding Archive (SEA).

1. Select an item or group of items.
2. Hold down the Shift key to substitute the alternate DD menu, and choose **Create SEA....**
3. When the standard Save dialog box appears, accept the displayed name or type a new one (keep the suffixal identifier **.sea**).

A *TeachText*-styled icon appears, to mark the compressed item as an application type. When the icon is double-clicked, the program creates an expanded duplicate of the "application."

Document

Combined.dd

Combined

DISKTOP

A multipurpose, Finder-oriented desk accessory, *DiskTop* accesses files, folders, and disks, while in an application and without requiring a return to the Finder, for such useful functions as Copy, Delete, Eject, Find, New Folder, and Rename. Equally important are *DiskTop.Extras,* for the Launch function, and *CE Toolbox* for installation in the Apple menu. The following brief tutorials should underscore the importance of this remarkable software.

    1. Choose **DiskTop** in the Apple menu, to open the main window.

      •The icons of all mounted disks are displayed, together with the number of bytes used and those remaining on each disk (Figure 274).

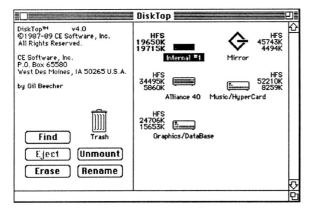

Figure 274. *DiskTop* Main Window.

    2. Click the **Find** button to display the Find Criteria dialog box.

      •The insertion point flashes in the blank Name box.

    3. Type **Disktop** (Figure 275).

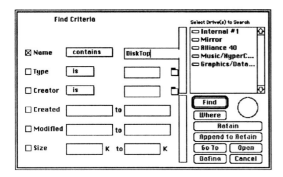

Figure 275. Find Criteria dialog box

4. Select the disk or disks to be searched.

5. Click the **Find** button.

•If the search is successful, a Files Window appears with a display of the found files and the message "Find completed" (Figure 276). If unsuccessful, the "No files found" message is displayed.

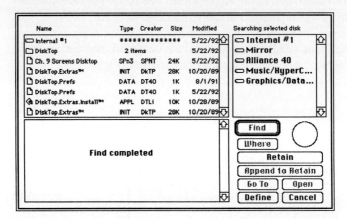

Figure 276 . The Files Window after completion of a successful search.

To bypass the main window and directly access the File Window, choose **DiskTop Find** in the Apple menu instead of **DiskTop**. When a wanted file contains commonplace words in its name that might bring up unrelated files, the search criteria can be further defined by adding the Type or Creator four-letter code. The File Window has pop-up menus for the display of default lists, and the user can freely add other codes or remove unwanted items from the menus (Figure 277).

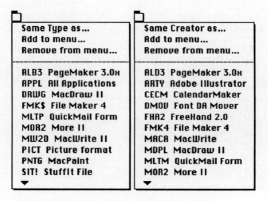

Figure 277. Type and Creator pop-up menus.

The final procedure is finding the exact location of displayed files.

1. Choose **Disktop Extras**™ in the File Window.
   - •The lower half of the screen displays the hierarchical icons.
2. Click the **Go To** button to display an alternate version of the main window (Figure 278).
   - •The located file, automatically highlighted, can now be copied, moved, deleted, etc.

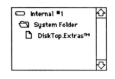

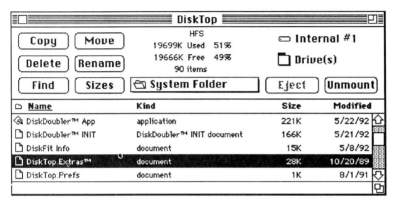

Figure 278. Alternate version of the main window, with the located file highlighted.

When **DT Launch...** is chosen in the Apple menus, the self-explanatory Launch window is displayed with its list of applications. When a program is selected and the **Docs...** button is clicked, the related documents appear (Figure 279).

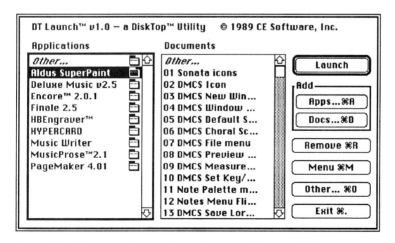

Figure 279. *DT Launch* window with application and document listings.

Norton Utilities

This outstanding set of utilities includes the indispensable *Disk Doctor* application (annotated below). When the *Norton Utilities* icon is double-clicked, a screen appears with button icons for accessing six tools (Figure 280). Among the other utilities are:

    •*Directory Assistance II.*—A Startup Document (INIT) that provides pop-up menus in dialog boxes. The menus contain file- and folder-related commands.

    •*DiskLight.*—A Control Panel Device (CDEV) which flashes an indicator icon in the menu bar during read/write activities.

    •*FastFind.*—A Desk Accessory (DA) to locate and launch files.

    •*FileSaver.*—Another, important CDEV that creates and automatically updates special files with information about all documents, applications, and folders on disks. This information optimizes the procedures for the recovery of damaged disks or accidentally-erased files.

    •*Floppier.*—A program to copy and format floppy disks, including bypass of bad sectors, and create and store Disk Image Files on hard disks, for unlimited copying purposes.

    •*KeyFinder.*—A DA which displays a screen containing all Keycap alternatives for a font.

    •*Layout Plus.*—A utility for customizing the Finder with regard to font, font size, icon spacing, and other enhancements.

Utilities
✓Main Menu

Norton Disk Doctor
UnErase
Volume Recover

Speed Disk
Norton Backup

Floppier
Norton Encrypt
Wipe Info
Norton Disk Editor
Layout Plus

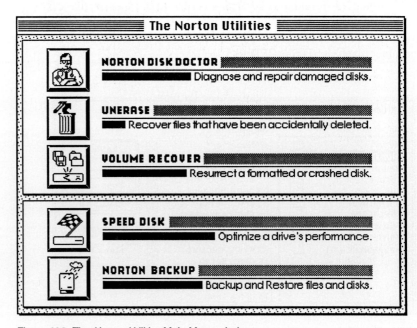

Figure 280. The *Norton Utilities* Main Menu window.

The importance of *Disk Doctor* cannot be overstressed, particularly in the event of a hard disk crash. Figure 281 shows the *Disk Doctor* status window before the automated disgnostic procedures are initiated.

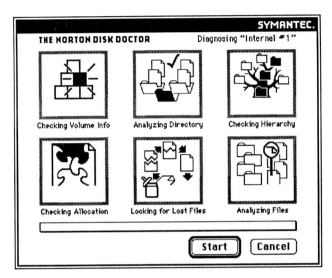

Figure 281. The *Norton Utilities Disk Doctor* diagnostic window.

When a problem is encountered, a dialog box is displayed with a diagnosis and a recommendation whether the problem can be fixed by clicking the **YES** button (Figure 282). If the problem cannot be repaired by the program, suggestions are offered for other corrective action.

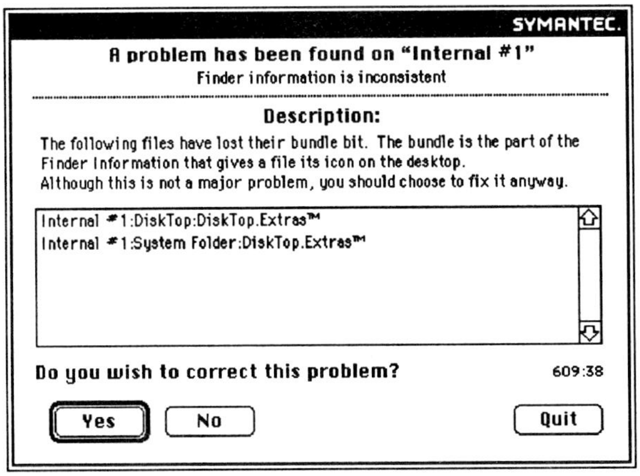

Figure 282. Dialog box with diagnosis and recommended repair.

Now 3.0.1

Some of the ten applications that make up this excellent collection are similar in function to those in *DiskTop* and the *Norton Utilities*. Three outstanding Control Panel Devices (CDEVs) are:

•*NowMenus.*—The dialog box provides check boxes which enable the automatic display of a specific menu and its submenu, without requiring a mouse click, as the Arrow pointer passes over the Menu Bar. After the selection is made, a click elsewhere on the desktop closes the menu.

•*NowSave.*—The dialog box has a scrolling window for listing the applications to be automatically saved. When the **Configure...** button is clicked, a dialog box opens with optional check boxes to save files by the number of minutes, keystrokes, and/or mouse clicks,

•*WYSIWYG Menus.*—The well-worn acronym "WYSIWYG" (What You See Is What You Get) is nevertheless a logical choice as a prefixal designation, since this clever tool provides the means to display the actual typeface of each name in the Font menu, including its size and style. Figure 283 shows the Control Panel with default selections, except that the default **Disable** is replaced with **Enable** and the Extended Keyboard **Control** key is the choice for toggling between normal (Chicago font) and WYSIWYG menus.

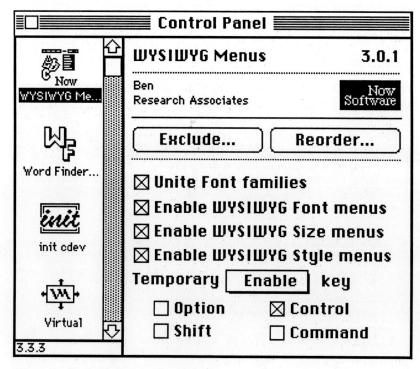

Figure 283. *WYSIWYG Menus* Control Panel.

The **Exclude...** button displays a dialog box for listing those applications in which *WYSIWYG Menus* will not be installed. The ingenious **Reorder...** button displays a scrolling window with the installed System fonts and united font families, in alphabetical order. Any font can be reordered by click-dragging its name to a new position in the window. (Figure 284).

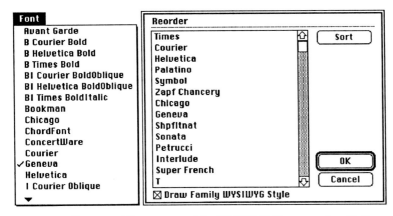

Figure 284. The normal Font menu and the *WYSIWYG Menus* reordered listing.

When the Control key is held down while the Arrow pointer is clicked in the normal Font menus, the enabled WYSIWIG menus and submenus appear as replacements (Figure 285).

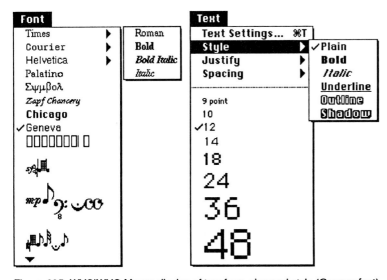

Figure 285. WYSIWYG Menus display of typeface, size and style (Geneva font).

PopChar

PopChar

This extraordinary Control Panel Device (CDEV) generates all the characters that are available in the current font and displays them in a pop-up menu at the top of the screen (Figure 286).

| Geneva 12 | PopChar 2.3 by Günther Blaschek |

```
  !  "  #  $  %  &  '  (  )  *  +  ,  -  .  /  0  1  2  3  4  5  6  7  8  9  :  ;  <  =  >  ?  @  A  B  C  D
E  F  G  H  I  J  K  L  M  N  O  P  Q  R  S  T  U  V  W  X  Y  Z  [  \  ]  ^  _  `  a  b  c  d  e  f  g  h  i
j  k  l  m  n  o  p  q  r  s  t  u  v  w  x  y  z  {  |  }  ~  Ä  Å  Ç  É  Ñ  Ö  Ü  á  à  â  ä  ã  å  ç  é  è
ê  ë  í  ì  î  ï  ñ  ó  ò  ô  ö  õ  ú  ù  û  ü  †  °  ¢  £  §  •  ¶  ß  ®  ©  ™  ´  ¨  ≠  Æ  Ø  ∞  ±  ≤  ≥  ¥
μ  ∂  Σ  Π  π  ∫  ª  º  Ω  æ  ø  ¿  ¡  ¬  √  ƒ  ≈  Δ  «  »  …     À  Ã  Õ  Œ  œ  -  —  "  "  '  '  ÷  ◊  ÿ
```

Figure 286. *PopChar* display window for the Geneva 12-point font.

Figure 287 shows the configured Control Panel for maximizing legibility, particularly when music or graphics fonts are to be displayed.

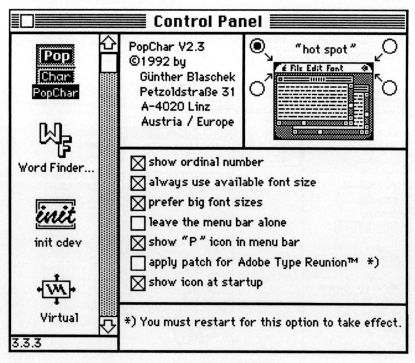

Figure 287. *PopChar* Control Panel with optional selections.

A TOOLBOX FOR MUSICIANS

QuicKeys 2™

QuicKeys 2 is another Control Panel Device (CDEV) that should be considered as one of the few quintessential utilities for Macintosh users, since it enables the assignment of diverse activities—file selections, menu choices, button clicks, etc—to single keystrokes The single-key assignments shown in Figure 288 indicate the use of Control key on the extended Macintosh keyboard. The Escape key is also available, but only for one assignment, perhaps stamping a current date or time in a document.

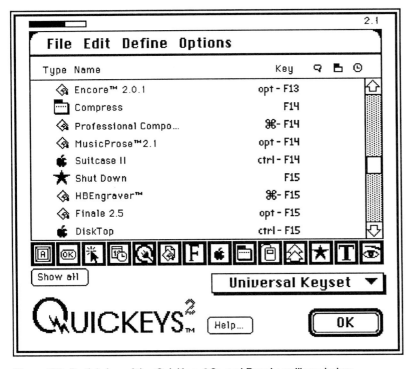

Figure 288. Partial view of the *QuicKeys 2* Control Panel scrolling window.

The horizontal Icon Bar in the Control Panel displays its category icons in the same order as their counterparts in the Define menu. When a Control Panel icon is clicked, the scrolling display changes to reflect only those key assignments which have been made for that category.

It should be noted that *QuickKeys 2* key assignments take priority over application-defined keystrokes, and that key assignments defined for the Universal Keyset apply to all currently running applications. When the same keystroke is assigned different definitions in other keysets, a cautionary dialog box is displayed for corrective action.

Figure 289 shows three of the submenus that are individually displayed when the related designation is selected in the Define menu. The choice of any listed item automatically inserts its name in a special definition window for assignment of a keystroke.

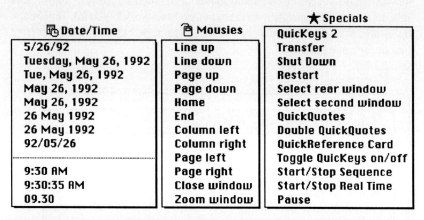

🖫 Date/Time	🖥 Mousies	★ Specials
5/26/92	Line up	QuicKeys 2
Tuesday, May 26, 1992	Line down	Transfer
Tue, May 26, 1992	Page up	Shut Down
May 26, 1992	Page down	Restart
May 26, 1992	Home	Select rear window
26 May 1992	End	Select second window
26 May 1992	Column left	QuickQuotes
92/05/26	Column right	Double QuickQuotes
	Page left	QuickReference Card
9:30 AM	Page right	Toggle QuicKeys on/off
9:30:35 AM	Close window	Start/Stop Sequence
09.30	Zoom window	Start/Stop Real Time
		Pause

Figure 289. Define menu Time/Date, Mousies, and Specials submenu items.

The Menu definition window is displayed when **Menu/DA...** is chosen in the Define menu and followed by selection of an item in a Finder or application menu, including Apple menu listings (Figure 290). The keystroke is then defined, the **OK** button is clicked to exit the window, and *QuicKeys 2* automatically saves the defined keystroke and activates it for immediate use.

Keystroke: ⌷ ctrl - F7

> **Menu**
>
> Select from menu   Keystroke: ▮ Unassigned ▮
>
> ● by Text: GOfer™ 2.0
>
> ○ by Position: 13
>
> ○ Look for menu by title: 🍎
> ○ Search all menus
> ● Only 🍎 menu
>
> While selecting from menu, hold down:
>   ☐ ⌘ ☐ Shift ☐ Option ☐ Control
> ☐ Don't complain if the menu choice can't be found
>
> (Timer Options) ☐ Include in QuicKeys menu   (OK) (Cancel)

Figure 290. Menu definition window with a DA ready for keystroke assignment.

Retrospect

The versatile *Retrospect* data-management utility is unique in its approach to backup and restore procedures. In the case of backing up the complete contents of a hard disk to other storage devices—floppy disks, removable disk cartridges, tape cartridges, and other hard disks—the user need only follow the sequence of instructive windows which, for the most part, only require the click of a button to carry each procedure to a successful conclusion. Thereafter, as needed or regularly scheduled, the same process is followed for the automated, incremental backup of those folders and files which have been modified since the last backup. Restoring this type of backup is equally simple: *Retrospect* recreates the folders and files on the source disk exactly as they were at the last backup.

Where individual folders and files are to be backed up or restored, the procedures require extra steps on the part of the user. And it should be noted that folders and files can be compressed to about half their kilobyte size during the backup, and that the restore process expands them to their original state. The following Tutorial illustrates the procedure for backup and compressing the folders and files on a hard disk to a set of floppy disks.

1. Double-click the *Retrospect* application icon to open the main window (Figure 291).

2. Click the **Backup** button to display the Source window (Figure 292).

Figure 291. The *Retrospect* main window.

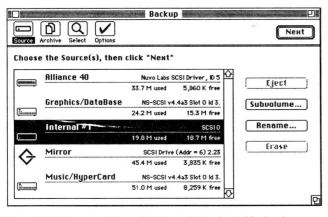

Figure 292. Source window with Internal #1 selected for backup.

Source

Archive

3. If the default (highlighted) Source disk is not wanted, select another one and click the **Next** button to display the Archive window (Figure 293).

•"Archive" is a generic designation for the intended storage media (floppy disks).

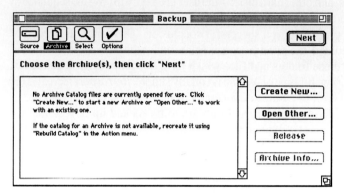

Figure 293. Dialog box for choosing the destination Archive.

4. Click the **Create New...** button to open the Archive type... dialog box (Figure 294).

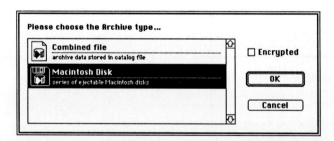

Figure 294. Archive type... dialog box with selected storage media.

5. Choose Macintosh Disk as the Archive type, then click the **OK** button to exit.

•The standard Save dialog box opens, where the *Retrospect* folder on the Source disk is highlighted as the default destination for the newly-created Archive catalog file.

6. Type the name of the Archive catalog file and click the **Save** button to exit.

•The file name should be the same as the Source disk or otherwise designated to mark the location of the present folders and files.

7. The Archive window reappears with a *Retrospect* floppy disk icon preceding the the newly-designated Archive file name (Figure 295).

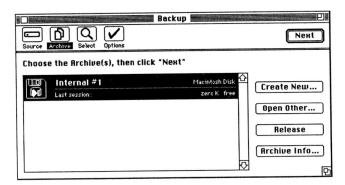

Figure 295. Archive window with the newly-designated file name.

8. Click the **Next** button..

• A status box appears, which counts the folders and files as they are scanned by the program.

• When the scanning is completed, the Browser window replaces the status box Figure 296).

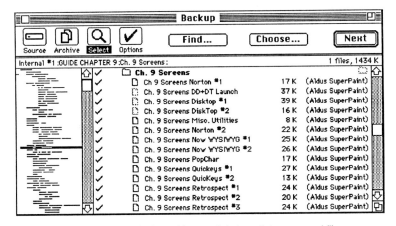

Select

Figure 296. The Browser window with a partial view of the scanned files.

9. The check marks indicate that the listed entries have been selected (by the program) for backup.

• Click the **Next** button to display the Options window (Figure 297).

Options

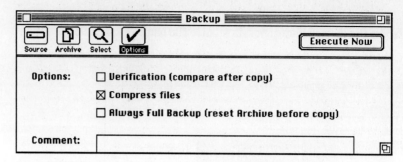

Figure 297. Standard Options window with **Compress files** selected

10. Click the **Compress files** box.
   •This option will compress file size approximately 50 percent.
11. Click the **Execute Now** button to begin the backup procedure.
   •The program calculates the size of the Source disk and displays a media request window.
12. Insert a floppy disk and click the **Proceed** button (Figure 298).

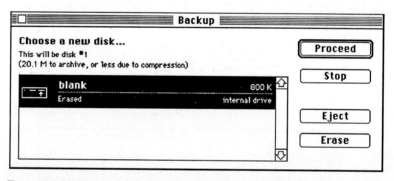

Figure 298. Media request window after insertion of the first floppy disk.

Retrospect displays a status box, while the files are compressed and written to each floppy disk, which indicates the number of kilobytes involved. Each processed disk is automatically numbered, designated with the the Archive file name, and locked. Whenever a disk is ejected, a prompt message requests the insertion of another one.

It is of course the responsibility of the user to have at hand an adequate supply of floppy disks, which should be numbered consecutively prior to insertion. The program will estimate the remaining number of disks needed to complete the job, but only in terms of file size prior to compression. In the case of backing up a sample of the author's Internal #1 Archive, during the preparation of this Tutorial, the first floppy disk contains 1418 kilobytes.

Suitcase II

Suitcase™ II

This well-known Startup document (INIT) conveniently accesses and manages resources—fonts, DAs, FKEYs, and Sounds. Two useful applications are bundled with the program: *Font and Sound Valet,* which compresses and automatically unpacks suitcase fonts or alert sounds; and *Font Harmony,* a program which renumbers fonts to resolve conflicts and, as an option, merges the style variations of a font into one family.

Font & Sound
Valet™

Six of the suitcases shown in Figure 299 were constructed with the Font/DA Mover, as the recommended procedure preceding the installation of resources by *Suitcase II.* These suitcases, designated according to category, contain many resources; the font suitcases, moreover, include all available typefaces and sizes.

Font Harmony™

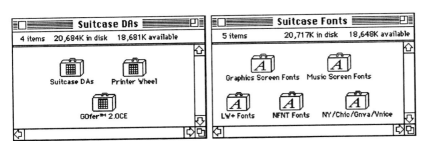

Figure 299. Desk accessory and font files constructed for *Suitcase II* processing.

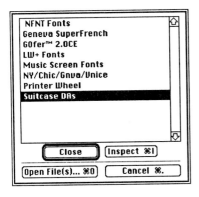

Font/DA Mover

1. Double-Click **Suitcase II** in the Apple menu to open the main panel.
   •The scrolling window lists the currently accessed files.
2. Click the **Suitcases...** button to display the Suitcases panel for closing, opening, or inspecting resources (Figure 300).

Figure 300. Suitcases panel.

3. Click the **Open File(s)...** button to display the dialog box.

4. Scroll to the "Suitcase DAs" folder and open it, select a desk accessory, and click the **Open** button.

•The newly-accessed desk accessory is listed in the mmain panel.

5. Repeat Steps 2–4 until the desired DAs and fonts have been accessed (Figure 301).

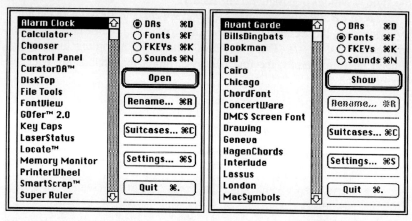

Figure 301. Some of the accessed resources in the *Suitcase II* DAs and Fonts main panels.

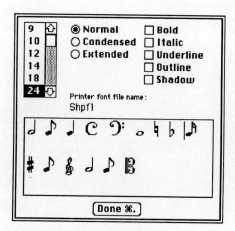

If a typeface is chosen in the Fonts main panel and the **Show** button is clicked, a dialog box appears with a sample of the characters. The list of selectable sizes, spacing-control radio buttons and boxes to change style are provided to view various configurations (Figure 302).

Figure 302. Font sample dialog box.

This concluding chapter provides tutorials for a necessarily limited number of indispensable tools which expedite desktop computing for users in general and musicians in particular. These tools, otherwise known as utilities, consist of small applications that are for the most part installed in the System Folder. The following overview is intended to provide related data as well as briefly summarize chapter content.

DiskDoubler.—An easy-to-use program which rapidly compresses files to a significant degree, thereby expanding the storage capacity of hard disks, floppy disks, and tape or removable cartridges. Manufactured by Salient Software, the current street price of version 3.7 is about $48.

DiskTop.—An excellent disk, folder, and file management utility while an application is open, with regard to such frequently necessary operations as Copy, Find, Launch, and Move. Manufactured by CE Software, the current street price of version 4.01 is about $63.

Norton Utilities.—A package of exceptional tools, particularly the *Disk Doctor* application which repairs crashed disks and problematic files. Manufactured by Symantec Corporation, the current street price of version 1.1 is about $98.

Now Utilities—Another outstanding collection of programs, especially *NowMenus, NowSave,* and *WYSIWYG Menus* which, respectively, automatically pulls down and temporarily freezes menu bar menus and submenus, saves during work sessions, and displays each font in its own typeface, size, and style. Manufactured by Now Software, the current street price of version 3.01 is about $83.

PopChar.—A unique program which can display all the available characters of the current font, while the user is typing text, for quick selection and easy click-insertion. Developed by Günther Blaschek (see Figure 280, above), who uploaded the program as Freeware (public domain), version 2.3 can be downloaded from CompuServe Information Service or purchased from various Macintosh user groups for a nominal fee.

QuicKeys II.—This rightly-celebrated program enables the assignment of simple, single-key macros for launching applications, choosing menu items, clicking buttons, and so on and so forth. Manufactured by CE Software, the current street price of version 2.1 is about $93.

Retrospect.—A superb backup and restore application, for use with different kinds of storage media, that for the most part only requires a button click in a progressive series of simple dialog boxes, to carry out the processing to a successful conclusion. Manufactured by Dantz Development, the current street price of version 1.3 about $146.

Suitcase II.—Another popular utility, that simplifies the management of desk accessories, fonts, and other resources. Manufactured by Fifth Generation Systems, the latest upgrade is version 2.1.1, which was released in 1992 as *Suitcase* (without the roman number) after completion of this chapter. The current street price is about $53.

Glossary

application. Any Macintosh software for manipulating information. Also referred to as a program or an application program.

archive. To store inactive files on floppy disks or other media.

arrow pointer. The basic Macintosh pointer shape.

authoring. The *HyperCard* user environment for creating graphics, fields, and buttons.

background. The basic template—picture, fields, and buttons— which is shared by a number of cards in a *HyperCard* stack.

backup. To make a copy of a document or program.

bitmap. Any graphic or font made up of dots.

brightness. The balance of light and dark shades in a scanned image.

browsing. The *HyperCard* user environment for non-editorial examination of stacks.

button. A clickable shape for choosing, confirming, or cancelling an action.

byte. Eight bits, which can represent alphanumeric characters, punctuations marks, and other symbols.

card. The basic *HyperCard* window for data entry.

cdev. The acronym for <u>C</u>ontrol <u>P</u>anel <u>Dev</u>ice. A program that is placed in the System folder.

CD-ROM. The acronym for Compact Disk-Read Only Memory. An optical disk for mass storage of information.

character. Any letter, number, punctuation mark, or other symbol available from the Macintosh keyboard.

choose. To select a menu command, usually by dragging.

click-drag. The sequential action when the mouse button is held down, the mouse is dragged elsewhere, and the button is then released.

clipboard. The Macintosh memory buffer which holds whatever has been last copied or cut.

command. An instruction to initiate a computer program action.

contrast. The tonal range of an image, between lightest and darkest.

compress. To reduce file size.

crop. To trim an image by repositioning one or more of its boundaries.

database. A file of information, created in a special application for sorting, permutation, or other processing of the data.

default. The preset option, preference, or value in an application.

DA. The acronym for Desk Accessory. A program which is available from the Apple menu in the Finder and/or applications.

desktop. The Macintosh working environment, consisting of the Finder menu bar and the gray area on the screen. In this book the term also designates the musician's working environment, where a Macintosh computer and its peripheral hardware, together with an optional MIDI keyboard and its accessories, are close at hand.

dialog box. The special box displayed on the screen, which requires a user response. Dialog boxes range from simple message or alert boxes, usually with OK and Cancel buttons, to bounded areas which contain various button shapes, scrolling lists, and so forth.

dither. The simulation of gray tones by grouping dots into large clusters of varying size.

document. The data file produced or used by an application.

dot. A unit corresponding to a single pixel or to a variable-size group of pixels.

dpi. The abbreviation for dots per inch. The number of pixels or printer dots in an inch, representing a measure of screen or printer resolution.

draw layer. The layer in a graphics program where discrete objects rather than a series of dots are generated.

EPS. The acronym for Encapsulated PostScript. A PostScript-encoded graphics and text format for printing an image, together with a PICT image for screen display.

EVPU. The acronym for ENIGMA Virtual Page Unit. EFPUs are proprietary measurement units (288 per inch) used in the *Finale* and *MusicProse* applications.

export/import. To transfer documents between applications, usually with special filters.

extended keyboard. The Macintosh ADB (Apple Desktop Bus) keyboard with extra keys (arrow, control, function, etc.) and a numeric keypad.

FatBits. The magnification view of an image, which enables dot-by-dot editing.

field. A specific text item in a database record or *HyperCard* stack card.

file. A document or an application program.

filename. The unique name that identifies a document, a folder, or a disk.

fill. The pattern or shade which fills a shape.

Finder. The basic desktop program which controls routine file management.

folder. A holding area for files (and other folders), represented by a file folder-shaped icon.

Font/DA Mover. The Macintosh utility program which installs, moves, removes, and creates new suitcases for fonts and desk accesories.

footer. A text block which is automatically printed at the bottom of each page.

format. Text attributes (font, size, style), justification, leading, margins, and so forth.

gray scale. The range of different gray values that make up an image.

grid line. A non-printing dotted or solid line for positioning text or graphics.

group. The multiple selection of discrete objects in the Draw layer of a graphics program.

halftoning. A scanner software procedure which represents the gray tones of an image by use of variable size dots.

handles. The small squares that appear in the corners and sides of a graphic or text object.

header. A text block which is automatically printed at the top of each page.

heterometric. The rhythmic structure of a melody in which one (or several) of the text lines has a different number of syllables.

highlighting. To visually distinguish text, a graphic, or an icon—usually by inverting the pixels from white to black or vice versa—to indicate that it has been selected.

histogram. A graph whose bars show the distribution of gray tones in an image.

Home card. The special card that serves as a pictorial index to *HyperCard* stacks.

HyperTalk. The unique scripting language that is available to *HyperCard* users.

I-beam. A cursor in the shape of an I, which replaces the arrow pointer or other shapes when text is to be entered.

icon. A graphic symbol which represents an object, a concept, or a message.

240

image. The product which results from scanning an original.

incipit. The beginning of a melody or a melody section, maximally the first seven intervals.

isometric. The rhythmic structure of a melody in which all text lines have the same number of syllables.

init. The abbreviation (initialization program) for a utility program placed in the System folder and designated there as a Startup document.

insertion point. The flashing vertical line which indicates where the next keystroke will insert or delete text.

invert. *See* highlight.

K. The abbreviation for Kilobyte, equal to 1024 bytes or characters. A measure of computer memory and the size of applications, documents, and disks.

landscape view. Page orientation where the width exceeds the height.

layout. The placement of page elements. *See also* format.

leading. The vertical space, usually measured in points, between two successive lines of text.

Line Art. A scanned image consisting of black and white lines.

MacPaint. A file format stored as black and white bitmaps, with a resolution of 72 dots per inch.

macro. A command that is composed of two or more other commands or actions.

marquee. The selection rectangle of moving dots.

Mb. The abbreviation for Megabyte, equal to 1024 kilobytes, Another measure of computer memory and the size of applications, documents, and disks.

menu. A list of commands in the menu bar.

message. A *HyperCard* command, frequently typed in the Message box.

MIDI. The acronym for Musical Instrumenta Digital Interface. A protocol for the communication among MIDI instruments or between them and the computer.

multimedia. In this book, audiovisual databases which include user interactivity.

object. A graphic, created in the draw layer, which is mathematically described as a series of straight lines.

offprint. A user-constructed pamphlet, derived from an electronic manuscript, in approximation of a separately-printed extract from a periodical.

open. To display a window by double-clicking an icon or a name in a list box, or clicking the Open button in a dialog box.

orphan. The first line (sometimes two lines) of a paragraph at the bottom of a page of text.

paint layer. The layer in a graphics program where a series of dots rather than discrete objects are generated. *See also* bitmap.

palette. A set of boxed symbols which represent tools, shapes, or patterns, for use in an application.

paste. The insertion into a document of text or graphics which have been copied or cut to the Clipboard.

Photo. A scanned image made up of different gray values.

pica. A typesetting measure equal to 12 points or approximately one-sixth of an inch.

PICT. The standard file format for object-oriented graphics.

pixel. A picture element of a screen image. *See also* dot.

plain. The basic or normal font style.

point. A typesetting measure, approximately one seventy-second of an inch.

portrait view. Page orientation where the height exceeds the width.

PostScript. The Adobe Systems page-description programming language.

preferences. The settings, default or user-selected, which govern specific ways in which an application works.

program. The code or group of instructions that instructs the computer how to perform a function. *See also* application.

QuickDraw. The proprietary graphics language, built into the Macintosh ROM, for screen display and printer output of text and images.

RAM. The acronym for Random-Access Memory. RAM is the volatile portion of the computer memory, where the retention of information is lost if the power is accidentally or deliberately turned off.

real-time recording. The more or less uninterrupted sequence of musical data into computer memory, during the performance of a MIDI instrument.

record. A group of related fields in a database application.

resolution. The number of dots or pixels per square inch, or lines per centimeter.

ROM. The acronym for Read-Only Memory, which designates System programs that can be read but not changed.

scale. To reduce or enlarge an image.

scripting. The highest *HyperCard* environment, where user programs are created. *See also* HyperTalk.

SEA. The acronym for Self-Extracting Archive, which is applied to a compressed file that will expand when its icon is double-clicked.

step-time recording. Note by note insertion of the score, while a MIDI instrument is played in tandem with computer-keyboard or mouse operation.

shareware. Software uploaded by vendors to information services, for user downloading and free trial. If the shareware is suitable for user purposes, the vendor expects to be paid a nominal registration fee.

sharpening. A process for enhancing the contrast between adjacent gray tones to boost clarity.

shift-click. Holding down the Shift key while the mouse is clicked, in order to select multiple objects.

stack. A *HyperCard* document of related cards.

string. Any specified sequence of characters, such as the numbers representing an incipit.

style. The variants of a normal typeface (the type style), or the grouping of formats (the style sheet) in a word processing or page layout application.

template. A specially formatted document which is used repeatedly.

threshold. The Line Art scanning level that determines whether a gray shade will be represented by a black or white pixel.

TIFF. The acronym for Tagged Image File Format. A standard graphics format for high-resolution (greater than 72 dpi) bitmapped images.

virtual memory. A technology that uses hard disk space to create more application memory than is available in installed RAM.

widow. The last one or two lines ending a paragraph at the top of the next page of text.

window. The enclosed area for displaying information on the Macintosh screen, which has a title bar, close and resize boxes, and usually two scroll bars.

Vendor Addresses

Adobe Systems, Inc., 1585 Charleston Rd., Box 7900, Mountain View, CA 94039-7900: *Sonata* (Type Library Package #21).

Aldus Corporation., 411 First Avenue South #200, Seattle, WA 98104: *PageMaker, SuperPaint.*

Apple Computer, Inc., 20525 Mariani Ave., Cupertino, CA 95014: *HyperScan, OneScanner.*

Blaschek, Günther, Petzoldstr. 31, A-4020 Linz, Austria: *PopChar.*

Casio, Inc. 15 Gardner Rd., Fairfield, NJ 07006: *CZ-101.*

CE Software, Inc., 1801 Industrial Circle, P.O. Box 65580, West Des Moines, IA 50265: *DiskTop, QuicKeys II.*

Claris Corporation, 5201 Patrick Henry Drive, Box 58168, Santa Clara, CA 95052: *HyperCard, MacPaint.*

Coda Music Software, 1401 E. 79th St., Bloomington, MN 55425-1126: *Finale, MusicProse.*

CompuServe Information Services, 5000 Arlington Ctr. Blvd., P.O. Box 20212, Columbus, OH 43220: *Macintosh Forum Libraries.*

Connectix Corporation, 125 Constitution Dr., Menlo Park, CA 94025: *Virtual.*

Cyan, Inc. P.O. Box 28096, Spokane, WA 99228: *Canary.*

Dantz Development Corporation, 1400 Shattuck Ave., Suite 1, Berkeley, CA 94709: *Retrospect.*

244

DriveSavers, Inc. 30-D Pamaron Way, Novato, CA 94949: *DataStream.*

Electronic Arts, Inc., 1820 Gateway Dr., San Mateo, CA 94404: *Deluxe Music Construction Set.*

Fifth Generation Systems, Inc., 10049 N. Reiger Rd., Baton Rouge, LA 70809-4562: *Suitcase.*

Great Wave Software, 5353 Scotts Valley Dr., Scotts Valley, CA 95066: *ConcertWare+MIDI.*

Light Source Computer Images, Inc., 500 Drakes Landing Rd., Greenbrae, CA 94904: *Ofoto.*

Linguist's Software, Inc., P.O. Box 580, Edmonds,WA, 98020-0580: *LaserFrench German Spanish.*

Lyons, Tim: 9211 Palmer Rd., North East, PA 16428: *Sound Scripter.*

Merel, Steve, 400 Ardmore Ave., Manhattan Beach, CA 90266: *Maestro.*

Microsoft Corporation, 1 Microsoft Way, Redmond, WA 98052: *File, Word.*

Mirror Technologies, Inc., 2644 Patton Rd., Roseville, MN 55113: *Mirror.*

Now Software, Inc., 319 S.W. Washington Drive, 11th Floor, Portland, OR 97204: *Now Utilities.*

Opcode Systems, Inc., 3950 Fabian Way, Suite 100, Palo Alto, CA 94303: *The Book of MIDI* and *MIDI Translator.*

Passport Designs, Inc., 100 Stone Pine Rd., Half Moon Bay, CA 94019: *Encore.*

Salient Software, Inc., 124 University Ave., Suite 300, Palo Alto, CA 94301: *Disk Doubler.*

Sigma Designs, Inc., 46501 Landing Parkway, Fremont, CA 94538: *L-View Multi-Mode.*

Symantec Corporation, 1201 Torre Ave., Cupertino, CA 95014-2132: *The Norton Utilities.*

Tandy Corporation, one Tandy Center, Ft. Worth, TX 76102: *Radio Shack, Realistic.*

Thunderware, Inc., 21 Orinda Way, Orinda, CA 94563-2565: *LighningScan, ThunderScan, ThunderWorks.*

Toshiba America Information Systems, Inc., 9740 Irvine Blvd., P.O. Box 19724, Irvine, CA 92713-9724: *Toshiba CD-ROM.*

TSP Software, 4790 Irvine Blvd., Suite 105-294, Irvine, CA 92720-9910: *Filevision IV.*

Yamaha Corporation of America, P.O. Box 6600, Buena Park, CA 90622-6600: *X-100.*

Warner New Media, 3500 W. Olive Ave., Burbank, CA 91505: *Audio Notes, "The Orchestra."*

References

Aker, Sharon Zardetto, et al. *The Macintosh Bible*, 3d edition, ed. Arthur Naiman. Berkeley: Goldstein & Blair, 1991.

Antokoletz, Elliott. *The Music of Béla Bartók. A Study of Tonality and Progression in Twentieth-Century Music*. Berkeley and Los Angeles: University of California Press, 1984.

Bartók, Béla, and Zoltán Kodály. *Transylvanian Hungarians. Folksongs*, English edition. Budapest: The Popular Literary Society, 1923.

Bartók, Béla. *Essays,* ed. Benjamin Suchoff. New York: St. Martin's Press, 1976.

———.*The Hungarian Folk Song*, ed. Benjamin Suchoff. Albany: State University of New York Press, 1981.

———.*Rumanian Folk Music*, ed. Benjamin Suchoff. 5 vols. The Hague: Martinis Nijhoff, 1967–1975.

———. *Slowakische Volkslieder*, ed. Oskár Elschek, Alica Elscheková, and Jozef Krésanek. 2 vols. Bratislava: Slovenskej Akadémie Vied, 1959–1970.

———. *Turkish Folk Music*, ed. Benjamin Suchoff. Princeton: Princeton University Press, 1976.

———. *Yugoslav Folk Music*, ed. Benjamin Suchoff. 4 vols. Albany: State University of New York Press, 1978.

Beekman, George. *HyperCard 2 in a Hurry*. Belmont: Wadsworth, 1992.

246

BMUG Inc. *BMUG Newsletter*. Berkeley, CA.

The Boston Computer Society. *The Active Window*. The BCS•Mac Magazine. Boston, MA.

Busch, David D. *The Complete Scanner Handbook for Desktop Publishing*. Macintosh Edition. Homewood: Business One Irwin, 1991.

The Chicago Manual of Style. Thirteenth Edition, Revised and Expanded. Chicago: The University of Chicago Press, 1982.

Choate, Robert A., Richard C. Berg, Lee Kjelson, and Eugene W. Troth. *New Dimensions in Music*. 7 vols. New York: American Book, 1970.

Fél, Edit, Tamás Hofer, and Klará K.-Csilléry, eds. *L'art polulaire en Hongrie*. Budapest: Corvina, 1958.

Hofstetter, Fred T. *Computer Literacy for Musicians*. Englewood Cliffs: Prentice Hall,1988."

Holoman, D. Kern. *Writing about Music*. Berkeley and Los Angeles: University of California Press, 1988.

Kostka, Stefan. *Materials and Techniques of Twentieth-Century Music*. Englewood Cliffs, Prentice Hall, 1990.

Lincoln, Harry B. "Musicology and the Computer: The Thematic Index." In *Computers and Humanistic Research,* ed. Edmund A. Bowles. Englewood Cliffs: Prentice Hall, 1967, pp. 184–93.

Prentice Hall. *Author's Guide to Electronic Manuscripts*. 1988 ed. Englewood Cliffs, New Jersey.

Read, Gardner. *Music Notation. A Manual of Modern Practice*. Boston: Allyn and Bacon, 1964.

Suchoff, Benjamin. "Computer Applications to Bartók's Serbo-Croatian Material." *Tempo* 80 (1967), pp. 15–19.

———. "Computerized Folk Song Research and the Problem of Variants." *Computers and the Humanities* (1968), 2:4, pp. 155–58.

———. "Some Problems in Computer-Oriented Bartókian Ethnomusicology." *Ethnomusicology* (September 1969) 13:3, 489–497.

———. "Computer-Oriented Comparative Musicology." In *The Computer and Music*, edited by Harry B. Lincoln. Ithaca: Cornell University Press, 1970, pp. 193–206.

———. "The New York Bartók Archive." *The Musical Times* (March 1981), pp. 156–59.

———. *A GRIPHOS Application of Bartók's Turkish Folk Music Material*. Stony Brook: Center for Contemporary Arts and Letters, State University of New York at Stony Brook, 1975.

———. "Ethnomusicological Roots of Bartók's Musical Language." *The World of Music* (1987), 29:1, 43–65.

Szabolcsi, Bence and Aladár Tóth. *Zenei Lexikon* [Music Encyclopedia], Budapest, 1931.

Index